HUNTING MEN

Other Books by Dave Smith

*Limited Edition

HUNTING MEN

REFLECTIONS ON A LIFE IN AMERICAN POETRY

DAVE SMITH

LOUISIANA STATE UNIVERSITY PRESS)((BATON ROUGE

Published by Louisiana State University Press
Copyright © 2006 by Dave Smith
All rights reserved
Manufactured in the United States of America
An LSU Press Paperback Original
First printing

Designer: Barbara Neely Bourgoyne
Typeface: Adobe Minion Pro
Printer and binder: Edwards Brothers, Inc.

Library of Congress Cataloging-in-Publication Data
Smith, Dave, 1942–
Hunting men : reflections on a life in American poetry / Dave Smith.
    p. cm.
Includes index.
ISBN-13: 978-0-8071-3182-4 (pbk. : alk. paper)
ISBN-10: 0-8071-3182-2 (pbk. : alk. paper)
1. American poetry—20th century—History and criticism. 2. American poetry—
Male authors—History and criticism. 3. American poetry—Southern States—
History and criticism. 4. Smith, Dave, 1942– 5. Poets, American—20th century—
Biography. 6. Poetry—Authorship. I. Title.
PS323.5.S595 2007
811'.5409—dc22

                                                                2006005952

The paper in this book meets the guidelines for permanence and durability of the Committee
on Production Guidelines for Book Longevity of the Council on Library Resources. ⊗

To Ralph G. Smith, Harry M. Cornwell, Bruce Speers,
John Woodfin Speers, and Robert DeMott, hunting men,
and for

Jeddie Smith
son, hunter, companion

Their boots print fields that understand their feet.

—JAMES APPLEWHITE, "Drinking Music"

This species is extremely shy. Sometimes they would rise when at the distance of half a mile from us, and fly quite out of sight. If pursued, they would return to the very keys of mud-flats from which they had risen, and it was almost impossible to approach one . . .

—JOHN JAMES AUDUBON, "The Great White Heron"

Contents

HUNTING MEN

Introduction

I take my title, *Hunting Men,* from a memoir-essay honoring men who taught me patience, observation, and willingness to rely on my senses, skills they used in hunting upland game birds. These mentors opened to me mysteries of a communication not merely instructive or informational. They lived by a code of unspoken but firm principles, and once in the field behind bird dogs like Freckles and Lady and Red, any crisis or conundrum, any action or idea, any fear or brave step, literally anything the mind could entertain was open for debate. That exchange made a companionship very like a family's; for me it has lasted a lifetime. Jokers, senders-up of each other, flayers of sham and pretense and hokum, these men had an inward strength that was character, the thing we want in hunting men. Out of all those days and hours spent walking and talking while the bird dogs criss-cross ground and swamp like feudal clerks after hidden taxables, the lessons are too many and too subtle to sum. This hunting was an education to me in nature's abundant beauty and a training in how to search, why it matters to search there. It was memory's storing-up of images that define the life of a place and, I think, of poetry. Hunting, a pastoral and sometimes violent activity, as a metaphor for poetry will seem sentimental to the reader who has raised and trained no bird dog and to one who has never tried a wing shot; it will seem even more offensive to one who has failed to locate a downed and crippled flyer while the dog trembles on point at another, whereupon a choice must be made to fetch or hunt on. And ludicrous will be the hunter's opinion that the harshest criticism leveled in that field comes with the scorning back-flicked glance of the dog whose perfectly ritual behavior has been perfect, and perfectly blunted by human inability to see and act upon the obvious when the sky is so blue and the world is so ripe.

My mentors, while hardly poets or even readers of what any audience for this book will take for granted, were, I am convinced, the initial and legitimate guides to my life with poems, those miracles of verbal invention and mystery-incarnation. They taught me how to practice finding right details, to think about what I saw or did not see from every perspective that influenced a field, its actors and circumstances and nature.

This book, however, is about poets and poetry, not the field of upland game. It studies a selection of male American poets, a choice that may provoke the reservations of gender-oriented critics. Whenever I have needed to refer to poets, I commonly use the masculine pronoun; it has been the most comfortable way since I have always been a male and there is no good point to do otherwise. But why, one might reasonably ask, have I not included considerations of poets who happen to be women?

The explanation is that poets who have most focused my reading life, and those who are most central to the context and narrative of personal discovery which makes this book's spine, are male. There are additional limits to perspective here: these essays, often written as reviews or given as lectures over a twenty-year period, have been modestly revised but not updated. For example, I do not speak of Stephen Dunn's poetry after his *New and Selected Poems, 1974–1994,* although it was followed by four additional collections, with *Different Hours* winning the Pulitzer Prize for 2000. Three of the poets, Dunn, Larry Levis, and William Matthews, have been my friends, which extends what I have to say toward memoir. I recognize that in my subtitle, *Reflections on a Life in American Poetry.* Still, readers should not expect the emphatic forward argument of the critical monograph or the fragmented mosaic of daybooks and journals. The book is more segmental than continuous but it develops, I believe, some continuous thematic interests apparent in each piece.

I begin with an essay on southern poetry which is a distillation of three lectures given on that subject (see my acknowledgments page for titles), and there I consider not merely whether a regional literature has value in a global readership but whether it actually, and definably, exists. Readings of Edgar Allan Poe, John Crowe Ransom, Robert Penn Warren, and James Dickey follow, each a representative southern poet who emerges from and builds upon his predecessor (an argument I leave fallow). Each, with the exception of Poe, bears a relationship to poetic modernism that, in America, took impetus and more from the Vanderbilt Fugitive poets. Poe is the first southern poet, though he seems seldom to have thought that, and thus the Fugitive progenitor (Allen Tate called him "our cousin"); Ransom and Warren were Fugitives; Dickey studied with Donald Davidson, another Fugitive.

The Fugitive tradition, flight toward an American possibility of new poetry and escape from the old poetry, always a yearning for spiritual authority, was the core approach of American poets who matured after World War II. A search for new structure continued in those poets coming to accomplishment after the Vietnam War, some of whom constitute this book's second section, beginning with Richard Hugo and ending with Larry Levis. In the third section, I turn toward autobiography with two interviews that speak about my own three decades of life in the life of American poetry and here I begin with "Hunting Men," my attempt to speak of what Faulkner called the pastness of every present moment we live. "St. Cyril's Dragon: The Threat of Poetry" intends an expression of poetry's character as I see it.

To those with reservations, I hope what I have to say proves persuasive or benign. Choice is the primary part of readership, electing or rejecting, coupled with adduced motives for either act, if the reader is not foreclosed by agenda or conviction. My reader will recognize, as I do, that in choosing, one is often prodded by that shadowy arbiter, taste, which may require turning away in silence and moving on, as the dog sniffing for the covey of quail does. I argue for what I like; I seek to explain that admiration.

꙳ ꙳ ꙳

Poets, indeed anyone about to publish a book, face publicists who always provide a form that seeks information, background and foreground alike, helpful to promote the author. What was your idea for this book? Applicants for grants, for admission to writers' colonies, for sabbatical leaves are routinely asked to describe the "plan" they expect to execute. These applicants, and I have repeatedly been one, typically compose a structural, thematic, philosophical, perhaps even logistical scheme, according to which a book will come trundling forth like Henry Ford's new machine. Appetite for this plan is so keen that teachers and critics often treat the books of poets as if they had been precisely laid out with T-square and stress tables. Poets affirm this ghost-idea in writing memoir-essays that recount the progressive development of a poem's idea. Poe's "The Philosophy of Composition" has a hand in this heritage. Appended notes to a book of poems, the legacy of T. S. Eliot, implicate a plan. Biographical statements in literary journals impute a plan.

By and large, such a plan, idea, or scheme is bogus. With few exceptions, the poet writes poem after poem. At some point, he begins to feel, an embryonic book exists, a discovery, and enough poems means the book is finished.

Enough, if he is a good poet, requires a structure, a tension mechanism sufficient to nudge the accumulated poems from a clutch to a cohesion. Having found some binding architecture, one almost always invisible in the way that stress forces are invisible on house or body, the poet revises. Or repeats. Or pads. The latter two actions represent the career of most books. In the case of Walt Whitman's *Leaves of Grass,* all three procedures may be observed, and to an extent far greater than for most of us. Western poetry holds it is good to revise; not to do so is either arrogant or ignorant or rebellious. Allen Ginsberg is reported to have said "first thought, best thought." James Wright said he revised because he did not assume his mind was coequal with the mind of God. A book of essays, even memoir-and-response, however loosely joined, also requires a plan.

My scheme gathers essays composed since my *Local Assays: On Contemporary American Poetry* (1985). Some, done as public lectures, permitted me positions occasionally liberated of strict evidence. The reader will find here little applied methodology, little political or aesthetic campaigning, and small contest for or against poetry's seasonally contested fashions. Yet they overlap in arguments and repetitive allusions; there is a line of poets relevant to my life. If I find in them an appealing vision, character, voice, or structure, I do not intend to advance a unifying thesis. While the span of my attention ranges from Anglo-Saxon lyrics to contemporary colleagues, I choose no systematic conclusion for the book. Were one reader to ask of another what I think, I should be pleased to hear, he thinks this, he thinks that, he thinks maybe. I am delighted by Whitman's amused question, "Do I contradict myself?" I am even more delighted by his defiant answer that to every American poet is perfectly well known. Humility, in reading poems, seems to me the primary tool for success.

In my essays on southern poetry, I am ambivalent, reductive, nervous, defensive, and didactic. Very well, says Whitman, I contradict myself. My life in the life of poetry has been like a swimmer's in and out of that flow, the murkiest, most deceptive, most native of this book's currents. Like the spinal twist and surge of a great river, southern poetry, and what it has taught me to respond to, has been a kind of native language. I think good poetry is inevitably regional. In what I have to say here, the adjective *southern* is lowercased and the noun *South* is capped to suggest a scheme or priority, but statements made about southern poetry vary as they assert a more or less uncomfortable pressure on a self I find in contradictory discourse with itself. The poet in the South, many readers of this book will certainly agree, exists as palpably as Holiday Inns and old railroad tracks; the southern poet may be another creature. Does southern poetry exist? Maybe so.

-◇- -◇- -◇-

I was southern before I became a poet. To say so declares factual information about birth and cultural environment. Regional identity is central to poetry's power. Great poetry cannot be divorced from an intimate, organic link to place. Dante's *Divine Comedy* leads directly to Florence, as Baudelaire walks the streets of Paris, as T. S. Eliot owns London. Place may be native landscape or the landscape one's imagination possesses. It is almost always a fiction comprehending a community to which one most belongs as well as the emblematic source of the poet's self-awareness, where he is most a self. Place may exist, as it does for me, almost entirely in one's head. There, I know a language sound, a way of behavior, a heritage, what the signs on the field mean. Beyond that, I bend, if not break, under definitions of what being a southerner might mean; words become unreliable. Homer speaks for all Greeks, making himself, as narrator, a tent within which the heroic and tragic abide, a community. Outsiders, if equally human, he treats as different but with equal respect, humility, and understanding. To do less is to be a provincial.

I was born a Virginian; for me, being southern is not a choice. But for any southerner, in thought and act there are multiple and various choices. Warren, the genius of southern poetry, was asked in his twilight by Peter Stitt if he considered himself a southern poet. "What else can I be?" Warren answered. There is both aggression and helplessness in that. He wasn't asked if he wanted to be southern, a question he may have answered quite differently. Indeed, what to be is the central question posed by southern literature. If Warren was southern by fact of history, his choices in what to write and how to write made him a poet of southern experience. He knew his sound was his identity. It marks difference between southerners and between those on the other side of the drawl line. *Voice,* a word now almost mystically blank as existentialism, means the poet's sound composed over a career of trial and error. It is the intersection where writers live intuitively and inwardly, the chief coordinate for who any writer is, southerner or not.

The naïve reader will think I mean only the accent whose distortions of "normal" speech indicate how a character sounds, hence where he is from.

Writers of southern fiction, even of magnolia romance variety, understand how orthography creates Gomer Pyle as quickly as dialogue begins. But I am not trying to define voice as habit's speech patterns. The poet has little to do with the drawl that so nominates the region; it is scarcely audible in a poet's repertoire. It may be the poet's environmental voice but it is not his chosen sound, which more often than not is figurative, rhythmic, imagistic, driven by repetitions in structure which advance meaning rather than dramatic event. The sound of southern voice is not a conversation, it is a model of consciousness given audibility (or even the absence of consciousness). The southern voice for the poet, whatever it may be for fiction, is a literary creation founded on models of narrative and song which promote awareness of self and community.

In the South the most significant model is the King James Bible. That southerners spend most of their lives in the rhythms of that work, from pulpit to Bo Diddley to reasons for weather cycles only partly explains what I mean. The English poet Philip Larkin yearned, as the southerner does, for something gone out of his life. In "Church Going," Larkin described a bicyclist nonbeliever who stops by an abandoned church. There he enters, as he says he often does, apparently compelled by what he cannot provide on his own, and pokes about, pretends to deliver a sermon, leaves a worthless coin, then departs pondering what this massive presence will come to. He knows, of course, and so observes "A serious house on serious earth it is, / In whose blent air all our compulsions meet, / Are recognized, and robed as desire." That hunger for serious life, what it is and how it speaks and how we may address it, is fundamental to southern poetry, more so I think than the wide river of folk humor from Brer Rabbit to Brother Dave Gardner which so influences southern fiction, a seriousness no doubt the consequence of Puritan history as that humor is the consequence of frontier loneliness. I once heard a learned man say every southern poet he had known wanted to be a preacher. Yearning is not the same thing as preaching. The literary form this yearning for seriousness takes is the poet's struggle to make language achieve the memorability, dignity, and authenticity, if not beauty, of books which tell us life has gravity, destiny is real. Poetry and redemption may yet exist, up the road somewhere we think, from first to last.

Anxiety over destiny and identity characterize Poe's southern voice inside poems that never depart from Anglican imitations. A lugubrious darkness in everything Poe did is not inherently southern, although he contributed that to the regional sound. Yet the intense somberness of the cosmically injured and isolated man, prominent in Dickens, who was only a few years Poe's senior, seems southern by way of immigrants from the British Isles who filled the South. The same tone is Larkin's. Poe's stories and poems are, above all else, ethical studies, however twisted, and we are not surprised to hear Allen Tate claim him as the southerner's "cousin." Poe's voice rose at the beginning when there was no southern literary past, no cultural community, hence no figure of self, a long way from 1945 when Tate, writing "The New Provincialism," says, "the renascence is over; or at any rate that period is over," and then he asks, "Will the literature of the South, or of the United States as a whole, be different from anything that we knew before the war? Will American literature be more alike all over the country?" Tate fears loss of a "southern" voice, his deepest identity. He adds that "no literature can be mature without the regional consciousness; it can only be senile, with the renewed immaturity of senility." Then a further point: "It has been generally supposed in our time that the limitations of the mere regional interest, which are serious, could be corrected by them for a 'Universal' point of view, a political or social doctrine would 'relate' or 'integrate' the local community with the world in the advance of a higher culture. What this culture is or might be nobody was ever quite clear about. . . . What it never occurred to anybody to ask was this simple question: What happens if you make the entire world into one vast region?"

Tate wanted to force the South into the high dreams of literary modernism, to form a culture of art in the Bozart, and yet in the debris of World War II he identified a regional literature as the better way. Grounded, he thought, in the struggle for a value scheme, a political construct less chosen than evolved, somehow naturally, by local communities, regionalism was: "that consciousness or that habit in men in a given locality which influences them to certain patterns of thought and conduct handed to them by their ancestors." Regionalism is thus limited in space but not in time.

To Tate, a region was people, not land or space. If they did not consciously strive to know themselves, to implement a progressive self and community, they were doomed to anonymity and cheapness. "A society without the arts," he said Plato had written, "lives by chance." A provincial man, locked in the present, lives in aberration. Citizens might assume a short or a long view, the regional. Equating regionalism with religion, a view that leaves little to chance, Tate added "regionalism without civilization [no serious arts]—which means, with us, regionalism without the classical Christian culture—becomes provincialism." The consequence, Tate argued, meant "the only acceptable literature that the South can produce must be a literature of social agitation, through which the need of reform may be publicized." His plea for a Christian orthodoxy rubs hard for contemporaries, but his demand for historical awareness and intuitive scrutiny is more agreeable, if biting, in days when the historian David McCullough says only the tiniest percentage of Americans can identify who fought in the Revolutionary or the Civil War. Without memory and without argument, as Yeats thought, there can be no art, no hope. Without hope, destiny is only a huckster's word.

Not long ago I had a letter from a novelist in North Carolina, which included a news report about dwarf-tossing, a sporting event unknown to me. I knew anything was possible in the South but suspected that I was having my leg pulled. Then my local news reported dwarf-tossing had been outlawed in Florida. Soon a follow-up article said a number of dwarves were protesting the new law on the grounds it discriminated against them and prevented them from working. No information was offered as to whether wins were based on distance, weight tossed, or stylistic skill, the sort of details that matter to writers, to those interested in how one could tell that story, how language presents, makes, and interprets both what happens and what we imagine. Poets think that way, which is why Delmore Schwartz wrote that in dreams begin responsibilities. Poets are dream-hunters. The dreams of any region, if psychotherapy has taught us anything, are universal but the costumes and dialect are site-specific. The good poem tells a single story of life and death, renewable and enacted. It is a special, privileged form of communication with an infinite capacity for formal innovation. Even dwarf-tossing has a plan, an idea of quality based on a prior and tempered judgment. Good readers, like good poets, rise to the poem's occasion; they trust instinct; they prepare; they adapt; they apply a kitchen sink of knowledge. Reading poems is, for me, like good days with hunting men who make interesting a life often unbearably grim, who know where the secrets might be. A poem knows, too. I have tried to be faithful to that experience of poetry in what follows. My success, if it occurs, will be to send readers to the books of the poets where the world, as they knew it, waits and is full of the delights of the unglimpsed and known.

I

Southern Odes and Others

There's a Bird Hung Around My Neck

OBSERVATIONS ON SOUTHERN POETRY

In the spring of 1935, at a group of writers gathered in Baton Rouge, Louisiana, to hold the Conference on Literature and Reading in the South and Southwest. Robert Penn Warren, then thirty-five years old and not yet a founder of *The Southern Review,* presided as conference chair, directing a sometimes edged colloquy between Allen Tate, Caroline Gordon, John Peale Bishop, John Gould Fletcher, a goodly number of journal and university press editors, novelists Roark Bradford and Lyle Saxon, literary lights now dimmed, and the English cultural entrepreneur Ford Madox Ford. When discussion turned toward distinctions to be made between writers who seem to speak for a region and those who do not, the Oklahoma folklorist B. A. Botkin, editor of *Space,* alluded to the practice of the *New Republic* magazine of publishing groups of poets by state. Mr. Botkin concluded: "I defy you to tell the difference, by the way, between some of these California and Southern poets—at least so that you and I or anyone can understand it. In fact, one of the things that strikes the outsider about Southern writing is that as soon as one stops writing prose and becomes a poet one ceases to be a Southerner and even poetic."

Mr. Botkin speaks to an audience, as he quickly acknowledges, which includes a number of the once Vanderbilt Fugitives and some fellow travelers —Robert Penn Warren, Allen Tate, Cleanth Brooks, Frank Owsley, Randall Jarrell—so he adds, "I know that the Fugitives will say that they conceive of the South not as a specific subject matter but as a way of living, an attitude, a tradition." Botkin wants to argue with this valuation of tradition because Oklahoma, he feels, has no tradition except that of being on the run from somewhere else. Besides that, it is hard to define an attitude. He provocatively quotes Tate saying tradition is "the knowledge of life that we have not had to learn for ourselves, but have absorbed out of the life around us—those ways of feeling, those convictions of propriety, those ways of speaking, of which the writer himself is *hardly aware* and from which he cannot escape."

To Botkin this defines a provincial literature and he responds that "taking things for granted, especially one's region, and setting attitude and manner, especially of one's region, above subject matter, above facts and reason, is provincial in the unfavorable sense." Southern intellectuals, like Americans in general, are notoriously sensitive about possession of an indigenous culture, with good historical reasons. They were especially stirred in the 1930s and particularly so by the prodding of Tate who, speaking for his peers, wanted home-grown accomplishment worthy of the respect of international modernists. Only months before Botkin's remarks, in the *Virginia Quarterly Review* of April 1935, Tate's essay "The Profession of Letters in the South" argued: "It must be confessed that the Southern tradition has left no cultural landmark so conspicuous that the people may be reminded by it constantly of what they are. We lack a tradition in the arts; more to the point, we lack a literary tradition. We even lack a literature."

Botkin and Tate might have agreed a southern poetry existed, but they would have thought it an inferior literature, compromised by provincialism that even then was synonymous with *southern*. Tate's definition of tradition, if not of regional writing, as mystical as whatever the South was, verges on Louis Armstrong's definition of jazz as something you cannot recognize so long as you have to ask what it is. Still, given impetus by the accomplishments of the writers of the so-called Southern Renaissance, a southern literature has been, by readers and scholars alike, deemed to exist. Assessments of its character and quality have become principal interests of conferences, graduate programs, university presses, and, still in some towns, book reviewers. All are engaged in documenting, as Louis D. Rubin says in *The Mockingbird in the Gum Tree*, "resemblances, the common subjects, themes, attitudes toward human nature and history shared by most of the writers."

Few in this industry of definition, including the Fugitive poets, have argued for the poor cousin of southern poetry, for to do so betrays the modernist impulse to "make it new" and looks, in any event, defensive. Fiction, by nature, enacts a narrative grounded in character and place. Prior to the Civil War, "southern" was a geographical description; afterward *Southern* became the index of a regional and a cultural myth whose replications would become a fiction's local identity. Southern fiction became the *it* produced by those who were *there*. But poetry, criticism has asserted, did not belong to that community or its "tradition." In 1976, Cleanth Brooks, as Louis Rubin reported in *Southern Literary Study*, told a gathering of scholars that "we are not getting a good deal of terribly good or striking poetry from the South now, and what we're getting is basically international, or Anglo-American." No one disagreed. Good poetry, Brooks felt, could not simultaneously manage regional identity and meet prevailing modernist standards for iconic quality; he was thereby agreeing with Botkin that one might be a southern writer only when not writing in rhythmic lines (a matter to which the English critic of southern literature, Richard Gray, nods when he argues that Poe, in fiction, is southern; in poetry, not).

To the individual poet in the act of writing, the existence of southern poetry, let alone whether he or she composes it, is a matter of indifference. Poe, a keen observer of his place and affiliation, seems hardly to have noticed such matters. Yet the increasing self-awareness fostered by the nineteenth century, with its fractured civic experience and memory, encouraged William Gilmore Sims, Henry Timrod, and Sidney Lanier to write poetry based in what William Carlos Williams would later call "the local," though he understood this as the regional that embodies the universal. That a living poetry can only be written by poets whose vision is informed by a living coherent culture is also the sub-premise of Tate's arguments. Such poetry comments upon a culture's life, shaping it by the imagination, which, in the *Biographia Literaria,* Samuel Taylor Coleridge says "struggles to idealize and to unify." This struggle very largely consists in dramatizing and seeking to understand the self in its chaotic relations, especially the self as artist, trying as T. S. Eliot says, to shore fragments against ruin.

Early southern writers idealized their society beyond known evidence, portraying the South as a ubiquitously admirable "community." A *polis,* it was sold as invariably a nice place to live in, both for aristocrats and slaves, run by gentlemen who could quote Homer in Greek, ride hard and hunt well, and bring in divine crops, human and otherwise. Men throve because they knew the evil in the world and the world in God's program; women throve because they produced. In *A Shaping Joy,* Cleanth Brooks found in this community a "sense of religious wholeness, . . . consciousness of human relationships, . . . tragic dimension of life." When the Civil War forced the industrial half of that century into battle with the agrarian half, with disastrous results at every social doorstep and level, the "community" emerged in the pages of white writers. It was a splendid literary image that muted or voided what contrary historical evidence plainly showed: much of the South was populated by slaves, barely freed people of color, lower-class whites, yeomen immigrants, wandering hustlers, and come-heres with the new power, a community rapacious and marginal, and brutal of necessity. Partisan literature, quick to praise the old way of agrarian self-reliance beset by cancerous consumerism, the putative cause of those non-belongers, by the advent of the twentieth century was in need of rehabilitation that would show the South as it really was, not as wishes would have it. This would lead to the Fugitive aesthetic preference for the concrete in literature, a suspicion of the abstract that fortified the criticism and teaching of John Crowe Ransom, as much as anyone the prototypical new poet in the South. Louis Rubin describes this image of community: "Southern society tended to cultivate the amenities. It placed considerable emphasis on manners, believed in noblesse oblige, cultivated the paternalistic concept of role . . . the Old South was precapitalistic and even feudal, and its symbols of aristocratic distinction were land and slaves, not money."

The twentieth century's new writing men were obliged to reexamine identity, the fundamental task for any writer, and now it meant asking what the South itself was, this geographical place that, according to history and living citizens, had once been a separate country not only in law but paid for by gouts of blood, a land more than 800 miles wide and 1,200 miles long, with a multicolored, multilingual, multicultural people. Who was the southerner? Chroniclers inevitably said what Louis Rubin said of the southerner, "He belonged." Some did. Some, less powerful, did not. In early decades of the century the region's literature took flight from a dead hand past; it bared its lies, urged by international modernists, with a backward yearning stare for truth, to resist provincialism at all costs.

Some of those men seated before Botkin in Baton Rouge had been, only a decade earlier, undergraduates declaring themselves "Fugitives" in revolt. They would never escape the name, but they would find their flight led to the conviction, which they would never recant, that art is always rooted in regional life. How else would *southernness*, a name for what they belonged to, and what they thought themselves bound to, manifest itself? Coming to maturity in the 1920s in the eleven southern states, a landscape of human survivors of an often horribly oppressive experience, these writers believed poetry might yet grasp a home place whose stories, told, might reveal a destiny, a purpose. But it would have to be the inner place of consciousness, as Wyatt Prunty has written, "an emblem of a happening" where a sense of *home* and value-toting selves chafed against the society of fact.

Nevertheless, if an idea of home sits at the core of southern literature, home seems hardly capacious enough as definition, and all definitions of this literature have proven slippery, whether racial, geographic, historic, philosophical, or aesthetic, whether borne forth by drawl, cuisine, gospel, jazz, or preference for narrative structure. Perhaps that is why James Applewhite reads southern poetry as the "art of musical, emotional, rhetorical intensity (from Poe to Faulkner to James Dickey) that is unable to state its premises and propositions as clearly as other regions." A distinguished poet, unusual in never having left his native North Carolina, he characterizes his region's literature by "Southern allegiance" (hinting choice, not inevitability), although its dominant "tone, landscape, atmosphere" arises, he says, from a "collective emotional miasma which left no space for individual speech."

Thus, the burden of provincialism which is, at best, deception by sentimentality, handicaps the southern poet who is unable to speak clearly because of "climate, history, mythology." Perhaps it is the Botkin in me that nods against weather as a maker of the southern poet and wants to resist the murderous charm of myth. Still, Applewhite seems dead on when he says the southern poet has pursued with equivocal success "that rare smoke of the soul's fire rising beyond the pines" and does so yet among "the Kudzu, used car lots, fundamentalist congregations, and slumber of Sunday-noon dinners." Botkin, I can hear him, asks if that distinguishes the grit bard from any American poet in other regions? I think the answer is yes, no, and maybe. James H. Justus, in *The History of Southern Literature,* asks, "Is there such a thing as a distinctly contemporary southern poet?" He seems to think so and provides a descriptive profile of his poem:

> a recurrence of rural subjects; a residual fondness for conservative forms and techniques; an easy habit of incorporating emotional diction and syntax into a poetic discourse that is otherwise perceived Standard; a penchant for order and control even in experimental efforts; a preference for the visually concrete and aurally sensuous image over abstract meditation; the importance of memory in altering, deepening, and extending compulsive scenic recall; and, unlike more aggressive postmodernists of their generation, a lingering reliance upon pattern, design, and wholeness despite a resigned recognition that both life and art are resolutely fragmented, disjunctive, and discontinuous.

Literature's business is to look through the particular to the universal, to speak with clarity that repeats, to use language to make characters whose lives compel us. Justus, running in fear of the provincial, describes only what good poets do, for any literature of quality is grounded in regional awareness, both inner and outer. If I am wrong then science fiction in *The Kingdom of Ur-62* is the equal of *The Canterbury Tales*. The very existence of the South and southerners, to judge by what newspapers say, stands in argument. Letters to editors routinely complain southern culture is little more than Chinese trash sold at roadside shops from Virginia to Texas. Opposing voices defiantly claim the South is different, looks so, feels so, sounds so. In Baton Rouge, Louisiana, where I live, we have two news-dominating crises. The first is a decades-old suit to desegregate public schools. The other argues whether to fly or not fly the Confederate battle flag over public sites. Both illustrate the continuing racial divide in American life; one emphasizes a mythical southern character. The distinction? In no corner of the United States except the South do people so experience, on a daily basis, the contending forces and the continuing end of the Civil War one and a half centuries ago.

Most of what is written of the South reeks of nostalgia. Distortion, as Flannery O'Connor proved, is an effective device for eccentric contrasts, for sending up colorful myths and entertaining lies that keep pop historians, visiting movie productions, and jive comedians in business. Excess may be only marketable style, yet our own scarcely recognized face in the common mirror speaks awareness of a culture's existence and values. That individual countenance is the fabled community, the past with consequences, in cheek and jowl the shadow of obligation, the whatever it is that feels like pity and respect and maybe awe. No writer can abstain from speaking the dense individuality in communal experience that is, finally, what differentiates the South from the rest. Toni Morrison, William Faulkner, and even John Grisham have more in common with each other than with John Updike, Joyce Carol Oates, Terry McMillan, or Ken Kesey.

If "southern" once implied a social vision whose comment was coherent, critical, and frequently unwelcome, a comment, since the Vanderbilt Fugitives and the tribes of Faulkner, bent on disabusing the southerner of excuses for regional and personal failures it aggressively chronicled, southern fiction now appears to be a more or less scathing, often ludicrous portrait of a society so backward, fumbling, self-destructive, and culture-less that H. L. Mencken's famous dismissal of what he called the Sahara of the Bozart seems more than kind. *Time* magazine, in 1989, quotes novelist Pat Conroy who jokes that every southern story opines, "On the night the hogs ate Willie, mama died when she heard what Papa did with Sister." If southern fiction is read dominantly by women in middle-class suburbs built around golf-course spas, as marketing studies argue, where is Conroy's other South? Is life in the South no more than comic outrage, violence, family evil, sex, death, grotesque and insipid cousins, a stupidity of tidal consequences? So say Willie, Mama, Papa, Sister, and every hog interviewed by *Time*.

This southern fiction appears to have shucked off what might be called that old style consciousness. The new Real South seems more outer place than inner. In 1991 Fred Hobson's *The Southern Writer in the Postmodern World* questioned whether "what was once natural [had] become stylized, what was deeply and painfully experienced [had] become ritualized?" He decided the "acute self-consciousness, an intense awareness of *being* southern" had shifted among the younger writers to a "relative lack of southern self-consciousness." If fiction does not maintain art's inwardness and argument with the self, if it tracks no shared community, no continuous identity, what art does that? Movies? Poetry? I hear Mr. Botkin, his seersucker suit rustling as he wipes his moist neck, call for recess and libation. Still, the matter does not so easily resolve.

Time, for all its venerable chronicle of the venal southern stage, did not mention southern poetry. No musophobists, *Time*'s writers seemed to feel poetry could not exist down there. Who would buy it? Who would read it? Nevertheless, in one recent year, the *Atlanta Constitution* reported Maya Angelou banked $3.5 million in poetry sales. Those strophes down home interest somebody, but it isn't the critic who can't describe how poetry relates to or critiques the landscape we live in. He's parked his Toyota pickup in the lot of Euro-theory that doesn't read fiction or poetry anymore. Necessary first-rate advocates for poetry in the South remain, well, slim and none. There are no prominent books on the subject. Rubin's *Southern Literary Study,* now almost forty years old, still seems definitive when George Core, editor of the *Sewanee Review,* quotes long-dead John Crowe Ransom saying "that modern southern poetry was not greatly different from the poetry of the rest of the country"; with Blyden Jackson, the black voice, concurring there are no southern black poets; and Cleanth Brooks explaining that "lyric poetry always has less to do with the social issues and the family." The argument is seductively syllogistic against a southern poetry: it is like all modern poetry;

all modern poetry is lyric; lyric poetry doesn't concern social issues; southern fiction concerns social issues. Ipso facto, indisputable, the logic reminds me of Warren's poem about Emerson: "All you have to do is not argue."

Still, there is contrary evidence, some circumstantial. Poets have published books of poems which bear all the markers adduced by Professor Justus (among them Professor Justice). Poets openly admit they regard themselves as southern. On April 23, 1985, the American Academy of Poets held a "Southern Poetry Symposium" in New York City, with New Hampshire novelist Russell Banks asking, "Where is the South and what are we talking about when we say Southern Poetry?" The exhibits included poets Charles Wright, William Harmon, David Bottoms, Cleopatra Mathis, and Robert Morgan. The senior man, Wright, said, "Sure. It's all gone, isn't it?" They all agreed, vanished, gone, poof. Then Bottoms observed, well, some of it wasn't gone, because they, these poets, and their memory-diving poems were there. "It's not gone completely," he said. Then Harmon remarked the South was mostly written words, and Wright, who lived in Laguna Beach for some years, said, "Everybody's a product of Hollywood," and that might have settled the matter, with the Fugitives having left the building and the country. But Wright complicated things when he supposed, "I've always considered myself a Southern writer—always will—whatever that means." It means what Warren meant when interviewer Peter Stitt asked if Warren still considered himself a southern writer and Warren answered, "What else can I be?" He understood plainly Stitt wanted to know what Warren belonged to and implied, correctly, it was in Warren's poems, just as Warren coyly agrees. The southern poet, like the poet everywhere, makes a tale of self enlarged with the other; he employs words to live more fully, starting with what is local, accepting, arguing with, and transferring a myth of being. The poem of the South is a dialectic for which a southern drawl is both signature of environment and stage apparatus.

What we most belong to is what we feel is threatened by the ubiquitous sprawl of communities that blur into the boundary-less and ugly run-on that once was our place, with defined character, before, say, Nashville became Music City Nowhere. But this phenomenon may have the odd merit of permitting a new enfranchisement of regional writers, those who heretofore possessed no voice and yet saw and felt a region unlike the sanctified version. Mr. Botkin might have agreed, holding his nose at a literature bound by "manner and matters," a literature whose memory of a society has

increasingly proven contradictory and untrustworthy and fragmenting of
the idea of real community. Botkin would have noted, acerbically and accu-
rately, there can be few southern poets left alive who have actual experience
of anything that smacks of the old *polis*. Perhaps that is why regionalism
itself is the problem. Its vision is alluring, necessary, and way too parochial.
The Fugitives, steeped in the modernist thinking that was avant garde and
determined to be international, did not think so. Scientific naturalism left
them little answer in the inner place to which poetry had always resorted.
Donald Davidson, the least of them, writing in "Regionalism and Natural-
ism in American Literature," did not believe regionalism was the problem.
He said: "Regionalism is not an end in itself, not a literary affectation, not
an aesthetic credo, but a condition of literary realization. The function of a
religion is to endow the American artist with character and purpose. He is
born of a region. He will deny its parenthood to his own hurt. Without its
background he is a homeless exile in the wilderness of modern life."

Davidson, not seeking to define the South or southerner, only its poet,
returns to the image of home, to the condition of belonging, to a character
intuited and thought changeless as the journey of the individual life is surely
not. His "condition" for art rests on an attitude of self-consciousness, but
one with a prior agenda. He equates regionalism with religion, an assump-
tion few contemporaries accept, but his conclusions explain why every poet
of the South from Allen Tate to Yusef Komunyakaa works with a common
obligation to civic attention and critique, and every one of them has proven
embittered by and isolated from his "place."

If this poet writes under a distinctive historical pressure that enforces a
common identity, and if his genre seeks a world more epiphany than epic,
his obligation and his material, his particularly employed details, must ren-
der the same verisimilitude art has always required for looking beyond the
home window. Perhaps this poet has not managed the comic perambulations
of fictioneers Harry, Barry, and Larry, image-makers for the new South, yet
like Coleridge's mariner he bears the good and bad news of community in
unified emblems poems exist to carry. Poems and poets have always made
statements. But statements, to the contemporary mind, have little staying
power, and poems seem disconnected from lives as they actually are lived.
Even so, in 1985, writing in *The Southern Review*, poet Applewhite said, "The
quintessential southern poet is typified still by enclosure within a burden of
emotion almost too intense for statement."

How that emotion might be turned usefully electric, like a river, how those statements might be made, what forms might suffice, have been questions the southern poet has had to engage in the common pursuit of identity that transcends regions. In the end the history of southern poetry, more viscerally complicated by history itself than in other regions, though ultimately the identity is not radically different, is one of form. To what does the poem's form belong? Two primary directions, taken with liberal definition, continuously appear, as rhythmic as waves and sometimes as self-opposing as surf, even sometimes in the same poet, always seeking intuitive belonging and deliberate rebellion. From the start, influenced by gothic traditions, black gospel music, rhythm and blues, tall tales from river cultures, even rock and roll, southern poems are made as either Anglican lyric verse with its authoritative conventions or as improvisational personal narratives with patterns of orchestrated elements, this last by far the most popular and, surprisingly, least region-specific.

The tradition of English verse so influential in the post–World War II years, and always the practice of Ransom and Tate, has continued in the mainstream poetries of Pulitzer winners Donald Justice and Henry Taylor and numerous others. Less constrained by metric loyalty but no less visibly participant in examination of the regional identity is a poetry made, variously, as song, meditation, or image sequence, its vernacular idiom often seeming composed more in contradistinction to than contradiction of an English tradition. Wendell Berry, Charles Wright, and Yusef Komunyakaa, very different poets, the latter two also Pulitzer winners, write an introspective and meditational lyric which is grounded in specific southern place but flexed by a voice more literary standard than definably southern. The character of southern poetic form, if it exists, appears most in the fusion of narrative momentum and lyric oscillation which characterizes the mature poetry of Robert Penn Warren and James Dickey.

From the early 1960s until the end of his life, Dickey, writing with an evangelical fervor, wed dramatic evocation of lives lived in the eye of nature to an expanded line, re-angling scenes of sexual pursuit, war survival, and competitions of the self for personal discovery. Reviving the Agrarians' deepest fears and showing nuances of the American primitivist movement, Dickey's pantheistic poetry, and the individual liberation it seemed to offer, shouldered free of many social problems, including that southern heritage of racial relations Wendell Berry called "the hidden wound." In later years

Dickey wrote poems so dedicated to realizing what he called "states of being" they could not manage, to most readers, literate statements, but he had early on identified making statements as the poem's need and, to do it with contextual credibility, he developed a narrative of fragments and self-catechism, a structure of subdued verse techniques, intense rhythmic momentum, and opportunistic assertion. In this, he was instructed by the poems of Randall Jarrell and of Robert Penn Warren.

Warren's *Collected Poems,* work of more than fifty years, begins in simultaneous imitations of Eliot and Thomas Hardy, two directions he never abandoned, emphasizing now the anti-verse of pell-mell meditation and then the careful minuet of received form. But in the blend of both, and both are sealed by what seems to have been his regionally inherited Puritanic self-scrutiny, he achieved historic sweep, a dense and symbolic portrait of man in his place, an iconic representation of the artist as the one who suffers to know and express the truth no one escapes. In poems both dour and suspiciously (to him) joyous, each wishing beyond all to "tell [me] a story," Warren seems, in the end, to have followed another poet, one he scarcely resembles, one his fellow Fugitives regarded as a woofer at best, Walt Whitman. Warren's view that a poem is democratic in idiom and matter succeeded in an art more personal and thoughtful, more ruefully and radically individual, one always memorial with the passion to remember as a service of civic inquiry and duty. But he would, I think, have been most pleased to think that in opening the poem, making it opportunistic in moral inquiry that insists on fair and equal scrutiny, he resisted provincialism. He became what he could not avoid. Warren said of being a southern poet: "You are what you are. I was born and grew up in Kentucky, and I think your early images survive. Images mean a lot of things besides pictures."

Well, what do they mean? Poetry, seldom written to teach or preach, permits readers to learn from images. Southern poems risk being little more than calendar art and pastoral consolation: fog on blue mountains, lone-standing horse in Carolina, proud church in Alabama meadow. Such images from Wendell Berry's *Collected Poems* are necessary to poets. Yet, unresisted, they cloy like fraudulent fuzzies that chatter in Maya Angelou's lines even as they chattered in the southern apologists from whom Fugitives fled. Poetry, to have a role in culture, must ferret out behavior's vectors and principles and effects; it must juxtapose a community-eroding present to a community-protective past. The poet needs the hard lens of naturalism and the soft lens of romantic yearning, ill-fitting spectacles at best. The southern poet likes that transcendent blink of vision commonly called "epiphany." He, or she, doesn't like what Scarlett learned, that a deep sigh of epiphany doesn't do much to stanch hunger, let alone disease in the Delta.

Vivid myths, tribe tales, tutelary lives set against implacable circumstance, with memorable images of dramatic moral engagement seem right for a poetry from which awareness and strength proceed, and these every region has. But triadic odes to hooty owl or to a God like a well-dressed CEO, arias to the Stars and Bars or to magnolia and Voodoo, whether in perfectly counted sonnets or long-lined conjures are no less parochial for their form. The regional poet does not succeed by staying at home but by exporting home across demarcation lines in poems whose art stands as undeniable as it is durable. The southern poet, like Coleridge's mariner, is inheritor of an inescapable consciousness of hard realities, racial hurt, economic despair, political bankruptcy, cultural amnesia, fouled environments, and grim futures. Readers will be fit, though few, as Milton says. Of that, he must take little concern, working as if only he knows what burdens him. But readers will know, and in known realities poetry matters. The way to be a southern poet, he discovers, is to try as fully as possible not to be one, to be only a poet writing

❧ ❧ ❧

One evening in the fall of 1960 I sat on the last seat of a Virginia schoolbus as we bounced in twilight toward Petersburg. The road was called "old 460," though it was a recent four-lane going east–west. I could see ahead the concrete line cut through the tobacco and corn of Virginia's "Southside," a place I saw as wholly different from my own suburban Tidewater. Although my neighborhood kept shoulder to shoulder the brick bungalows of World War II's survivors, with gravel drives and chain link yard fences, many homes abutted farms that traced back to Revolutionary War families, the fields and poor black hands doing business as it had always been done. Our mothers planted flowers only to see coveys of quail get more benefit than they did. We loved Elvis, fast Chevies, drive-ins, and would go to college, prosper more than our parents; we were the start of the "me-generation."

Dusk settled on acres of crops as we moved west into orange sun low ahead, wisps of fog filling slopes of fields. It was August, hot. The smell of earth, manure, horses, and cows washed in the open bus windows. I still see that country: thick slabs of green, then dark-shadowed phalanxes of whiskery pines, green again, then intermittent swamp, bog, or dark-water of pond, but also weather-washed barns, abandoned cars, trucks, rust-burned, and houses so far apart I wondered how they lived without neighbors, what grocery stores they went to, what schools, if they ever saw a movie. I thought the life there was plain, unlike ours, certainly as boring as the hours we passed on that bus. I felt I would run from there as quickly as I could get my thumb out for the next car. But, oddly, I felt also a strange attraction to this place and life that puzzled me like a just-discovered country cousin.

I was on that bus for a reason. With the rest of my high school football team, I was suited up for a preseason scrimmage against Petersburg High School. I recall only two things about that evening. The first, perhaps irrelevant, is that Petersburg High had a fullback who was said able to kill, or at least maim, anyone who tried to tackle him. I was a small defensive linebacker whose role was to tackle, so I had interest in that. It provoked in me a meditative attitude. Coach Shotgun Brown insisted we ride in silence, convinced that he had learned in the big war to work himself up to feats of bravery by *thinking*. He wished us to do that. I watched the passing fields with fearful interest. In fact, that fullback did not kill me that night. And I proved, at least once, capable of a tree-felling tackle. The cost was a spinal annoyance I feel on some occasions, but the gain was that brooding trip through country I had not really looked at. I have forgotten what mayhem felt like in Petersburg, but I have kept images of "Southside." I recall the way my cleats would lift from the metal floor of the bus and then, rhythmically, clatter down again every time the wheels went over tar strips that bound together sections of that concrete highway. For almost 100 miles I rode with my warrior colleagues through the dead world and I smelled its tranquil country, contemplated oncoming disaster, and pledged fidelity to my team. Thud, thud. A year later I found myself, just as frightened, at the University of Virginia, where the second book my English class read was Robert Penn Warren's novel *All the King's Men*.

I had never heard of Warren or his book. I knew nothing of the deep South, mid-South, even the upper South, nor of change coming so rapidly automobiles altered it as you watched. With a car, a man previously stuck in fields could drive to Norfolk, the largest U.S. Naval port in the world, and take his life in his hands with all the city threw at him, bright sins, pleasures, bustle, living. Or he might drive inland, or South, and he'd find things much as they must have been when Yankee troops disembarked from gunboats off

North Carolina beaches, marching north to occupy my area early in the Civil War, and to stay there forever. This was an agrarian, nearly feudal society. Inch by inch it yielded to the pressure of mobile Americans. Now little villages along Route 460 have their McDonald's; their television dishes bring in the planet's other side; there's everything to buy in discount shops; public transport stops; there's not much feel of disconnection from the world; there's not much sense of their life as different. In 1960 that highway was a river that ferried people out of a darkness called the South.

Even thirty-five years later I can feel the first fifty pages of Warren's novel return me to that sleepy, uncharted place of otherness. I didn't know *All the King's Men* had begun as a verse play; some long part of the opening scene, anyway, was a poem. I wouldn't have known what a poem was. I didn't know anyone quite like Warren's people, Sugar Boy, with his .38 Special, driving the Cadillac and stuttering, Willie Stark, the Boss, riding shotgun, Lucy, Stark's wife, Tiny Duffy, Tom Stark, the boss's son, and Jack Burden, moody journalist-narrator watching the landscape inside and out. But Virginia was operated by Harry Byrd's political machine and somebody every day bitched about or furiously defended the Byrds. We all knew, even I knew, about *them*. Warren's people must have seemed like what I knew; they must have started me paying attention to what language does to you unawares. As I sat in Alderman Library reading my blue Modern Library edition, my feet tapped to the touch and sound and push of the words in the paragraphs, a kinesthetic pulse page after page. Here's what I mean:

> To get there you follow Highway 58, going northeast out of the city, and it is a good highway and new. Or was new, that day we went up it. You look up the highway and it is straight for miles, coming at you, with the black line down the center coming at and at you, black and slick and tarry-shining against the white of the slab, and he heat dazzles up from the white slab so that only the black line is clear, coming at you with the whine of the tires, and if you don't quit staring at that line and don't take a few deep breaths and slap yourself hard on the back of the neck you'll hypnotize yourself and you'll come to just at the moment when the right front wheel hooks over into the black dirt shoulder off the slab, and you'll try to jerk her back on but you can't because the slab is high like a curb, and maybe you'll try to reach to turn off the ignition just as she starts the dive. But you won't make it, of course. Then a nigger chopping cotton a mile away, he'll look up and see the little column of black smoke standing up above the vitriolic, arsenical green of the cotton

rows, and up against the violent, metallic, throbbing blue of the sky, and he'll say "Lawd God, hit's a-nudder one done hit!" And the next nigger down the next row, he'll say, "Lawd God," and the first nigger will giggle, and the hoe will lift again and the blade will flash in the sun like a heliograph. Then a few days later the boys from the Highway Department will mark the spot with a little metal square on a little metal rod stuck in the black dirt off the shoulder, the metal square painted white and on it in black a skull and crossbones. Later on love vine will climb up it, out of the weeds.

The language and images I knew then were all here: idiomatic speech, the hyperbole of *Hot Rod Magazine,* the hard-boiled journalist's irony, lingoes Warren easily catches, the feel of inevitable doom, a weight of vivid life in that plain and relentless place that seems to have no beginning or end; it's a *now* that we float through on wheels. I doubt Warren was interested in anybody's particular story as he started writing, but he *was* interested in the poetry of the moment and life that is always *there* so it speaks when you are ready to hear it. He begins with lyric repetition and pastoral scene that always starts the epic setting out on the journey of souls. His prose is nearly blank verse, language designed for momentum and meaning-weight, full of memorable images. For example, again from Warren's opening passages of *All the King's Men:*

> this is the country where the age of the internal combustion engine has come into its own. Where every boy is Barney Oldfield, and the girls wear organdy and batiste and eyelet embroidery and no panties on account of the climate and have smooth little faces to break your heart and when the wind of the car's speed lifts up their hair at the temples you see the sweet little beads of perspiration nestling there, and they sit low in the seat with their little spines crooked and their bent knees high toward the dashboard and not too close together for the cool, if you could call it that, from the hood ventilator. Where the smell of gasoline and burning brake bands and red-eye is sweeter than myrrh. Where the eight-cylinder jobs come roaring round the curves in the red hills and scatter the gravel like spray, and when they ever get down in the flat country and hit the new slab, God have mercy on the mariner.

I feel, oh boy how I feel, the irony of pity for the mariner, an allusion to Coleridge, but at the time I probably wondered what a seaman was doing on that road. Now what strikes me is abundance, things, not just people and places, that have passed out of our knowing in only thirty-five years. Warren needs to be annotated for contemporary readers to see what he sees: rough road, not smooth interstate, an automobile that cost more than small farms, arrogant power hauling Louisiana's head of state, a machine that sucks down leaded gas for a quarter a gallon, smelly, rank breaths, no air conditioner to cool or keep the countryside out, 80 pitiful horses that throb for the audacious cruising speed of 40 m.p.h.; and because farm air rushes over the riders, bully hot, they are glad to be hair-whipped, blown. When they roll through spaces unpeopled, Jack Burden sounds the fecundity and oppressiveness of it all—boys dreaming of stock car racers, girls secretly, erotically naked under prissy clothes, that little ship of fools passing through the valley of death marked by those tiny squares, seeking at the end of the slab of highway, the small town that is the southern community, "the sad, valentine lace of gingerbread work around the eaves of the veranda, and tin roofs, and where the leaves on the trees in the yards hung straight down in the heat, and above the mannerly whisper of your eighty-horse-power valve-in-head (or whatever it is) drifting at forty, you hear the July flies grinding away in the verdure."

Even to an unliterate dreamer like me the myth and ooze of southern literature rode up: heat, languid landscape, incipient sex even in the children, the struggle to flee destiny, press of thanatos that is destiny, all of us rolling—you can hear the muffler rumble—toward a pastoral and innocent (as a surprised cottonmouth) community where families go about their business. The density and cumulative lyrical prodding of this language awakened in me a historical mind, an awareness of people's life-marks on the visible, or maybe the entanglement of human living in natural force that seems so hidden, until it isn't. Then, I didn't know what poetry was. I started to find out, in 1974, when I was teaching at a small college in Missouri. The librarian gave me a discarded book, Warren's *Selected Poems New and Old, 1923–1966*. Everything changed. Warren's poems shocked me. Life's struggle inside the violent beauty of his saying.

NOT TO BE TRUSTED

Delight is not to be trusted.
It will betray you.
Delight will undo the work of your hand
In a secret way. You

Cannot trust delight.
As I have told you,

It undoes the ambition of the young and
The wisdom of the old. You

Are not exempt. Though it yet
Has never undone you,
Look! In that bush, with wolf-fang white, delight
Humps now for someone: *You.*

Southerners know Warren's puritan foreboding, pulpit tension, the push of biology and contingency. In his poem it is symbolic, or allegorical; in his prose it was mythic. From him, I learned how dullness in scene masks deep contention. Route 460 may be just a road for BMW Sunday drives, life there now flatly dead as it was omnipresent and hostile to our elders, who got away to jobs and suburbs, who would not again take up backbreaking farm life. But the fingerprint of that south was there in rhythmic cadence and image; Warren showed it to me. His words had the feel of rapacious change, the brutality of being other, the struggle with endless pasts still permanent as cow pies, that singing of the exile in his own land.

This language was not dialect and drawl, but dialogic enactment of consciousness, the act of citizenship. Warren works with pulse and ebb, momentum and sweep of phrase, suspensions, layers, strings, all loosed like epic invocations. His diction is mixed, plain enough for stoop understanding, only tucked inside a chord-striking formality, sometimes elegiac and sometimes odic. You have to learn to speak Warren like a foreign tongue, though it is the language you breathe; he surprises. I could hear it. I didn't know it was poetry, or did what poetry was supposed to do. Poetry was in books written by the dead. He woke an auditory imagination in me, an appetite for images, teaching me life is not the subject of poems—it is the essence of poems, the blood Emerson said spurted in Thoreau's sentences. *All the King's Men,* my first encounter with southern poetry, gave me permission to become what I already was. Warren helped me to know how to think and to see, but mostly to speak.

Thirteen years passed before I read his poems. I read the prose my school taught, predictable names—Faulkner, Conrad, Joyce, Dickens, O'Connor. I liked William Styron, who grew up in my home area of Tidewater, Virginia. So we had writers, too! My place was the village of Churchland, then in Norfolk County. The county, in the early 1960s, disbanded to avoid desegregation, was annexed part into the new city of Chesapeake, part into old Suffolk. We were called "Truckers," which my children find amusing;

shipbuilding, commercial fishing, and truck farming were local industries. Farmers raised edible crops and *trucked* them to boats for markets up the Chesapeake Bay. Churchland disappeared in the 1970s, blitzed by strip malls, subdivisions, and roads to ferry commuters fleeing desegregated schools and black cities. It was doomed by interstates and cheap cars. Lying only thirty-five miles from Newport News, taking Route 17 you passed over three salt rivers, through tobacco and soybean acres to reach that buzz of the city that built aircraft carriers and submarines and great ocean liners. Newport News ran into Warwick and Hampton and Phoebus and Poquoson and fringe villages. They had been distinct places. Borders existed on colored maps, on street signs, and in the fistfights of loyalists. William Styron and Dave Smith came from that new South.

Louis Rubin called Styron the last "southern" novelist because he wrote in the manner of Faulkner and Joyce. He exposed failure in people he loved. When I was on active duty in the U.S. Air Force, the book editor of that local paper told me I could not review Styron's play *In the Clap Shack* because Styron was, simply, not to be reviewed, not after his second novel had said such ugly, unfair things about locals. In his first novel, *Lie Down in Darkness,* his language is the South's; his people are those hurt by and hurting the South of postcard fiction. I grew up on the edge of Styron's World War II Cape Cods and piney yards for yeomen and merchants, starched kids, the sham of dreamy goodness masking lives losing focus. Styron was our exiled poet, driven out for telling how the pastoral dream was as hopeless as the Navy's dead fleet on the James River. Who belonged to what? Poems pulled off our scabs, was the way Warren put it. Styron is special to me, heroic, and a writer who went to elementary school with my now dead eye-doctor. Riding the train to Styron's place in *Lie Down in Darkness,* his narrator told me what I knew of character inside me, character in my place:

> Stirring, the novelty salesman looks drowsily out of the window and grunts, "Where are we?" and you murmur, "Not far from Port Warwick, I hope," and as he turns on his side to sleep some more you finger your copy of the *Times-Dispatch* which the newsboy sold you an hour ago, and which you haven't read and won't read because maybe you have things on your mind; and instead you look out once more at the late summer landscape and the low, sorrowful beauty of tideland streams winding through marshes full of small, darting, frightened noises and glistening and dead silent at noon, except for a whistle, far off, and a distant rumble on the rails. And most likely,

as the train streaks past the little log-road stations with names like Apex and Jewel, a couple of Negroes are working way out in the woods sawing timber, and they hear the whistle of your train and one of them stands erect from his end of the saw, wiping away the beads of sweat gathered on his brow like tiny blisters, and says "man, dat choo-choo's goin' to Richmond," and the other says, "Naw, she goin' to Po't Wa'ick," and the other says happily, "Hoo-ee, dat's a poontang town, sho enough," and they laugh together as the saw resumes its hot, metallic rip and the sun burns down in the swarming, resonant silence.

The elegiac, incremental push and drag dance of sentences here memorializes that permanent, near-untouchable place Warren awakened me to. Styron showed me it was neither ideal nor unified, only what I belonged to. And what the black voices of truth's witness belonged to. *Lie Down in Darkness* travels the same ground where I lived a decade later, and took a bus ride in to play ball. Like Warren's, this rhythmic, mythic journey through death's region takes me home to that unknown we keep having to define. Styron's language is a poetry of uncertainty, change, violence, all in the wail of that train. His tableau is pastoral; his poetry is elegiac. But in 1963, reading Styron for my class at the University of Virginia, I would not have known this. If I had, I'd have avoided it for being poetry with its hidden, edgy messages.

◦ ◦ ◦

During the summer of 1965, following graduation from college, I tended bar at Virginia Beach. I'd had a failed marriage. My father was dead, my mother gone somewhere, my friends burrowed into romance or law school or just distance. Once I woke up next to a woman from Michigan whose name I didn't know, whose hand-replacing metal hook rubbed my neck. That day I quit, went home to my grandmother's house, then sold boys' underwear for Sears. I drove an old Plymouth whose back seat I slowly filled with beer cans. Vietnam was coming. I'd applied for Air Force Officer Training School. The fervor for Kennedy's Camelot was gone now and I knew myself entirely adrift.

My grandmother was an orphan. She had not finished high school. I don't believe she ever read a complete book of any kind. For some reason she brought home with her groceries an issue of the *Atlantic Monthly* which carried James Dickey's "May Day Sermon to the Women of Gilmer County, Georgia, by a Woman Preacher Leaving the Baptist Church." Was it a poem?

A folk tale? A short story in lines? I read it, puzzled. I could not say what it was or meant, but I felt power, a life I'd lived and seen around me and voices I could hear any day if I walked back into the Churchland Baptist Church where years earlier, and often, I'd invited God into my soul. (He apparently had enough souls and left mine unclaimed.)

> Each year at this time I shall be telling you of the Lord
> —Fog, gamecock, snake and neighbor—giving men all the help they need
> To drag their daughters into barns. Children, I shall be showing you
> The fox hide stretched on the door   like a flying squirrel   fly
> Open   to show you the dark where the one pole of light is paid out
> In spring by the loft, and in it the croker sacks sprawling and shuttling
> Themselves into place as it comes   comes   through spiders dead
> Drunk on their threads   the hogs' fat bristling   the milk
> Snake in the rafters unbending through gnats to touch the last place
> Alive on the sun with his tongue   I shall be flickering from my mouth
> Oil   grease cans   lard cans   nubbins   cobs   night
> Coming   floating each May with night coming I cannot help
> Telling you how he hauls her to the centerpole   how the tractor moves
> Over as he sets his feet and hauls   hauls   ravels her arms and hair
> In stump chains: Telling: telling of Jehovah come and gone

I didn't burst from my chair. I didn't shout. But I felt the surge of recognition, even a release of enigmatic energy, its incantatory language swelling me. I knew the gospels behind the poem's advice, knew its sermon form, the thumping catalog of nouns and verbs that would not explain this brutal genesis but would leave it vibrating before me. Still, I didn't acknowledge this or any poem's claim on me. I became a high school teacher, a football coach, afraid of poetry. Two years later, in 1967, I went to graduate school and was given a copy of Dickey's *Poems, 1957–1967.* I read it thoroughly, annotated it in different colors, and for years would look at its language every day. Living in St. Louis, my wife and I went to poetry readings at Washington University. Donald Finkel and James Merrill seemed like poets, demeanors learned, ironic, and measured. I did not know how to hear that music. They put me to sleep. Then I saw Dickey read. He was cheered by the crowd from the first word. He clowned, he cooed, he entertained, he probed. I listened. It might have been a tent revival. Dickey presented himself as a regular guy, an athlete, a joker, cool and perceptive, yet he made words ring and dance. It seemed to me everything he said fit me. He spoke of personal experiences

I would have hidden. He celebrated himself as, I would later understand, Whitman had done. There was a great joy in his poems; he reveled in sex, death, human excess, the hunger to transform oneself, the driving will to be—just be—openly and eagerly. I was mesmerized. If poetry had this force, then I wanted it.

I also very much wanted to write like Dickey. Perhaps I wanted to be him. Later, when I went into active duty in the Air Force I knew he had done that, too, and twice. I wrote a master's thesis on *Poems, 1957–1967,* a document so muddled that I have not reread it in more than thirty years. I wrote poems, published in small magazines, imitating Dickey, tossing off his adjectival phrase, blending violence and epiphany too easily, or I bellowed lines in the huckster tone of his "Power and Light," which begins "I may even be / A man, I tell my wife . . . " I published a book with so much bad Dickey in it, I tried to buy all the copies. I should say bad Dave Smith trying to sound like good Dickey. His poems taught me how to compose a tale, where to start and end, what to emphasize for development of the sub-narrations. He showed how a poem rises to symbol out of plain experience, how appetite for big vision is worthy, how the need to change form after you succeed is immaculate. From Dickey I learned the poet wants to make "statements" which are only sometimes didactic lines. I glimpsed what I would learn harder from Warren, that honesty demanded by the language and image is how you tell the real poem from poetic contraptions.

I learned, too, that I had to wean myself from his powerful influence because I did not want to sound like inferior Dickey; moreover, I didn't see things as he did. For my thesis, I had occasion to contact him and he proved a solicitous correspondent. In later years he asked me to his house, praised, encouraged, befriended me. I kept distant, fearing this Leviathan might swallow me in a blink. When, as his guest, I read poems at the University of South Carolina, he introduced me, drunkenly praising me in butchered sentences. Later he gave me the hand-scrawled page, each sentence exactly as he had butchered it aloud. He made other comments, uglier, I wouldn't hear until after his death.

I wrote about his work, praised a capacious, original imagination that was as southern, if also patrician by birth, as pigs' feet. He was a force not bound by aesthetic shibboleths. He did not share the naturalistic view that makes a man tremble to see how little a thing he is, but instead embraced contingency and mystic connections. He adored raw Nature and gladly took an imagined place in it. He wanted to believe he was fully what he and it were made for. He was unburdened by guilt, history, sordid family sagas. Dickey's poems overleap tight-lipped verse and its pieties. His journeys by the dark wood road compose a romance of self-reliance as formidable at its best as Melville's, one shaped by Whitman's buoyancy. There have been few American poets whose life and art so outrageously boiled. His muscular poetry believed life feels good most of the time and most of the time we want more of it. His courage was a will to survive and sing, a warrior's valor, with Whitmanic delicacy, confidently promising life is worth everything. Parables of the man who will not be denied his chance, his poems brawl and sprawl and spout, untidy, undomesticated. A poet immersed and uncensored, experience and determinism both yearning to come out into glory, he links the southerner to Emerson and thus is, quirkily, sometimes the least southern of poets. A comedic genius binds him to folk mythology and tall tales all the way to Mark Twain. He knew what he was up to, cultivating an identity southerners had naturally and meant to escape: crude, vulgar, oafish, a redneck Thomas Wolfe all over again. But, literary as they come, Dickey had been Donald Davidson's student at Vanderbilt; he, like Warren, would speak from a regionalist ground. He became the bridge from the Fugitives to what might come afterward.

Maybe Dickey's most durable gift was unswerving determination to find ways words could be remade, revived. His early and middle poems speak a language as angular as dialect, and initially as hard to grasp. His middle and best work piled up haunting phrases in tight stanzas. When he reconfigured his style, one critic wrote that Dickey had found a meter, perfected it, and dropped it, lapsing into failure. His so-called anapestic trimeter was made more by eye than ear. His desire for a cool, loose style in his late poetry betrayed him to theatrical narration and then translation of European surrealists, a hermetic speech for undecodable chaos of the interior. Yet even in *The Eagle's Mile,* his last book, poems were acts of ambition, intuitive, buoyant, more boyish than manly, more infectious than rebellious, more determined than anxious. He meant to boost courage, to shade fears. Dickey spoke to a southern code his readers understood between the words, in the rhythms. Not too much courage, honor, high sentiment, and not too much corn pone either, but some, enough, and no apology for bared appetites, and last a preacherly love of final things. He practiced southern identity rituals and called out "I may be a man," even as he cringed in the basement, drinking. Dickey was malicious, selfish, terrified, unscrupulous, manipulative. So what, if words made hope? They did in "At Darien Bridge" from *Helmets:*

> I stand and look out over grasses
> At the bridge they built, long abandoned,
>
> Breaking down into water at last,
> And long, like them, for freedom
>
> Or death, or to believe again
> That they worked on the ocean to give it
>
> The unchanging, hopeless look
> Out of which all miracles leap.

Robert Penn Warren, William Styron, and James Dickey all had a gift that so quickens southern writing one almost forgets to acknowledge it. They knew how to tell a story. They touched people with symbol, intensity, grace, innovation, plain interest. Charles Wright, now the senior southern poet, has often said he cannot tell a story and so stands outside the tradition. His collection *The Other Side of the River* belies his disclaimer. Telling the tale is not definitively southern; how it's told may be. Wright's refusal of "narrative" may simply be a self-protective comfort zone, but it may, also, be one of the uses of manners, usually taken as a show of respect for individuals. Wright has always resisted, at least openly, the personal revelations contemporary poems practice. His art is grounded in the European views of Ezra Pound and T. S. Eliot. But manners, a code of behavior, evolve when people want not to be approached too openly. Life in defeat—and, suppressed, the southerner's history—proves complicated, contingent, its textures rough. Manners protect against slips, mistakes. Ritual behavior becomes a context, a kind of story within which other stories take place. Charles Wright, a mystic, keeps his eye on the largest story that subsumes all the manners, rituals, behaviors, rhythms, increments of being, but his process is to peel things apart rather than pile them up. As lyric as that may be, even it is a story of depth and layered experience, of known multiplicity and process, of truth that ends not in results but awareness. Wright, as mystic and lyric poet, has no end to his story, but that is not the same thing as having no story.

Warren and Dickey composed tales that were psychologically credible, regionally accurate, and symbolically resonant myths which permitted statements of meaning, comments about southern life, which no lyric could sustain. Both were, I think, determined to do for the southern story what Robert Lowell did with *Life Studies*. To tell the story of the self and its immediate kind with actual names and feeling meant rejecting even the manners a poem's form consented to. These poets give permission to the next poets to examine the events of their personal lives, to foreground having lived in particular time and place and fact that result in formed identity. Allen Tate was a southern poet viscerally tuned to Anglican verse; he offered no new alternative. But Tate knew, and said, the South would have to create a literary culture where none existed. The Fugitives answered that call. Warren, twice winner of the Pulitzer Prize in poetry, and Dickey, winner of the National Book Award in poetry, were the makers. In their wake have come southern poets who extend the line with innovative form and life stories. A. R. Ammons, Donald Justice, Yusef Komunyakaa have all won Pulitzer prizes. Fred Chappell won the Bollingen Prize. Charles Wright has won Pulitzer, National Book Award, National Book Critics' Circle prizes, everything offered except the Nobel. All writing about the South.

The southern poet now is female, black, Hispanic, Vietnamese, and Chinese. Whatever the poet's heritage, the South, as speech and behavior and consciousness, informs the poetry, shadowed by the line that prepared their way, always telling the tale of individual life within community. Dickey and Warren and Wright seemed to me, as I grew aware I belonged to a line, formidable and inescapable, their figures not to be matched. When I first met Dickey I was twenty-four. When I met Warren I was forty-two. Now, at sixty, I am amazed young poets in the South know my books but may not know the names or books of predecessors whose struggles to tell their story prefigure today's tale. These young poets have not yet ceased to think of themselves as regional; they yet understand what William Carlos Williams meant when he advised poets to use the "local." But if the southern poet should become as extinct as a passenger pigeon, identified by no place, simply a voice broadcasting in "received standard" whatever world we all happen to live in, he, and we, will have come to what Tate feared, the death of the provincial, which is to say of the individual. The deeds and the shadows of the dead will not then intervene for good or ill, who were both bulwark and resource. They argued for the destiny they knew, and wanted, as each poet does in art's obligation. This obligation embraces and is embraced by other communities, or it is only lullaby and self-deception. When a National Book

Award judge told me her vote must be cast for "her people," she told the smallest story on the tongue of the parochial spirit, its weakness the cheap courage of membership. "What is a man but his passion?" Robert Penn Warren asks, and what is a culture but passion braided, a story of the largest pattern, the fullest meaning we can imagine? Warren tells us how poetry claims importance. Ending *Audubon: A Vision,* he writes that a poet may, even in the grapple of romantic yearning and natural process, tell a local story that matters, the story all children ask of their mothers, the good story of where we come from and go to:

TELL ME A STORY

[A]

Long ago, in Kentucky, I, a boy, stood
By a dirt road, in first dark, and heard

The great geese hoot northward.
I could not see them, there being no moon
And the stars sparse. I heard them.

I did not know what was happening in my heart.

It was the season before the elderberry blooms,
Therefore they were going north.

The sound was passing northward.

[B]

Tell me a story.

In this century, and moment, of mania,
Tell me a story.

Make it a story of great distances, and starlight.

The name of the story will be Time,
But you must not pronounce its name.

Tell me a story of deep delight.

Edgar Allan Poe
and the Nightmare Ode

When I left home for college at the University of Virginia, I must have imagined history was something confined to textbooks and roadside commemorative markers, which occur in Virginia nearly as often as azaleas and daffodils. Among the splendid benefits of college, nothing outweighs being awakened to the presence of the past as it has shaped and changed one's life. In 1963, that terrible year of President John F. Kennedy's assassination, I lived in a cottage next to James Southall Wilson, founder of the *Virginia Quarterly Review* and a Poe scholar. He was also husband to the formidable granddaughter of President Tyler, a woman who outweighed and out-harrumphed everyone whom she encountered. Wilson seemed to me, and I think he was, in accent, in courtesy, in a passionate and delicate rose gardening, and in languorous tales about Poe, an embodiment of the southern gentleman, the type of man our parents, preachers, and teachers invoked freely for moral edification. Professor Wilson also stood in for the world of southern refinement, principle, and neoclassical culture ubiquitously proclaimed as our due heritage, a world, alas, more lost than present. He was scarcely like the men in my family, for whom being a southerner meant only raising the Stars and Bars with a liquid rendition of Dixie.

Some among us believe we find ourselves in men whom history isolates for our models. Once, dawdling by the serpentine wall which Mr. Jefferson, as we were taught to call the university's founder, had built with slave labor, I exchanged pleasantries with a man who had written books I read in my classes, a man named Faulkner. Almost daily I walked to class by the brick pavilion where Edgar Allan Poe had lived in 1826. Poe was a greater southern presence to me than William Faulkner, for I had read Poe's stories and poems as far back as memory went. My schoolteachers had been aggressive in noting that Poe was a Virginian like all of us, not merely a name in a textbook. Through Poe and Faulkner I learned I was not wholly outside a history fabricated only by textbooks. I was of it and of them.

I don't think I much considered what I was until my first-year English class read Robert Penn Warren's *All the King's Men,* a book intensely aware of "southernness." I seem to remember *where* I read almost every page. I felt I was reading about family, not so much in the characters as in tone, pressure, intensity, a kind of inevitability. Mine was the sort of family made mobile and almost prosperous during the Second World War. I spent summers with my grandparents, often taking Sunday rides in a green Hudson automobile, meandering through the woody burgs of Yorktown and Williamsburg. These were places people lived in, not the toy villages they are now. I played on Virginia's much bloodied battlefields, but I did not trouble myself to know exactly whose blood was spilled or why.

Even as I began to see myself connected to others in the southern story, I slowly became aware I also stood outside the official Virginia history, the class model of whom we were supposed to be, for I belonged to no patrician family, had attended no prep school, hardly knew what an Episcopalian was, let alone a Catholic, and could point to no cultural ancestry which I possessed or whose loss, with family ground, shadowed me. I grew up in a subdivision whose backyards debouched (a word I got from Allen Tate) onto farms that had always been there, farms tended some by tractors, some by black laborers with names like "Snuff" and "Peanut." They worked for the parents of my adolescent friends. They seemed to think my name was "Mistuh." Those farms are gone. Those who called white people "Mistuh" are gone. Not gone with the wind but with the developers who bulldozed eighteenth- and nineteenth-century properties and village squares and schools, who made shopping centers, who made our Baptist Church an anachronism like Philip Larkin's church in "Church Going." Change in the South, welcome where it liberates, is the relentless bastard of greed, though it may bring us new roads, toothache relief, and fresh writers. Its peculiar violence, characteristic of a place in metamorphosis, leaves the southerner orphaned, intensely aware of *being there* and simultaneously *not being there.*

That awareness precisely characterizes Poe's writing, as actively in his poetry as in his fiction. Poe's university room, in 1963, was marked by a plaque that made it officially historic, yet a student lived in the room. I don't believe

I ever saw its interior but I had seen others and it was not different, only a room in which a young scholar lived. If I had to think of long dead and here memorialized Poe, despite wiser teachers, as a disembodied creator of tales rather than a man, I could in those days also think of him as alive behind that door, a student with a university life not radically unlike my own. In this way, too, I was in and out of southern history. It did not occur to me that Poe might have felt the same although he had arrived only one year after the university opened for business. Poe was in the business of understanding a relationship with the imminent past.

Today, the memorializers at the University have erected a barrier to this awareness. An impervious Plexiglas door seals his room, into which the monied visitor, always a coveted pigeon, may gaze as if into Poe's very soul. What the visitor will see is historically correct: a wooden bed, a small desk, a few chairs, a rug, and a scatter of living's accouterments. Oddly, a raven (almost certainly *plastic*) is perched on a branch as naturally as if it were a poster of the Beatles, or whatever group the young now adore. No stereos, no rack of books and tapes, no knickknacks, no letters from home, no photographs of mom and pop and favorite girl. The room's black and white prospect is sterile and chilling. They have buried Poe in plain view to a greater extent than Poe himself managed. University administrators everywhere seem to believe history is only a containable pollutant, but one is shocked nevertheless when a university so boastfully dedicated to the human and individual truth reveals its lack of comprehension. Undefiled, tourists come and stand and look for Poe as if he were Elvis or Madonna. Probably some have read Poe; others have seen the horror movies. Reflected in the glass, their ghostly faces stare back as they, like exiles, strain to see in to Poe, the bard of our nightmare of dispossession.

To be banished from the garden is western civilization's most painful sanction. It is recorded in the Genesis case of *Adam and Eve* v. *God*. It is recorded in a long literary tradition of gardens and exiles. The intellectual historian of the South, Lewis P. Simpson, has articulated what the garden image means in *The Dispossessed Garden*. He calls it a "pastoral plantation" and defines it as "a secure world redeemed from the ravages of history, a place of pastoral independence and pastoral permanence" and "a homeland of the life of the mind." Simpson believes there was little modernist alienation in the antebellum southern mind which, as he says, "was cut off from what affected the general stream of literary culture because of the involvement of the Southern man of letters in the politics of slavery. He could not participate in the opposition to society which distinguishes the function of the man of letters in Europe, and in New England, where it marks in important ways the writings of Emerson, Thoreau, and Hawthorne."

The antebellum mind viewed the Jeffersonian garden as encompassing, perhaps engendering, a civilization whose classical and Christian values link individuals to a supernatural continuity, a community of souls. Yet the garden was to be lost to the encroachments of the modern world, to commercialized values, a dispossession and outage dramatized by civil war and so intensely felt it became the signature of southernness. The southern literary voice is that of an outcast, an orphan, an outsider cut off from the communal support and, importantly, that communal definition which he once had, as an individual if not as a writer, and which henceforth, if he has it at all, is carried like a threatening headache. Or a pastoral memory. Or myth. James Joyce causes Stephen Daedalus to declaim, on Irish soil, this modern, nationalist pathology: "History is the nightmare from which I cannot awake." *Alienation,* of course. From one end of the South to the other, that is precisely the condition expressed and indicted by the literary voices.

The nightmare of half-being, half-knowing is that of *not* being and *not* knowing: the state of dispossession. Until the twentieth century's somewhat over-grandly called *Southern* Renascence, this regional literature occupies only the garden of half-being and half-knowing, a netherland of knightly gentlemen, asexual ladies, and a contract heaven. The divorce from reality experienced by protagonists is a denial of history, an orphaning. When the denial's lie festers sufficiently to invade the body of society, sickness requires treatment; writers begin to probe the actual, becoming aware and, more importantly, making a readership aware that historical conditions of ignorance, poverty, defeat, pain, brutality, hopelessness, self-delusion, and isolation from community have configured the South as different from that heritage which is an American ideal of positive change and credible hope.

That idea empowered Jefferson to raise a university in the garden, to foster an enlightenment whose headache was slavery. The black man was, as Simpson persuasively argues, "the gardener in the garden," and therefore as much founder as Jefferson himself. But if it was the founding hand, the slave's hand was inevitably the absent hand that left the ideal garden to seed and riot. And who more than a slave was the orphan dispossessed of his site of redemption? Who more than an orphan could chronicle the simultaneously personal and cultural nightmare of outage?

The nineteenth century offered this role to England's Charles Dickens, for whom the tale of the orphan stands as emblem of his age. The same experience went to his American peer, Edgar Allan Poe, born barely three years earlier. Poe, it may be said, was also a gardener, transplanter of the English garden of verse into the virgin American soil. From the first poems he published at age eighteen to his last, and in his remarks on form, Poe coveted an invariable, mechanistic prosody which might with force yield up a predictable life, stable and evident, historical, perhaps even compensation for what his own life lacked. His essay "The Philosophy of Composition" argues a dogmatic methodology he says led him to improvisation (if this be contradiction, I call on Whitman and Emerson for sufferance) and to an impression of platonic beauty which "The Raven" seems to many to have achieved. Even T. S. Eliot, no admirer, conceded Poe sometimes made the true magic of poetry. But Poe's rational blueprint of process tells us only what he thought *about* the poem; it does not tell us much of what he used to *think* the poem, or why.

"The Raven," unequivocally the most famous of Poe's small body of poems, must stand among the most famous *bad* poems. Americans are fond of saying they do not read and do not care for poetry. It may be so. Yet they commonly recognize Poe's bird as the subject of a poem by a weird guy who drank himself to death. Written and published in 1845, in print steadily for nearly a century and a half, the stanzas of "The Raven" are flashcards of sound instantly familiar to us all. We may not know Whitman, Dickinson, Frost, or Eliot. But we do know Poe. We know "The Raven." Baltimore's professional football team is named for it.

A poem that might have been designed by Benjamin Franklin, "The Raven" purports to be explained by Poe's "Philosophy of Composition." Poe wrote his essay for crowds smitten by his bird. Interestingly, he does not justify poetry with morality, as Emerson and Whitman would have done. He pretends to expose the poet's trade. Some recent criticism has seen "The Raven" as a parody of Romantic poems of personal discovery. Perhaps. What Poe leaves unsaid peels, layer by layer, toward two questions answerable only by speculation. The first asks why "The Raven" has for fifteen generations commanded the imaginations of people who have often enough known it to be howlingly bad in its excesses, a poem, as someone said, for those who do not like poetry. The second question, less obvious, perhaps one which has not occurred to the majority of readers, asks if Poe is a southern writer. They are related questions.

That "The Raven" is a bad poem is and will remain unacceptable to many readers. Poe people are not swayed much by rational argument. Were they, the plot alone would convict Poe. A man sits late in a storm; he laments a lost lady love; a bird not ordinarily abroad at night, and especially not in severe weather, seeks entrance to the human dwelling; admitted, the bird betrays no fright, no panic, no trauma at all, its attitude entirely focused on its host, as if it had arrived either by invitation or some ritual of nature's clock; a guest in any event; the bird then enters into a ventriloquial dialectic with the host and is domesticated to become an inner voice, the voice of the *innerground* as opposed to *underground*, a word with special meaning to the American spirit with its reasons to run, to hide. The poem's action then ceases.

Poe surely knew this one-man back lot production for the smoker it was. His embrace of gothic machinery includes a terrified, obsessed man, an inhospitable, allegorical midnight in December, a "gifted" animal, extreme emotional states, heavy breathing of both cadence and melodramatic signifiers (*grim, gaunt*), the presence of inexplicables (perfume, Pallas, bird), all to portray a psychic battle in the consciousness. What Poe assembles is a version of saloon theater for the mind's ear. But his poem's form emerges from the unbuckled ways of the ode, the loosened metrics of which Poe knew in the prominent work of Keats, Shelley, Coleridge, and Wordsworth, transatlantic inscribers of the pastoral garden. Poe made his living, such as that was, as a magazinist, or journal editor, and his slush pile of submissions would have been full of imitators of the English poets. Odes attracted people because, as Gilbert Highet has said, they "soar and dive and veer as the wind catches their wing." And because readers look to them for public pronouncement of truths, which they neither want nor expect to see contradicted. The capacity for passion, personal experience, ambitious public utterance, and a celebrating finish defines the ode. Boosterism, self-infatuation, and lyceum podium performances of nineteenth-century America made Poe and the ode a natural match.

Poe was drawn to what was left of the Pindaric form of the ode with its systemically recurrent parts. The classical ode, both Horatian and Pindaric, implies fixity and continuity. The form manifests noble purpose, dignity of subject and demeanor; it is ordinarily a public address with an encoded civics lesson. The same explosions of social change which scattered emigrating people over the globe loosened the metrical grasp of this lyric form until it has become, in American practice anyway, not readily different from an elegy. Indeed, as comedians know, ode is a word suspect to both poet and reader, a synonym for what Ezra Pound meant by "emotional slither." Once, perhaps, the ode celebrated and the elegy grieved. Both have become, in some measure due to Poe, less specialized in use. It is possible to view most of today's lyric poems as odes.

Poe was attracted to the ode because of its classical rigor but also because it represented a daring shift, begun by the English Romantic poets, which gave the form a singularly interior expression. Paul H. Fry in *The Poet's Calling in the English Ode* points out that Allen Tate's "Ode to the Confederate Dead," in which Tate stands at the cemetery gate but cannot enter, cannot be among that historical order there, especially permits the poet to dramatize a moment of *being there* and *not being there,* an awareness of visionary discontinuity prerequisite to pastoral. With "abysmal frustration," Fry says, the ode writer at that gate discovers there is "no threshold at all between the self and what is unknown, or other"; the ode of all forms "most boldly and openly tests the possibility of calling in the Spirit." The intent of the ode is to marry the poet's voice with the God-voice in order to manifest reality—life, death, afterlife, whatever. The ode-voice celebrates all that it summons because, whatever its registers of discourse may be, it praises a "belonging-to" quality.

Poe's strategies, largely braided tropes of reiteration and interrogation, are distantly related to the Pindaric triad movement, but also to the Horatian personal monody. I don't mean to follow Poe's descent from either, or to examine the micrometrical features of his poem. A single stanza shows the chains of repetition Poe takes from the ode. His famous first stanza, sixteen of ninety-six lines, clusters in a quintet plus a hemistich (bob):

> Once upon a midnight dreary, while I pondered, weak and weary,
> Over many a quaint and curious volume of forgotten lore—
> While I nodded, nearly napping, suddenly there came a tapping,
> As of some one gently rapping, rapping at my chamber door—
> "'Tis some visitor," I muttered, "tapping at my chamber door—
> Only this and nothing more."

He called the meter "octameter acatalectic," with alternation of "heptameter catalectic" in line five and "tetrameter catalectic" in the bobbed sixth line. In duple feet of tetrameter, trochaic (louder) or iambic (softer), lines have norms of sixteen, fifteen, or seven syllables. Full lines are broken by a mid-caesura; halves of each line link internally by rhyme exact or slant. The lyric half-line surges against the longer rhythm of the full line. The full line assumes a prose rhythm in a unitary sprawl and self-containment. The sound of each stanza is like a contained body of water into which a weight is dropped, causing a wave excitement that floods outward. When the wave reaches and rebounds from resistance, its energy surges dash at each other. Narrative events create new waves. The result is psychic chaos, an unstable pace stumbling, almost, upon itself, imitating panic, queasiness, and fear that falls to a rhythmic trance which Poe felt exposed the reader to, and dispossessed him of, tranquility. He relies on the catalectic, or broken pattern, a missing syllable that "bumps" our reading. The poetry lies in his ballad half-line, in comfortable lyric expectations, mnemonic power, and the narrative momentum to tell a plotless story, one entirely interior and psychological. He telescopes that line into the ode's regularity to record a personal complaint trimmed of the form's meditation over imponderables such as art, beauty, life, and death. The subject of his dark ode would be lost love, ultimate dispossession, furnished with classical allusions for eternal resonance.

Readers have always liked this bird of adaptations, clunky and jury-rigged, seeming almost as daring as Poe thought it, as it is, in the drama of the nightmare of lost belonging-to. "The Raven" reverberates not with the usual flight-to-vision celebration but with the thrill of despair, isolation, and the utter futility of lovely words. The nightmare vision made the poem an allegory of the self in darkest terror (or is it the *darkest* self?). That terror, Poe had reason to know, arrives when a man loses his woman. But his parable of loneliness nudges the reader beyond the problem of an absent lover, which is only exterior drama. Robert Lowell, in "Skunk Hour," pointed to the more crucial interior drama, echoing Milton: "I myself am hell; nobody's here." This condition of individual hell seems apt description of an orphan's self-awareness. It does not require a leap of imagination to read Poe's poem as the figure of the dispossessed garden, the eroded southern culture, in which Poe seeks to know what, in any real sense, belonging is. If the poem centers the bereaved lover, it emphasizes his plight as outsider. Poe finds himself alone in the time and the season of human intercourse at its lowest ebb, a time, indeed, when we remind ourselves that we had better mend our ways, or else—as Dickens's Scrooge learns so painfully.

A knock at his door should bring Poe a human visitor, if any, an emissary from the community. Yet there is only darkness. And then the Raven, the predator. And a predator who seems to know Poe is doomed to an absence of intercourse, a silence, to words which echo without effect. Poe understands this runic moment, and he declares that even the predator bird will abandon him, as life has done, as hope has now done. Now Poe's poem is nightmare, the individual isolation that horror movies have turned to ghoulish marches of the living dead. If Poe's bird seems deadly, incantatory rhythms which evoked the birdspell are the forbidding stanzas that clank forth and enchant us as if the feathered guest were enacting a chthonic ritual. The Raven, in fact, makes no move after it arrives. Its only threat is its natural blackness. It seems eerily content. Merely a bird, this is a creature familiar to odes like Keats's "Ode to a Nightingale" (1819) and Whitman's "Out of the Cradle Endlessly Rocking" (1859). Yet how different Poe's bird is from, say, the nightingale so sweetly caged. Poe's discursive form stands in the very breath of his creature, and he is safe to glimpse but not engage the threat. Having summoned the Raven, Poe cannot deny or repress it: the bird sits in the forever of that last stanza, a curse neither expiated nor escaped. It is, as the English poet Ted Hughes would make clear with his fabular *Crow,* a living nightmare.

I had better, at this point, say a nightmare of alienation. But alienation from what? The simple answer is Lenore, the woman who is always *there* and constantly *not there.* Here Poe perceived something useful about odic form. The ode, in celebration, is usually a public form. But we do not think of "The Raven" as either public or celebration, so private is its agon from start to finish. Again what is dramatized is what doesn't happen, the human visit: a moment of social cohesion. An opportunity for reunion with the community fails, but a visit occurs that shifts the abandoned speaker toward public experience. The erotic, aesthetic, social, and familial resonances Poe celebrates in missing Lenore may be read altogether as the essence of that community. It will be missing *eternally,* for Poe cannot lift his soul "from out that shadow that lies floating on the floor" and that in-escape is the nightmare of alienation.

Doubtless, for most readers, Lenore, whomever she might have been and may be in her *is-ness,* constitutes the drawing power of the poem. We have all loved and lost, felt our hearts break, felt ourselves abandoned. The testimony of balladic country-western music, ubiquitous in America, depends upon that. Yet few country western songs last in anyone's consciousness as "The Raven" has done. Poe's addition of a nearly voiceless but intimidating bird employs Gothic machinery to touch unresolved fears of what we project under the bed or behind the darkened door. Worse, Poe's bird has the power of knowledge—it knows *us*—and this makes the world a far more slippery place than we had thought. It exposes the inside otherwise hidden. That is a problem for Poe because any inside without connection to an outside (community) leaves merely emptiness, a desert. No self can supply love's support, community sustenance, or the hope we once drew from an outside system. Poe's terrible fable sticks with us because no matter what our intellects conceive, our hearts believe we are alien, each of us, and there is a god-bird that knows it, too.

But alienation from Lenore seems, finally, not the whole of Poe's trouble in "The Raven." The narrator, persona, speaker, surely Poe himself as every biography has suggested, is paralyzed, room-captured, divorced from books, ideas, perhaps even poetry, and in the last stanza from the goddess of wisdom, who has until this minute has sat like Virgil over Poe's bower. But not Pallas now; now the Raven. Why? Can being dumped by hard luck account for such despair? Poe has a modern's existential attitude. He has understood the relentless industrial rapacity which Dickens made into a character more draconian, destructive, and irresistible than any since Milton's Satan. Poe, like Dickens, had lived with that monster in Richmond, New York, and Baltimore. Some have argued that Poe pilfered his bird from Dickens. The fact is they shared the century's dispossessed life and the alienation of hard times.

Poe loved women who died, often violently, often diseased. His mother went first: he was two. His father, David Poe, had already abandoned the family. Poe became in life what he would always be in his writing, an orphan. He was raised in Richmond, Virginia, as the ward of Scottish businessman John Allan and his wife Frances, a sickly woman who would die while he was yet a moody boy. He had a crush on Jane Stanard, mother of a childhood friend, but at the age of thirty-one she went insane and died. Poe had suffered the deaths of three women he loved before escaping his teens. His foster father, Allan, remarried and had children by his second wife, who had little interest in Poe. While Poe might be raised more or less as the squire-son of a rising burgher, he was not Allan's blood and his days were numbered. He knew himself orphaned from every perspective.

Poe's letters show that he believed the Allans afforded him only marginal status as a family member, status he thought waned daily. Proud, intelligent, needy, trained to expect the rewards of class and position that Allan seemed now determined to deny him, Poe, at eighteen, went to the University of Virginia where he was undercapitalized and forced to suffer his inferior circumstance. No gentleman in fact, he was pushed outside the society there, and he left school. Returned to Richmond, he found there was nothing for him, no home, no family; he embarked on one of his secret journeys. Wandering, turning up, writing, editing, trying to establish a domestic community, then drifting off—this was the pattern for the rest of his life. In every relationship and circumstance he proved to be the outsider, the orphan.

No one feels the powerful attraction of *being there* and *not being there* more than the orphan. Poe, Melville, and Whitman dramatized it. Jay Gatsby knew it. Americans are all orphans, all, at one point, come-heres; all, the scheme said, equal in opportunity. The idea of a fresh start, a better way, a redemption that is a national possibility supports the very imagining of the "new world." Foster father Allan used his chance to make it, and would trumpet that, were he with us, possessing a Kiwanian spirit equal to Walt Whitman's. But with Poe the shimmer of hope in the morning sun seemed to turn leaden early on. It grew heavier all his life. Like Gatsby, he could not declare a belonging-to. Nor could he, unlike Gatsby, lie about the world. He could not take Whitman's abundant road. Every intercourse with the social world failed. Compelled to tell truth, there is nothing more obsessive in his tales than the urge to lay out what was inside all men. His truth, however, was nightmare.

If we read "The Raven," despite its absence of specific local details, as an "awareness" of the psychic life of an American in 1845, we see that Poe has conjured the nightmare of the individual cut off from history, abandoned by family, place, and community. He experiences personally what the South will experience regionally and the country will, down the long road of military belligerence, experience emotionally and mortally. Though he means to celebrate the lost Lenore, he most intensely celebrates union with community, identity with a place and a people which Poe simultaneously *has* and *has lost.* In 1845, he certainly spoke for many southern whites. Paradoxically, he also spoke for the slave paralyzed in his garden and also dispossessed. This is still the nightmare. Poe celebrates the imagination that suffers and knows simultaneously, ultimately the plight of an artist who stands in for everyman. This figure in the lost garden, knowing its lostness, without explanation, feels the change that is hopeless and continuous, a state of being that will find expression in America's favorite song, the ballad of the outlaw, the renegade, the cowboy in black, the rebel without a cause.

"The Raven" is the drama of the nightmare awakening in the American poetic consciousness where there is no history which is not dispossession, little reality to the American promise, and nothing of consequence to place trust in except the song, the ode of celebration. Poe knew that he stood, like Allen Tate, who called him cousin, at the gate to the answers. But he could not go beyond it. Like Tate, he sought to form a culture where none existed. He began with English poetic baggage, but too often it failed him. "The Raven," whatever failure it may be, succeeded as the croaking and anguished southern nightmare ode, a crisis of allegiance and alienation, and we have been, some of us, finding ourselves in it ever since Poe began hearing "Nevermore."

John Crowe Ransom's
Lyric of the Holy Grail

CAPTAIN CARPENTER

Captain Carpenter rose up in his prime
Put on his pistols and went riding out
But had got wellnigh nowhere at that time
Till he fell in with ladies in a rout.

It was a pretty lady and all her train
That played with him so sweetly but before
An hour she'd taken a sword with all her main
And twined him of his nose for evermore.

Captain Carpenter mounted up one day
And rode straightway into a stranger rogue
That looked unchristian but be that as may
The Captain did not wait upon prologue.

But drew upon him out of his great heart
The other swung against him with a club
And cracked his two legs at the shinny part
And let him roll and stick like any tub.

Captain Carpenter rode many a time
From male and female took he sundry harms
He met the wife of Satan crying, "I'm
The she-wolf bids you shall bear no more arms."

Their strokes and counters whistled in the wind
I wish he had delivered half his blows
But where she should have made off like a hind
The bitch bit off his arms at the elbows.

And Captain Carpenter parted with his ears
To a black devil that used him in this wise
O Jesus ere his threescore and ten years
Another had plucked out his sweet blue eyes.

Captain Carpenter got up on his roan
And sallied from the gate in hell's despite
I heard him asking in the grimmest tone
If an enemy yet there was to fight?

"To any adversary it is fame
If he risk to be wounded by my tongue
Or burnt in two beneath my red heart's flame
Such are the perils he is cast among.

"But if he can he has a pretty choice
From an anatomy with little to lose
Whether he cut my tongue and take my voice
Or whether it be my round red heart he choose."

It was the neatest knave that ever was seen
Stepping in perfume from his lady's bower
Who at this word put in his merry mien
And fell on Captain Carpenter like a tower.

I would not knock old fellows in the dust
But there lay Captain Carpenter on his back
His weapons were the old heart in his bust
And a blade shook between rotten teeth alack.

The rogue in scarlet and grey soon knew his mind
He wished to get his trophy and depart
With gentle apology and touch refined
He pierced him and produced the Captain's heart.

God's mercy rest on Captain Carpenter now
I thought him Sirs an honest gentleman
Citizen husband soldier and scholar enow
Let jangling kites eat of him if they can.

But God's deep curses follow after those
That shore him of his goodly nose and ears
His legs and strong arms at the two elbows
And eyes that had not watered seventy years.

The curse of hell upon the sleek upstart
That got the Captain finally on his back
And took the red vitals of his heart
And made the kites to whet their beaks clack clack.

In 1977 I received a call from a courtly gentleman at Kenyon College who invited me to read my poetry there. I was quick to accept. Making arrangements, he inquired if there was not something he might do in advance to make my visit pleasant. Surprised because such a solicitous kindness was most unusual, I answered with a lame joke that he might produce Professor Ransom for dinner. A silence followed, then the man gravely replied that Ransom had died in 1974. It was instantly clear the gentleman felt both Ransom's presence and his loss so palpably that he could assume I hadn't known of the death, especially as he knew I was a poet many generations younger than Ransom, perhaps so much younger that I did not know the fate of the poet many hold responsible for the way colleges even now teach literature. Did he know I must have had a tenderness for the literary man that my caller was loath to declare gone? Lame my joke may have been, but I had asked for a hero I knew to be dead.

John Crowe Ransom's poems are among the most civil and, as the Latin master poet A. E. Housman might have put it, *civilizing* of our age, though there is now cause to assert their appeal, even perhaps their existence, is a matter of some doubt. As a matter of cold fact, teaching a recent graduate seminar in the poetry of the Vanderbilt Fugitives, a literary posse of whom Ransom was the head sheriff and founding member, I learned that only Ransom's *Selected Poems,* published by Alfred Knopf in 1969, was still in print and that only in some several hundred hardcover copies. But that woeful circumstance did not deter me. I phoned used bookstores all over the country to locate copies, starting with the Kenyon College Bookstore. The kind woman there also informed me that Mr. Ransom was long dead; she said she couldn't recall the last time anyone had asked for his poetry. I got nearly the same answer everywhere, though I managed in the end to turn up a copy here and a copy there until I had my goal of fifteen. Nevertheless, this exercise convinced me that it is a black irony that the man who taught Allen Tate, Robert Penn Warren, Cleanth Brooks, Randall Jarrell, Anthony Hecht, and James Wright how to think about poems remains, however present, increasingly absent in American poetry. I believe he is worth hunting up.

Ransom was many things, a remarkable man, as inscrutable as most are idiosyncratic. He emerged from rural Tennessee, the son of a Methodist minister, and he was, as Andrew Lytle, last of the Fugitives, wrote, provided by that background with a sense of wholeness in man, meaning one with an awareness of a community of folk and their histories, a man whose relationships defined him, whose values had been absorbed as much from southern culture, which his student Allen Tate thought more than imperiled, as from a lifetime of book reading. His advocacy of ties between the communities of literature and people (I want to say principles), most famously in *The World's Body,* made him a critical voice exceeded in eminence by no American except perhaps T. S. Eliot. Almost single-handedly he gave the South self-respect when no one else had, or could, setting loose a flow of intellectual energy that created Fugitives, New Criticism, and southern poetry. It also drove him north, exiled from the South. Ransom the critic, professor, and editor does not interest me here. Ransom the poet does.

It may surprise people to hear Ransom was a quarterback of his high school football team, a lifelong sports aficionado. His image, insofar as he has an image, remains that of a retiring, timid college don. His teaching career began with a Rhodes Scholarship to Oxford University. He had not intended to teach anything, let alone poetry writing and criticism, but on his return to the states, for economic and family reasons, he went that way. He had come of age in the dawning of Vanderbilt University's new hope for the South. World War I called him to military service, an obligation young men used to feel more strongly than an obligation to make money. Ransom went to France, an infantry lieutenant in the most individually violent war Americans have experienced, with the possible exception of the Civil War (many of whose veterans were still living neighbors when Ransom shipped over). In the tides of intellectual change sweeping Europe, of which war was the stormy surface, Ransom got a hard baptism. He knew well the images of a world in collapse which T. S. Eliot so famously inscribed in *The Waste Land*; brutality and inconsequence surrounded him.

He knew the specters threading modernism and European intellectual life. It made the pastoral outlook of the Tennessee hills to which he yearned to return seem heavy baggage for his dualistic nature. His poems depict a lifelong struggle to accommodate a deeply conservative spirit with a relentlessly forward-looking intellect. He simply could not accept the mythical South that others such as his colleague Donald Davidson clung to. His personal struggle forged a style so individual it was remarked that any three unrelated lines on a scrap of paper washed up on the proverbial desert island would show the writer could be none other than John Crowe Ransom. Allen Tate said of that style "an imitator would have made a fool of himself." It was a most pronounced literary sound, an arch Anglican verse, out of step with the drift of poetry toward the personal, written by a poet who had every reason to agree with Eliot's idea that the man and the poet occupied different houses. Still, Ransom's poetry seems now, somehow, essentially and evidently the man, Ransom: genteel, meditative, courteous, eclectic, smart, loving, but with character any Marine would admire. To him, irony, that deployed marching order of the twentieth century, was as natural as October.

Ransom's irony became the tongue inside everything his poems had to say. On the page it functioned as lens, a filtration scheme, a costume, a shape. Ransom was a man of intense feeling recognizable, though tautly repressed, by his extraordinary discipline in many poems about women betrayed, children dead, the corpses of the loved ones lingered over by those who are left. He was courtly in the old southern way that isolates moments when the self needs protection, moments that ask and offer and enforce privacy; decorum, he believed, should not permit pandering with sensational or even scandalous matters of family doings. This was what Robert Penn Warren meant, in part at least, when he urged, in *Democracy and Poetry,* the poet to develop a "responsible self." Irony, the testing attitude of the ungulled, meant restraining from the subjectivity of human experience; it meant hard form and resistance to temptation; it required giving the poem dignity, grace, memorability, order that might endure the roughest human matter, for he did not shrink from what a man is capable of, he only distanced it enough for examination. The range of Ransom's irony includes wit, egg-headed puns, learned allusions, imitations, satiric comments, and more—all of which keep Ransom the poet enshadowed, as he might have said, so that the reader may be worked upon by the art of words, not a rhetoric of personalism. Howard Nemerov found Ransom's poetry to possess an "elegance" and nicely defined this as: "a means to precision of statement, more especially a means to control of tone: it implies manners, or style—the general code, that is, by which particular choices are made, by which objects are arranged in one order rather than another. At a deeper level the quality insists even abstractly and generally that order and choice always matter, whether the world is reasonable or not."

Ransom, impelled and excited by the century's changes, rapacious and deconstructive, wrote poetry to work out personal solutions in moments fecund with sub-voiced moral, political, cultural statements. He learned from John Donne's poems of interior jousting and assaults, Thomas Hardy's too. His young disciples, the Vanderbilt Fugitives, but mainly Tate and Warren, learned from him. Ransom's inability to abide the didactic poem, however exquisitely true might be its say, led to irony making his statements. He wanted people accurately portrayed, in contradiction and complexity; he wanted the fluidity and mysterious pressures that life actually has; he wanted local and naturalistic drama, but subdued to art. The language of his poems, corruptive of the monistic view of his heritage, was made up of archaic vocabulary and colloquial phrase and a directness of sentence preternaturally clean, a blend of mixed dictions which left him customized verse forms, recognizable all right but somehow like nothing else in the genre. Minor in scope, miniature in structure, his poems nevertheless bite in their hunger for tranquility. He might have dealt in the psychology of responsibility, obligation, and blame so common to the engaged poets of the postwar years, but he did not. He dramatized by parable, reserving himself and his authority.

The obliquity of approach and style to which Ransom confines himself also seems to have prohibited him from exploring a good measure of southern experience, though the South had been his homeland during much of his adult life. He never wrote about black life in the South, or the yet living evidence of atrocious slavery intertwined, inevitably, with his life as he grew to manhood during the worst years of segregation. Perhaps he felt warned away from all that by the debacle of *I'll Take My Stand,* essays in part defensive of a brutally racist society. But, by implication, one finds little record in his poems of the South's pervasive violence; no description of the waves, black and white, migrating to Detroit, to Chicago; no mention of flight from farm and field edge to villages and then to towns, people fleeing as they got less and less for a life of grinding labor. In the South it was all changing: work, worship, education, laws, ways one man knew another's respect. The ballyhooed new future offered neither wages enough to feed families nor prospect of keeping things as they had always been. There is nothing of people failed by the brutality of southern mills or hopeless schools or lack of hospitals, roads, what is now called "infrastructure." Drugs, alcohol, or whatever new insidiousness might be, ignored.

The world portrayed by Ransom can't be easily set for comparison beside either the reflexive portraits of being by Faulkner or Erskine Caldwell because it isn't really a world at all; it is style, and Ransom's style invites us away from the worst. His poetry can seem, often enough, the fiddly preoccupations of an old man lost in comforting dreams of a netherland, at least that's so in the proximity of revealing, worrisome poetries published in recent decades. The casual reader who stumbles upon Ransom may wonder what in God's name would *he* make of the fleshy lacerations of Sharon Olds or the vicious assaults of rap ballads?

That reader would, I suspect, stand surprised soon enough. Ransom's style hides the toughness of a mind that knew final and irrefutable vulnerability and violence and death which none shall survive. He might have said, as his younger southern colleague Flannery O'Connor did say, that violence was one of the ways people have got to Heaven. He had been the son of a preacher but was early disabused of Heaven's promises; when he spoke of life's darkness it came slant. Philip Larkin learned a bit of trade from him. Perhaps Randall Jarrell gave the most accurate assessment of Ransom's poems when he said that they "are produced by the classical, or at worst semi-classical, treatment of Romantic subjects." Jarrell called Ransom's poetry a war "of Feeling and Power" and noted his ironic strategy was armor with which a campaigner might survive in an uncivil world. Jarrell was dead right when he wrote:

> His poems are full of an affection that cannot help itself, for an innocence that cannot help itself—for the stupid travelers lost in the maze of the world, for the clever travelers lost in the maze of the world. The poems are not a public argument but personal knowledge, personal feeling; and their virtues are the "merely" private virtues—their characters rarely vote, rarely even kill one another, but often fall in love.
>
> The poems have none of that traumatic passion for Authority, any Authority at all, that is one of the most unpleasant things in our particular time and our particular culture.

Yet Ransom loves most the potential of each individual, which is the Romanticism Jarrell detected, and a faint strain, perhaps, of shoofly Emerson and Whitman. Every poem seems dedicated to the proposition that however bad the world undeniably is, the heart of a man remains a wonderful (literally), unpredictable, instructive organ. Not surprisingly, then, abuses to love constitute the primary manifestation of Ransom's great tale. Love's enemies, betrayal and death, are Ransom's favorite characters, both wrapped into one in the actor who literally plucks out the heart of his worthy opponent in Ransom's delicious "Captain Carpenter," which Jarrell thought was the poetic equivalent of Kafka's "Metamorphosis," and which may be the most violent poem of the century. Because he was one of Ransom's undergraduate acolytes at Vanderbilt University and then as a transfer student at Kenyon College, Jarrell (who was Peter Taylor's roommate in Ransom's house) knew the fearful anxiety which trembled behind the firm and lyrical facade of Ransom's poems. Jarrell understood why Ransom was a fabular, not a social poet, one whose song, more melodic than narrational, described affairs of the heart in an anonymous voice stained by sorrow. The place of this poem is usually unlocated and pastoral because it is not an actual anywhere, but is rather the interior ground of consciousness. There occur the most dire and most personal violations of the individual soul, not as news-making events but as the losses of self, the steady pruning away of powers of individuality.

If Ransom's poems are as pastoral as Robert Frost's, who engineered publication of Ransom's first collection, his farcical psychodrama "Captain Carpenter" seems the sort of mean historical jest Frost loved. First published by the thirty-six-year-old Ransom in the third issue of *The Fugitive* (1924) then included in his finest volume, *Chills and Fever*, the poem is a study in brutality, a tale of personal combat. Because Ransom was considered a leading southern intellectual, some were tempted to read this tale as another, spicier, rendition of the noble Confederate giving his all for the lost cause. Ransom regarded the Captain as "an old hero who dies with his boots on," but he declined to see him as a doomed southern warrior. To be precise, Captain Carpenter is no one we know. A mid-level officer of an unnamed army, modern to the extent he carries pistols and archaic to the extent he goes on horseback, the man seems to take his military duty so lightly he is distracted, if not waylaid, by "ladies in a rout" among whom there is one who, with a sword, "twined him of his nose for evermore." The Inspector Clouseau of his battle group, the Captain appears by destiny bound to encounter *bad* opposition. Barely three ballad stanzas into the sixteen-stanza poem, he meets a "rogue that looked unchristian" and he attacks. But not well; both of his legs are broken.

Captain Carpenter is a screw-up with good intentions. His defeats amuse us but they are costly; worse, they are continuous; they are campaigns against mysterious forces such as "the wife of Satan" who "bit off his arms at the elbows," a "black devil" that took his ears, and another who got his "sweet blue eyes." Trimmed, he is ready to fight. He spits a challenge:

> To any adversity it is fame
> If he risk to be wounded by my tongue
> Or burnt in two beneath my red heart's flame
> Such are the perils he is cast among.

Ransom, who loved his jests, must have delighted in his warrior's near-malapropism with that *heartburn*. What he surely most loved, however, was the Captain becoming, finally, pissed off after "threescore and ten years." Mr. Ransom did not permit identification of the old warrior with himself, even a shadow self, yet for both this is an act of temporary settling up with the nettlesome and, alas, invincible otherworld. Drawing on the Anglo-Saxon tradition of epic heroes from Beowulf to Galahad, and on the American folk heroes from Davy Crockett to John Wayne, caging them in the commonest lyric stanza, Ransom ends each line with the ascending rhythm of childish pleasure. In whiffs of song, he sends his man to battle the biggest, baddest villain in town:

> It was the neatest knave that ever was seen
> Stepping in perfume from his lady's bower
> Who at this word put in his merry mien
> And fell on Captain Carpenter like a tower.

The mincing and delicate footwork of the stanza's first three lines, dominantly iambic, archaic in diction, idiomatic in tone, smoothly set up the vaudevillian tumble and thump of the last line. You can hear the drum in the pit. (Those with no ear for southern speech should know that both "bower" and "tower" are spoken as monosyllables with the force of a rising foot.) But as Yogi Berra said, it ain't over 'til it's over. Knocked to the dirt, the ninety-year-old battler still has "the old heart in his bust / And a blade shook between rotten teeth alack."

For readers who might insist upon the Romantic triumphs of good souls so often afforded by escapist entertainments, Ransom is not the man. His Captain's combat for life ends when a villainous little knave simply "pierced him and produced the Captain's heart." But that isn't the point. The poem proceeds three stanzas more to allow the narrator, never a participant, to declare overt curse on the undefeated opponents of this determined, brave, ineffectual man.

> The curse of hell upon the sleek upstart
> That got the Captain finally on his back
> And took the red vitals of his heart
> And made the kites to whet their beaks clack clack.

The whole poem is transparently fable, grossly comic, cartoonishly built of off-the-shelf literary conventions exaggerated ludicrously to satirize violences we give ourselves to in the name of whatever idealistic cause flames us today. Ransom keeps the gore squarely before us. No offstage Greek blood for him. What, then, is our proper response to such an evil world? Are we to imagine Ransom thinks the Captain should have kept his challenge to himself, been more prudent? Was he only inept? Without doubt Ransom values a man who persists in principled, if misguided action. Americans like the Captain have had to fight in self-defense as well as in self-deceptions. Wars have been fought for glandular motives a well as for freed people. But Ransom defeats his Captain as handily as did any opponent, though he makes a solidarity with that man, for it is none other than himself, padded and hidden by the coolly deflective, persuasive costuming effects of his entertainment, itself sent up in that last double-beat, wryly bellicose "clack clack."

"Captain Carpenter" anticipates the unremittingly funny and bloody sorties of a troupe of English comedians in the 1974 film *Monty Python and the Holy Grail,* in particular a nearly infamous combat of knights in the forest. The film shows England's King Arthur, without subjects yet in A.D. 932, journeying to claim his royal identity. When he encounters a black knight in the wood, a figure young people today know as the "Darth Vader" of our cinema-saturated age, we confront our darker sides. The good king, so ludicrously innocent that one castle's defenders catapult cows at him, doesn't have a clue that men are intellectual dualists; he knows only the black knight blocks the way and, fairy tale or film or poem, a man must win the way to savor life. The good king has no choice but to undertake combat with the dark self. Mixing the medieval and the modern, as Ransom had done it in "Captain Carpenter," the film's battle is funny and grotesquely flesh-rending. When the black knight loses one arm, he deems it "but a scratch" and soon loses the other, his blood spurting as from an opened water hydrant. "Pansy" he calls the king, his extreme circumstance naught to him, humping the ground, legless and armless, a portrait of courage in a man self-convicted of imprudence, stupidity, foolhardiness. The satire depends on exaggeration and flat tone in delivery, much like the narrator of the medieval French epic

The Song of Roland, who with his sword halves a man and his horse, then observes "that was a mighty blow!"

There is hard symmetry and oblique moral comment given in that gruesome waste of flesh occasioned by testosterone-driven men. When King Arthur's troops cry "Run away!" in the face of great harm, we laugh, but we do not think *we* would run. Each of us, we know, in some private manner, pursues a grail as compulsively as Arthur does. Our own outrages may deserve such mockery. If Monty Python's crowd behaves with transparent silliness, and if unspeakable offense becomes macabre joke, it is amusement that works only because we know we have had and may yet have the courage to do such fighting. We can take up hard obstacles to the way through the wood when the way must be taken. Python's humor is an ironic morality lesson in lesson-making. Yet, as splendid as it is, *Monty Python and the Holy Grail* may lack something Ransom's "Captain Carpenter" has.

"Captain Carpenter"'s backhanded, buffoon-like humor, its quiet gravity, its balloon of viciousness did not make me suspect, when I first read the poem in college, that this was a myth-mocking portrait of a world gone anarchic with self-deception. If I was insufficiently learned to know why I was charmed by a ballad of violence, I saw, or rather felt, the contest of a man hunting for self-definition. I was reading this poem as a U.S. Air Force sergeant just discharged in 1972, with Vietnam's theater of the absurd still open, and the Captain could seem less literary figure than people I had known. His poem was a news report. Most men fought in Asia unprodded by the motivations of securing home, family, or cultural ideas, but all began in the old way of honor that required putting on a uniform. Ransom's poem is built around an idea a lot like *semper fidelis,* one venerated by and also mocked by the ballad.

The end of old ways hurts, and hurts most the hero. The Captain links in one image athletes, soldiers, and frontiersman, all of the line who strive mightily in our steads, even Jesus the carpenter. But the Captain is willy-nilly reduced to a heap of rubble. No reason given, no consolation, and isn't it a pity, though sweet the saying of that pity. Ransom doesn't moralize; he doesn't say to emulate the great ones. He simply indicates that the end seems to be the same whatever we do, men are reduced, diced, and by a dicey world. "Captain Carpenter," I think it likely, no longer makes a lesson of adherence to a code. Perhaps the young can't see the joke once the ideas of manhood, virtue, and sacrifice for community have no substance for them. They can't see the king as hero. Ransom could not go that far with his captain.

From Ransom's first collection, in 1919, *Poems About God,* he investigates what makes a hero, or unmakes one. His was a venerating imagination trying to yoke the good past to a weakened present. He knew language, which breaks more bones than sticks and stones, is in fact the grail. The poet, its pursuer, was his covert hero. He taught that to Robert Penn Warren, who, mocking Milton in "Folly on Royal Street Before the Raw Face of God," asks, "For what is man without magnificence?" Warren's synonym for magnificence was passion, and he wrote, "Passion / is all. Even / The Sleaziest." The Captain, decimated but undefeated, shudders with the passion a good poet can get into a lyric, by which I mean (though Warren may not have agreed) something like a whole truth, complex and contradictory, as it enters an image or moment. Admiration for Ransom's passion lay behind my feeble literary joke when I asked to meet a dead, but not absent, poet at a reading I was engaged to give that one evening at Kenyon College, in Ohio.

In the curious way the dead have of continuing present, Ransom refused to go entirely offstage when I had arrived where he had been part of literary skirmishes as the founding editor of the *Kenyon Review.* My host, Ransom's surviving faculty colleague at Kenyon College, took me to a supper arranged in my honor, offering me sherry and classical music. Then he placed me with a lovely woman, somewhat older than I was, and informed me she was Ransom's daughter and would be my dinner partner. To allay my nervousness and make conversation, I recall, there fell a chance to ask this engaging woman if she had read Thomas Daniel Young's just-published biography of her father. She blinked at me over the merest instant of baffled hesitation and sighed, "Why no, I haven't. Why should I read it? Pappy never did anything." To this day I summon my own blank gaze back at her and know the uncertainty I felt about what I should do next. I thought Ransom's poems had done much to tell southerners who they might be, or choose not to be. Thinking manners required assent, I said nothing. It would be years before I met Ransom's daughter, the novelist Robb Foreman Dew, and realized my dinner partner had been an impostor, charming as all get out, playing for my host a jest invented to match my own from that first phone call.

Ransom, I think, would have liked all this well enough, for he was the sort of man, as I was once told, who liked to laugh, whose worst offense was that on occasion he might sneak off to watch a Cleveland Browns football game without telling his wife. Hardly the brooding, dour, fallen-on-the-thorns-of-life sort of poet my generation flocked to, Ransom showed how the mind could make poetry of the tweak and bite of ironic control. He had become, exiled in Ohio, dissevered from his country, his weather, his place where answers had deep roots and eccentric soundings. So he had made that alternate country, one the Irish poet Yeats would say was not for old men, a pastoral land of ideas and ideals in mortal contest. I did not dally long at Kenyon, but it seemed to me Ransom was subtly present and doing there, rather than subtly absent and moribund. This was something of value in behavior from a man generally counted as a founder of the New South, whatever that phrase may mean. I think, after all, that must be how the roistering and valorous Captain Carpenter would have seen the matter, anyway, and what could be better, as the poet John Crowe Ransom once asked of a sealed, delivered, and still hateful letter about so much that would not change?

Warren's Ventriloquist

J. J. AUDUBON

James Weldon Johnson is said to have written his autobiography in five sepa-
rate versions, a comic idea which, upon reflection, will startle few writers.
Who are you? life asks a writing man. Robert Penn Warren's poetry, as in-
tensely as any contemporary poet's, grapples with this question. His answers
are shifting, multiple, contingent upon circumstance. He said in *The Fugi-
tive's Return* that the greatness of an art lay in its ability to create and hold the
single image of a man. He knew a life is a history, a narrative, a journey for
which the final redemption of meaning seldom, if ever, comes convincingly
to the traveler. Yet he believed in poetry's redemptive life-telling that con-
fronts fate, and he celebrated that in his strangely blended and iconic poem
Audubon: A Vision, a poem of lyric voice performing narrative tasks.

 Audubon: A Vision seems a curious, aberrational poem however it is ap-
proached. In her review of the book, Helen Vendler, a most reluctant ad-
mirer of Warren's, called it an elegy and a parable. Others have called it a
narrative and a history in verse. *Audubon* purports to be a chronicle of the
life of the American naturalist, artist, and entrepreneur John James Audu-
bon, who lived from 1785 to 1851. The poem is spoken by an omniscient but
hardly indifferent narrator. Its final moment, however, is given undeniably
to, and is abruptly spoken by, the poet Robert Penn Warren who, almost
defiantly, assumes an autobiographical post. If *Audubon's* pedigree seems
an odd intercourse of the pastoral elegy and the frontier tall tale, the book is
perhaps circumscribed only by recognizing it is an autobiography disguised
as a biography disguised as a legend disguised as a narrative poem, all serv-
ing to forge the image of a man, and a language in which he can exist.

 What drew Warren to such an in-folded, layered work? His early verse
was indebted to the authorial effacement of modernists T. S. Eliot and

Thomas Hardy who, in 1928, published his last book, *Winter Words.* Then a Rhodes Scholar at Oxford, Warren had been writing poems with John Crowe Ransom since 1921, and as Allen Tate's roommate at Vanderbilt, he gleefully illustrated *The Waste Land* on their dormitory wall. Modernist that he was, he did not easily accept himself as subject or speaker of his poems. There is no overt autobiography which might have offered us, as James Olney says in *Metaphors of Self,* "the symptomatic key to all that he did and, naturally, to all that he was." He refused the self-explaining statements such as poets are apt to make about the writing of poems—Poe's "Philosophy of Composition," for example, or fastidious Tate's "Narcissus as Narcissus." Yet Warren's first book, published in 1929, was a life-study, *John Brown: The Making of a Martyr,* and life-study would be Warren's interest, whatever the genre he favored, over a remarkable seventy years of writing.

Unlike Hardy, who wrote his own biography and published it in his second wife's name, Warren often stated vigorous opposition to seeing his life rendered into biography. Yet he cooperated with Joseph Blotner, whose *Robert Penn Warren* appeared in 1996. This "life" has, regrettably, too little of Warren's life in it. I am tempted to say that all we have, truly, of an indisputable Warren life waits in the collected interviews, *Robert Penn Warren Talking,* but any Warren poem is an autobiography of a speculative, alert, self-measuring consciousness in an enigmatic world. His lives are never merely well-recorded historical events. Each poem is a visitation of a life engaged in a struggle between an interior self and an exterior determinism; the struggle is always to observe a self who possesses and employs knowledge. It would be pretty to say this life was Warren's own. Pretty but perhaps not wholly accurate. The life he offers is neither autobiographical nor biographical, but dialectical and hypothetical, a living in, and of, words that compose a man. *Audubon: A Vision* is Warren's starkest rendering of that story.

James H. Justus tells us, in *The Achievement of Robert Penn Warren,* the problem in Warren is always "an adequate selfhood, a breaking out of the debilitating sense of incompleteness and fragmentation. The price," he says, "for that integration of self is not the loss of certain spiritual certitudes, but their hopeful and sometimes desperate testing." Such testing is, of course, directed at self-repair and self-creation and a full individuation requires living into consciousness. The Audubon of Warren's poetic biography passes precious little life, and what appears is far more cerebral than physical. No historian or student of Audubon has claimed the man owned the introspection Warren attributes to him in this poem, yet Warren requires, and gives him, a life of both significant deed and knowledge in order to demonstrate the value of humane ideas. Audubon's life, embodying the competing attractions to art's individualistic pursuit and community's self-compromises, and moreover displaying the embryonic struggles at the frontiers of country and imagination, seems in retrospect an ideal vessel for Warren's vitalizing.

It apparently looked otherwise to Warren. Published in 1969, the year I entered the United States Air Force and dead in the middle of the Vietnam War, *Audubon: A Vision* had proved difficult for Warren to write. He had started it in the 1940s, worked desultorily on it, but could not come to the "frame for it, the narrative line." Rumors have indebted Warren to both Eudora Welty and Katherine Anne Porter, who had themselves employed Audubon. Finally, as Warren said, he determined to write the work in "snapshots of Audubon," and he claimed that *Audubon*'s form came to him in a sudden rush while he made up the bed. It is an amusing suggestion of a craft-driven modernist's negotiations with Romantic inspiration.

Warren's narrative preparation and skills were established facts—a "long foreground" as Emerson said of Whitman's first work—well before *Audubon* became a gleam in his fancy. His seventh book, *All the King's Men,* had won the Pulitzer Prize in 1946. His eleventh, *Brother to Dragons,* published in 1955, was a verse tale, much admired for its historical, philosophical, and moral probing of Thomas Jefferson's murdering nephews and juxtaposed to our national conviction of American righteousness. If Warren's form trouble seemed mitigatable by his abilities, Audubon's factual life was openly, indisputably available. The young explorer Jean Jacques Audubon, bastard son of a French sea-captain and his Haitian mistress, had been treated by at least nine full biographies prior to Warren's work. Several were published in the 1960s when Warren's creation simmered, and it seems at least likely Warren would have read them. Audubon's *Ornithological Journals,* long in print and reissued in 1967, would have given Warren as much self-perceived character and as many dramatic life events, boldly embroidered if not invented, as a novelist might require. If Warren had ten Audubons to choose from, why was there a form problem? In fact, searching for a narrative line may have deflected Warren from recognizing that was not his difficulty at all. The trouble was a voice appropriately modulated.

Predictably terse, Warren's comments on the making of the poem imply he lacked not so much a formed knowledge of Audubon as a feel for the inner man. The poem moved rapidly forward when, as Warren said, he began to see Audubon as "a man who has finally learned to accept his fate. The poem is about a man and his fate." Warren, at the time of publication, was then sixty-four, with two children roughly the age of those America had watched the Chicago police bludgeon the year before at the Democratic Convention. Many recall how those years produced moments of decision, suddenly made, upon which entire lives seemed later to have followed. Warren's form problem apparently diminished as he came to feel drawn closer to Audubon's inner life.

Warren's attraction to Audubon's life story reaches deep into his sources of identity, beginning with a sense of a shared Kentucky origin. Beyond that, Warren's passion to live and work by the imagination and his feeling for the artist as both exile and frontiersman made Audubon a powerfully attractive ancestral model only two complete life-spans behind him. Audubon must have looked to Warren like the exemplary American success story as it ought to be, rather than as it so often became—a tale of consumptive and exploitative greed that makes heroes of Gatsbys.

The point of Warren's original interest in Audubon will probably never be known, but he shows awareness by the mid-1930s. Always compelled by history's actors, Warren, during his tenure at Louisiana State University in the late 1930s, could hardly have been ignorant of Audubon. Lewis P. Simpson, in a brief note on Warren's residences in Baton Rouge, observes that Warren so enjoyed driving his car, even over then primitive roads, that he didn't hesitate to purchase property twenty miles out from the university, commuting to his academic duties. Only slightly farther to the northwest was the river village of St. Francisville, where Audubon had lived and painted the portrait of Miss Elizabeth Pirrie in the fall of 1821. Long synonymous with America's nature world, in Louisiana Audubon is virtually the emblem of an ancestry that is itself identified with raw vitality of creature and place. Bird prints, elaborately framed survivors of his great portfolios, grace living rooms, law offices, and dental parlors. Zoos, schools, and roads bear Audubon's name. Audubon, the old man, must have seemed to Warren, in 1936, as immediate as did that new man, Huey "the Kingfish" Long, and Audubon's effort to live as an artist must have been especially telling to Depression-era eyes.

When Warren left Louisiana for Minnesota in the fall of 1941, he remarked that no place would ever look the same—indicting the rank frontierism of poverty politics. He was also noting the relatively unchanged beauty Audubon had known. It might be hard for a man to make a life of art anywhere, but Audubon had done it in swamps and in circumstances still visible in Louisiana. Warren knew Audubon was far from ordinary. He was a come-here immigrant who landed in the east, lit out for the west, and developed a talent for representational art. He also had the ability to organize people and resources to realize his talent's potential. Who was ever more American than Audubon, the entrepreneur marrying art and business? He spent desperate years but in the end, as Hollywood would script it, Audubon triumphed. He wanted and got it all: his girl, Lucy, children, money, fame. He proved wrong the ubiquitous doubters and naysayers, the privileged and the established, becoming even before Poe our favorite icon, the rebel whose cause was a driving passion for an art turned to a vocation, and a vocation that amounted to an autobiography of the New World man wrestling out an appropriate relation with determinist Nature. Before Audubon's portfolios, paintings of birds seemed lifeless abstracts. Audubon put birds into living scenes, made them realistic, dramatic, and with background contexts gave them a life story. Finding species theretofore unknown, he expanded the new world's American language with art, sometimes consciousness itself.

In *Robert Penn Warren and the American Imagination,* one of Warren's best readers, Hugh Ruppersburg, admires "the dialectic of idealism and pragmatism" that *Audubon* pursues. But, fuzzily to my mind, he says Audubon "seeks to lose himself" in frontier wilds: "He desires merger with nature, the loss of self, transcendence to an identity larger than his own—nature's. He learns in the forest that such a merger is unattainable: he inhabits the real world, of which the wilderness is a part. His thwarted desire for merger transmutes into a desire to preserve the wilderness of his vision in artistic form. Art becomes his means of merger, of transcendence . . . ." I am inclined to think Ruppersburg merely trapped in hyperbole until he remarks, "It is the ideal which matters." Not the life aspiring to a gritty balance of ideal and actual? Where in Warren is the ideal so privileged, the same ideal that, like the zealot of good cause, becomes so often our worst enemy? Audubon doesn't want to be lost, to transcend anything, or to merge with anything—unless of course his passion for painting represents that merger. If so, it is odd that the poem unequivocally minimalizes practice of the art. Audubon's painting is mentioned only twice. This Audubon does not draw or paint; he watches, and we watch him *watching.* Or he scouts, hunts, conducts business, and is said to learn to define himself against the world. "The world declares itself,"

Warren writes. Audubon can declare nothing until he has a language of inte-
grated being, a real self. The evidence of that self may be the painting, but we
see little of it. Or it may be the growth of consciousness, and there is a deal of
talk about that. How else is Warren to give this Ulysses an uncounterfeitable
signature? How retrieve from the deadness of time and his ten life-stories an
Audubon whose speech might redeem an American spirit, a form problem
indeed?

Warren's solution was, at any rate, under his nose and it was imagistic,
if not cinematic. He recognized in Audubon's bird portraits the artist's ma-
nipulation of foreground and background, the paradox of time and distance,
bountiful wildness and rapacious civilization. He saw how Audubon con-
trived the illusion of life's movement to survive and even to flourish in the
most natural contingency and circumstance. Audubon had painted birds
from corpses he killed, putting them in realistic contrast to symbolic land-
scapes, a procedure that served as an opportunity to reveal Audubon's growth
of consciousness. Warren knew, as Joseph Conrad had written, that art's in-
tention must be to "render the highest kind of justice to the visible universe."
And, snapshot to snapshot, each idiosyncratic in length and subject, Warren
caused a figure of Audubon to stand still, to watch, then leaped him years
ahead by exposition, image bridges, even quoted passages from Audubon's
journals, always emphasizing helplessness of phenomena before determinist
fate. But Warren had also learned from Conrad that for the greatest artist
"justice to the visible universe" is not enough. To Warren, the great artist is
"one for whom the documentation of the world is constantly striving to rise
to the level of generalization about values, for whom the image strives to rise
to symbol, for whom images always fall into a dialectical configuration."

Because Warren's problem was the tale of the inner man, he needed a
strategy to draw out the dialectical configuration he knew Audubon's life
story carried. Typically, poems of the life story begin and end in a defined
place, survey events, and occupy a large stage of time, providing context that
manifests struggle sufficient for a life's redemption of historical anonymity.
The Divine Comedy, The Prelude, Song of Myself, Ted Hughes's *Crow,* and
Elizabeth Bishop's *Geography III,* however diverse in strategical imperatives,
remain life story dramas. Warren once chastised John Greenleaf Whittier
for failing to submit his poems to life tests, for an "unconditional surrender"
to pure emotion, which meant Whittier and his poems didn't know life fully
enough. What Audubon knew, and it was adequate, had been described in

a scene in the *Ornithological Journals* called "The Prairie." Maria Audubon's edition of the journals notes that the incident occurred in the spring of 1812, in the upper Midwest plains, when Audubon was thirty-seven years old.

Warren transposes this scene to "The Dream He Never Knew the End Of," section II of the book's seven parts. At 197 lines, it represents nearly half of *Audubon*. No other event in Audubon's life is given in anything more than shorthand exposition by contrast. Although Audubon said his journals were "food for the idle," they reveal him to have been a man of discipline, one greatly busied by a career to which he was utterly devoted, roving over the American frontier as few did, or could, obviously delighting in abundant experiences of every sort. Why, then, did Warren choose to represent his life in a single anecdote portraying Audubon as, so it seems, accessory to murder?

The answer may lie in recognition of responsibility that a man assumes for the life he walks in. To Warren, the quest for language is always a self-definition. Warren's poem begins with definitions of Audubon. Part I locates young Audubon mythically, historically, and chronologically by lies attached to his name and origin, by describing his passion for the woods and its mysteries, by his lack of language. Audubon remains a stiff and standoffish character, however, where definitions, distancing and controlled as they are, revealing as they do Audubon's recognition of "How thin is the membrane between himself and the world," fail to make an Audubon "self" knowable. Part II, therefore, cuts to Audubon in action, seeking a night's shelter at a cabin he has come upon in the woods. Admitted by its resident hag, he feels himself threatened by her and her two crude sons. Guilty of uncivil, inhospitable, and ugly behavior, but not of actual assault, mother and sons are hung to death, and left hanging, by Audubon and three conveniently arrived quasi-regulators:

> The affair was not tidy: bough low, no drop, with the clients
> Simply hung up, feet not much clear of the ground, but not
> Quite close enough to permit any dancing.
> The affair was not quick: both sons long jerking and farting, but she,
> From the first, without motion, frozen
> In a rage of will, an ecstacy of iron, as though
> This was the dream that, lifelong, she had dreamed toward.

Watching her about to die, the narrator (in a droll pun by Warren) "becomes aware that he is in the manly state." A brilliant anecdote of loneliness, fear,

lust, murder, and complicity becomes, because of Warren's gift of conscious-
ness to Audubon, an allegorical window through which a great life story
springs. But whose story is it? Audubon's or Warren's?

This narrative of evil and slippery justice telescopes a man's life to a sin-
gle event about which all else, before or after, must orbit like lesser stars. It
prepares for multiple readings, some of which Warren simply does not fol-
low—Audubon's responsibility for three deaths, for example, and the Ameri-
can Adam's hypocrisy. Some are faint soundings—the fairy tale victim of the
woods, a creation myth, a Narcissus myth, the artist's individuation legend.
What is given conflates the gift of Audubon's biography and impressionis-
tic portraits of the woods world. Except for "The Dream He Never Knew
the End Of," Warren abandons narrative structure nearly presumptive for
a life story and makes his *Audubon* out of forms of rhetoric and lyric in the
manner of a pastoral elegy. He does so to emphasize the dialectic of a man
who passes through crisis to control. Warren's problem all along has been to
establish and sustain a voice which must carry a life tale without the abjured
narrative chronology.

The unusually static structure of *Audubon* chains images to initiate
rhythmic movement for that life voice. Warren's snapshots frame, isolate, and
project continuity of image and event relationships; they support interpret-
ability. Like panels in a morality play, these variably constructed moments
arrange stage furniture to contextualize an action that is suggested only, not
actual. With Audubon we watch a marvelous bear, a bee-glade, a perfect blue
of skies and ponds; we hear a thrilling tusked boar and the oceanic roar of
buffalo. To that extent, we experience a life Audubon measured in his jour-
nals as "in all conscience *perhaps* as good as worlds unknown." So genuinely
sweet seems this life, as a "walk in the world," that Audubon risks forgetting
the rude lesson of the hanging tree. He may imagine life is ever bountiful
even as he dreams of Lucy's lips that "gleam in the bright wind," but it is
exactly then that he "cannot hear the sound of that wind."

The reader can hear it well enough, however, for the voice of Warren's
narrator strategically moves from liquid evocation of beauty to an intense
and gravelly register that is naturalism's counter-voice. This dual sounding
directs us as clearly as Little Red Riding Hood's path. Braiding a pastoral
celebration of nature with an abrupt, chopped, sometimes choked lingo of
brutal, muscular consonants, of broken syntax, and of phrases sawed off to
hover in white space, Warren carves a style that seems as documentary as

his snapshots. Refusing the authority of an autobiographical "I," his panel poems yoke objectivity to a management of time and space by line signals and gestures readers of poetry are never quite prepared for, especially readers who expect the silky traditional voices. Warren baits us with a life story we already know, and may envy, only to overwhelm us with the drumming death-wind news all flesh is heir to.

The narrative of a life story assumes a unified pattern, even a metonymic shape that extends empirically backward and forward as it mimics chronology and implies paraphrasable meaning available only in comprehension of the whole. Thus, the narrative shape subordinates lyric, image, and what Warren, after Conrad, called "dialectical configuration." Lyric, conversely, emphasizes the immediate image, here and now, as a carrier of transcendent opportunity. Subordinating narrative to lyric pressurizes art visually. It also invests discrete moments with density and may impart hypertrophic significance to a single experience. Warren's life of *Audubon* does precisely that.

Most of what a man lives, like much of what passes for poetry, is surface, convention, the rounding off and filling-in, the fitting into expected form that is interstitial between moments which are everything. Art being long and life short may encourage aberrant symmetry in poetry, but in life's beginning, middle, and end we feel the truest pattern exists. We may not trust the song of happy experience, but we cling to its hope because we have had moments of joy which validate the hope for more. Audubon's boyhood, his loneliness, his feelings about paintings, travel, a favorite landscape, even his dreams all arrive at a paltry sum, as Warren says: "He died, and was mourned, who had loved the world." What he left behind were the paintings that collectively express "the dream / Of a season past all seasons." According to Warren the maker/watcher, this was enough. Or it ought to have been enough, for anyone's life story known through the detached perspective of time and space comes to little more. And yet, that little more matters.

Readers of poetry regard all pattern-breaking suspiciously. Had Dante abandoned his terza rima at any point it would have meant a no-confidence gasp from his audience. The establishment of the voice telling the life story carries the authenticity of life. Warren wanted that voice to register a lyric response to Audubon's fate, but he chose to violate reader expectations of the life-story form which legitimately might have emphasized greater balladic, metric, grammatic, and aesthetic regularity. The points of violation, or imbalance, are so extensive that they constitute a kind of anti-poem, as the poem is itself a mélange of genre strains. If we expect Audubon's long life spread visibly and symmetrically, Warren gives us several days. If we expect unity of time and place, Warren introduces a Northwest Orient airliner passing over the head of a narrator standing in no defined place. If we take Audubon to represent nature's exquisite beauty and permanent succor, Warren's imagery is blunt in denial with a portrait of a sky like "the inflamed distance" where the dawn is "redder than meat." Nowhere is Warren more undermining of expectations than in the most elemental unit of poetry, the line, whose rebellious and confident note is evident from the opening section of the poem (line function tends to be mirrored in Warren's stanzaic improprieties).

Beginning in medias res, his voice catechistic and surging against the left margin, rebounding, noisy with its alliteration, boisterous and yet controlled, if barely so, Warren flares the stage lights upon Audubon:

WAS NOT THE LOST DAUPHIN

Was not the lost dauphin, though handsome was only
Base-born and not even able
To make a decent living, was only
Himself, Jean Jacques, and his passion—what
Is man but his passion?

Saw,
Eastward and over the cypress swamp, the dawn,
Redder than meat, break;
And the large bird,
Long neck outthrust, wings crooked to scull air, moved
In a slow calligraphy, crank, flat, and black against
The color of God's blood spilt, as though
Pulled by a single string.

Saw,
It proceed across the inflamed distance.

Moccasins set in hoar frost, eyes fixed on the bird,
Thought: "On that sky it is black."
Thought: "In my mind it is white."
Thinking: "*Ardea occidentalis,* heron, the great one."

Dawn: his heart shook in the tension of the world.

Dawn: and what is your passion?

Each of the first four stanzas comprise a single sentence broken across lines as jagged as rocky ground. Pronouns have been pruned away; sense momentum has been decapitated for felt instability at line's end, sometimes a dizzying interrogation. The sentences three times bark "Saw" and are then immediately tamped by details ensconced by commas, forcing the reader to pull forward against line inertia. By the time he has juxtaposed watching Audubon to the great heron, lyric tension winds so tight what Warren calls "the tension of the world" throbs. The sonic character of an opening in hymn meter, what we might have expected, so radically differs from Warren's that you can hear the life whoosh from the words. Consider my rough revision:

> I was not the lost dauphin though
>   handsome was only Base-
> born and not even able to
>   make a decent living, was
>
> Only myself, Jean Jacques, and my
>   passion—what is man but
> his passion? Saw, eastward, over
>   the cypress swamp, the dawn . . .

Had Warren chosen colloquial iambics, the stanza would have gone no better, I think:

> I wasn't any lost dauphin, handsome,
> just badly born, not able to make a
> decent living, only myself, Jean Jacques
> my passion—what is man but passion? I . . .

The slackness in both decasyllabics and hymn meter points up the force with which Warren's improvised sound conveys rhythmically the drama of consciousness that is to come. Imagistically, sonically, literally, the first scene stands Audubon outside of nature's kingdom and gives him Adam's task of naming the creatures. The voice is not Audubon's; it is not Warren's. It is the voice of the biographer, hieratic and indisputable, correct for the prologue that sonorously marks this triadic moment with man, creature, and God.

This voice is the composition of an unusual line signature, one Warren evolved almost entirely after *Promises* (1957), what might be called the first of his major collections of poetry. It is especially unusual in establishing an identity in the free-verse idiom which typically sacrifices line signature for content. Any two or three lines by Warren are readily recognizable as his. Line employment in *Audubon* is not radically different from Warren's late work, but it is pared to a functional minimum that assaults unsuspecting readers.

Readers have historically expected narrative verse presented in a conventional metric of more or less insistent regularity concluding in patterned sound identity, or rhymes. Modern poets, however, early abandoned rhymes and lines of recurring numbered elements, whether syllables or stress, or both. Arguably, this led to a weakened conception of what lines do. The line, generally, advances external action, describes scene or circumstance, and embodies in various ways the mind's consciousness. Lines are thus declarative, imagistic, or rhetorical.

The declarative states, informs, accumulates information. It is built ordinarily in standard English word order (subject, verb, complement) and seeks completion in thought or action, tending to make a statement which may be a full or a partial sentence. This line minimizes connotative suggestion while enhancing narrative or discursive movement, and thus may be either a dramatic or a rhetorical line. Where the declarative line tends to completion, the imagistic line tends toward continuity, or spillage, and it seeks resonance in enjambment. The "poise" of a line in the grid of a poem's actions reflects juxtaposition of two imperatives: movement toward depletion and movement toward renewal. An enjambed line is an opportunity for multiple, even contradictory meanings in the hovering instant of line's end. Expression arises from the reader's expectation either sustained or altered by the intrusive white space. Line manipulation affects syntax, momentum, spatial experience, connotation, and even cognitive resolution while it establishes controlling cadence. Once established as a normative length, the line is usually continued to avoid violations offensive to either the ear or the eye that seeks symmetry, the imperative foremost to poetry.

Warren throughout his life wrote poems in traditional lines, but from *Audubon* on, a period of almost thirty years, he worked a line against conventional symmetry, one heard by some ears as inflexible, rough, clumsy. He wanted to make dramatic and visually immediate the mind's struggle for consciousness. A violent rhythm to narrate referential information would have many benefits, but they would hardly seem to be lyric pleasures. His line fully performs the functions that define what a line is, but it is idiosyncratic with violent chunks of staccato speech that isolate its speaker. It resists symmetric syllable count, prefers a cluster or "jam" of stressed words, extends sinuous sentences over surprising distance and abruptly butts them against equally rude short or half lines, often interrupting with query, expostulation, or what Stephen Dunn calls the poet's "wisdom statement," one that feels like a commentary arbitrarily placed in the poem. The effect Warren seeks is a vital surge of energy that cannot be contained by conventions; he wants colloquy, a mind in noisy debate. The effect of such language is power for the poem. Nothing is ever ended, done; what is said can never be wholly false, deceptive, or solipsistic. Nothing said is trivial. The line structure defiantly emphasizes the cerebral and speculative action of the watching poet but so identifies it as a part of the manly action of his "doing" that even the static part of his nature becomes significant to the whole of living. Because such lines mimic speech more than literary convention, they gain the power of surprise, the muscle of mental aggression, an opportunity for rebalancing emphasis, and may enhance the poem's shift from transmission of external to internal information. The simultaneously individual and communal nature of lines establishes tone, what the writer thinks, and voice, the idiom through which the writer speaks. Warren's lines mean to create immediacy, movement, vigor for a form which is dominantly inactive, one that risks reader boredom without the illusion of character alteration and engagement.

But what can that mean? Warren has done nothing. The watcher is invented, a string of words only. And Audubon, evidence suggests, may well have fabricated all or part of his tale. If so, is this only much ado about nothing? I think it is more. *Audubon: A Vision* is an entertainment first, but an entertainment in the testing of moral response. Audubon does not actually kill the woman or her sons, any more than he sleeps with them. He does not abuse their hospitality. He does not, as Ruppersburg seems to think, betray Nature. He does not flee in fear. But the woodspeople are dead; the regulators have gone; he is left with the burden of what he has and hasn't done, what he has and hasn't seen, what he knows and doesn't know, what the world is. He has a view of things and a language is composed to express, indeed to embody, that view. Again, what kind of poem would it be in heroic couplets. And what if it were in elegiac quintets? Or in any form perfectly symmetrical and confidently continuous. One doesn't feel it could work any other way. But that is, perhaps, only because we have the poem as Warren made it, and this way is the brooding, male, violence-dreamed shape of the life that must have purpose or it is nightmare only. Warren has, that is to say, gambled, as all artists must, with a form that might create its own living character.

Perhaps the most dazzling gamble in *Audubon: A Vision* is Warren's choice of an ending. Audubon dies in his bed, and time, which contains him, flows on; meaning continues, and contains the beautiful birds who "cry / In a tongue multitudinous, often like music." We seek to be equal to that. The ending is natural and follows the normal life story, even allowing for a certain blare of ripening gold light and drum-roll of chill wind. Both the pastoral and the funeral elegy is served by Warren's celebration of the hero who goes before and redeems our best understanding. To know him, we see, is to know one's self, a gesture of linkage which increases our sense of purpose in a world so visibly whirlpool-like. But Warren is too much the man here on this ground to leave his gaze on the outer world, however mythically reverberant, for the immediacy might be lost. Audubon's story is a man's life, and an event of crushing consequence in that life, and a life lived in the teeth of one singular event. Isn't it possible that any moment in any of our lives could have the same weight, hence the same grand beauty? Warren, recognizing this in the closing section, "Tell Me a Story," pleads for his own life story and for that singular life-defining moment, that fulcrum upon which meaning tilts.

Unlike the broken, grinding edges and wheezy, corrosive hinges of the lines in the first six sections, lines in this final unit are self-contained, syntactically complete, barely and slowly spilling one to the next, like a soothing fountain. The shortness and the spare jab of unmodified information create a sense of the essential, the final, and the dignified. This voice, one conceives, is capable of *knowing* what it asks for—time and distance and delight, all of which are aspects of *direction,* that which the great geese in naturalistic process already know. So we arrive at what Audubon came first to, his kinship—not a merger—with the geese in a world whose laws, knowledge or none, are inflexible and written before we have the first question to ask. But if we are like Audubon, and like the migrating geese, we are not them, are never to be them; nor are they us. Their fate is determined, to go; our fate is to know, or try to know. And where we cannot truly know, we can and must seek the story, the shape of a life that might be lived, and in knowledge. James Olney writes, "In speaking of autobiography, one always feels that there is a great and present danger that the subject will slip away altogether, that it will vanish into thinnest air, leaving behind the perception that there is no such creature as autobiography and that there never has been." This must be the greatest impoverishment, to have no autobiography, for where there is no story of self, there is no self, and no other, or none that matters. Worse, perhaps, there is no hope, no possibility of future life. If we are to exist, Warren's *Audubon* seems to argue, it must be in some awareness like Audubon's, with consciousness alert, sensing the membrane between us and the rest, testing its strength. In telling our stories, whether as confession or a poem's dramatic enactment, we are all in the position of James Weldon Johnson trying to get life right. The older a writer grows, the more he wants to make his unique life seen and known, which, paradoxically, reveals how his life is like another's, and that symmetry, in the end, opens the rough door to the illuminating value of *Audubon*.

James Dickey's Motions

Much has been written about James Dickey that is misinformed, silly, or plainly wrong, especially about the latter half of Dickey's career. The critical profile ranges from a venomous, apparently political opposition to a syco-phantic cheering. In *A History of Modern Poetry,* David Perkins writes tersely of Dickey's "Southern narratives" to imply facile local color, which some readers think characteristic of Dickey's poetry. Charles Molesworth and Neal Bowers view Dickey as a charlatan and boor, extending Robert Bly's early attack on Dickey's poetry for its socially and politically objectionable agen-das. At the other extreme, Robert Kirschten, in *James Dickey and the Gentle Ecstasy of Earth: A Reading of the Poems,* concludes with a partisan chant when he writes, "Long may James Dickey be the slugger of creative daring and commitment to poetry so that we may continue our circle and sing."

The southern poet, like the region's indigenous cottonmouth water moc-casin, does not travel well and plays poorly even at home, tendencies that are distinct limitations in national endeavors. James Dickey has often been treated by his press as exactly what Bly's essay called him, a "great blubbery southern toad of a poet." Moreover, both in his poetry and out of it he has assisted the persistent view of the *southern poet* as oxymoron and not least by playing the role of the brutal sheriff in *Deliverance.* One thinks of Donald Justice or A. R. Ammons to note how different and how melodramatically poetic has been the role Dickey has played.

A Georgian who lived most of his adult life in South Carolina, Dickey made his career in the 1960s and 1970s not merely with rhythmically fresh poems but also in critical reviews, often corrosive, of poets favored by one contingency or another. His success, and pleasure in his success, seemed unrestrained at his frequent stops along the poetry reading circuit, a circuit his dizzying pace and voracious appetites helped to make a feature of the life of poetry in the United States. Indeed, Dickey's personal conduct as traveling bard generated an apocrypha about him like that of Dylan Thomas. Dickey cunningly and rightly counted on notoriety to carry his poetry to an audience usually indifferent to academic poems, but his outlaw image among the academics has affirmed the southern poet as inferior and crude. That is, of course, poetry and politics. In his self-professed desire to be, and to write, unlike other poets, Dickey opposed everybody but thumbed his nose with particular animosity toward the eastern academy. The figure he cut was large and arrogant. He does not compromise or apologize for excesses.

If Dickey was the sheriff, he stood also, uncomfortably for many, too close to *Deliverance*'s sodomizing and murdering mountaineers, who were, after all, southerners. But Dickey's fiction and poems proved compelling to readers who wanted a sense of lives without the self-criticism and the warp that entailed. Audiences who turned out in hundreds to hear Dickey found in his work stories of men who seemed to have the true grit, tales not found in surreal fantasies, in metric cosmologies, in confession, therapy, or counter-culture meetings. Dickey's poetry affirmed the life of his readers, though it was imperiled, dangerous, abrupt. Mostly they were post–World War II, middle-class, upwardly mobile people who understood the ironic T-shirt that said "And Then You Die."

Yet what most distinguishes Dickey's poetry, early and late, is an unwillingness to abide that coda. He speaks frankly from inside a male, individual, joyous experience. "The Performance," "Walking on Water," "At Darien Bridge," not his most celebrated poems but each a chronological step in his art, are stations toward the roaring joyride of "Cherrylog Road," and the apotheosis of "May Day Sermon to the Women of Gilmer County, Georgia, by a Woman Preacher Leaving the Baptist Church." Mystic lift-off from an ordinary situation is the trope employed in every successful poem by Dickey. Before the ash of mortal circumstance, he offers what religions have always offered, what "The Salt Marsh" has:

> . . . your supple inclusion
> Among fields without promise of harvest,
> In their marvelous, spiritual walking
> Everywhere, anywhere.

It is even the joy of truck drivers hymned in "Them, Crying" because they feel for *"Those few who transcend themselves, / The superhuman tenderness of strangers."*

Dickey's poetry is far from ignorant of the dead, hurt, maligned, abandoned peoples who are the common interest of lyric American poetry, but his investigation and investment have nevertheless been in personal, transcendent joy. His poems seek a good time on bourgeois terms. They are scarcely marked by the gloom of the American poet's self-conscious rehearsal of personal problems from Lowell's New England institutions to Sharon Olds's sexual arias. His *story* is upper-tier southern, a search for life after success: up from the fens of suburbia, a university affiliation, discovery of imagination's open gate, praise for writers who warred and survived, wisdom scrupulously-to-be-examined, books at the heart of it all, teaching fame, more books. Had Randall Jarrell played football instead of tennis, he might have been this poet.

With the publication of *The Whole Motion: Collected Poems, 1945–1992*, Dickey included early uncollected poems, evidence for what Emerson, in his note to Whitman, called a "foreground." Poems gathered under the title "Summons" show how Dickey labored from his first published work to make a different sound. This early poetry shows little of the southern self-awareness and *mea culpa* whose breast-beating Faulknerian tones made the "burden" of consciousness which appealed, and does appeal, to generations of academics. That it might not attract a general reader, Dickey saw well enough. He was not a successful advertising man in Atlanta for nothing. He set out to transform the pastoral lyric by combining it with a heroic quest for a self who is, as Fred Hobson has described him, "the unburdened Southerner." Hobson, writing of Barry Hannah, seemed to echo Cleanth Brooks in citing the disinclination of lyric to attach to any specific landscape and purview; i.e., there is no such cat. Hobson says in *The Southern Writer in the Postmodern World* that "not only do family and past mean nothing to him, the South and his identity as Southerner, he insists, mean nothing to him either. The South of his remembrance . . . isn't mysterious, isn't violent, isn't savage, isn't racially benighted, isn't Gothic or grotesque, isn't even *interesting*."

Even so, the trajectory of Dickey's quest, both what he thought and how he said it, moved from outside to inside, from narrative anecdote to states of being as lyric. The scene, typical of the pastoral, has been the wood world or the sea world, Nature, because it hosts the unknown and, traditionally, nurtures the spirit. Dickey, like Emerson, like Poe, like Keats, has gone outside to find answers to questions echoing on the inside. As with all romantic and lyric poets, the problem was to make intuited consolation, the joy of asserted consequence, credible to readers. What he has done, it now appears in his seventieth year, is to have commanded a formidable rhythmic shift whose expression baffled more than it may have dazzled.

The landscape of the South has everywhere become an ugly memorial to greed and profit, every town and village marked at ingress and egress by the fecal-like stain of fast food dispensers, gas stations, auto lots, the Hell-road of neon. Suburbs rise overnight, leaving instant slums which themselves breed every conceivable social ill. Yet a past still alive is everywhere, too, like last living daughters of Confederate veterans, or my own grandfather, who died at age eighty-eight this past winter, a man who without benefit of a formal education became an aeronautical engineer, who as a boy had hoboed a train to Chicago to see an actual automobile. Wherever there is a Wal-Mart, there's the past, the Arkansan Sam Walton come out of fields to sow appetites and goods, if not ideas whose end we can't guess. Before this world was the Agrarian ideal of classics-tutored imagination, even morality, which has been lately expressed by Walter Sullivan, who says, "Life lived on the farm is more authentic than life lived in the city, because the rural experience teaches the nature of reality." Loss of the farm, much observed by Dickey's poems, distressed teacher Sullivan and pupil Dickey.

Fred Hobson is probably correct that writers from the South increasingly attend to a new, urbanized experience, the life they are actually living. But they are hardly disinterested in the life they are part of, a culture stories and poems show is more, not less, violent, broken, disintegrating, *present*. It may not be inhabited as much by professional southerners as by people who seek identity *now,* people defined by the consequences of place. That culture the Fugitives found so severely altered by the "burden" stands now with the newest of the new Souths. Poets who matter, if they exist, are part of the interrogation conducted by the moral imagination. Ransom stroked and cooed. Tate fussed. Davidson nattered. Interrogation in the South has had a rich place to examine, and interrogation, literally, is poetic act of Robert Penn Warren.

Dickey's voice, from his first poems, possessed a ventriloquial ability very like Warren's and was capable of calibration for effect, at times admonishing, assertive, even evangelical with a range of wailing, wall-bursting rhetoric. The cast of characters through whom he has spoken, while not infinite, displays operatic versatility: a king, warrior, hunter, fisherman, fish, bird, boar, wolverine, leopard, quarterback, musician, woman preacher, lifeguard, etc.

Being mysterious conduits for inner speech, his poems send to a wobbly world messages of health, solidarity, and continuity evinced in engagements with natural force. His "nature" revery stands on authority for speech from an intuited scheme of order as known to Milton as to Poe, but now in jeopardy. In his visionary role, Dickey urges cultivation of what Whitman would have called "athletic" virtues for renewed vitality.

This has, I think, brought Dickey's poetry to a gulch it has not always transcended. The lyric poet hasn't the equipment for scope, for patient portrait of social ills or their remedies, which is necessary for the epic chronicler of national states (one reason for the contemporary argument about whether lyric can be successfully political). Yet against all risk the lyric poet feels he must contend for the biggest stakes. Dickey once told me he hadn't and wouldn't ever write "anything small." Although *small* may have meant physical length, I understood it to mean poems not adequately ambitious to speak of and for the imperiled soul of the tribe. Dickey's most regional "big" poems record the end of old ways (hence, perhaps, of "southernness"). "Hunting Civil War Relics at Nimblewill Creek," "Snow on a Southern State," "Sled Burial, Dream Ceremony," "Slave Quarters," and "Two Poems of Going Home" suggest what I mean although the foremost example is "May Day Sermon to the Women of Gilmer County, Georgia, by a Woman Preacher Leaving the Baptist Church."

The will to assume a civic voice seems more prominent in poems which appear in *The Eye-Beaters, Blood, Victory, Madness, Buckhead, and Mercy* (1970), where the short lines and crisp stanzas Dickey had refined in his middle work yielded to poems whose visual shapes were irregular and whose aural experience was erratically loud. "Apollo," "The Strength of Fields," "The Olympian," and "For a Time and Place" assumed the speech of the republican broadcaster of answers. It is, I think, the wrong role for Dickey who seems here bathetic and transparently bad. He is bad because he abandons his rhythmic delicacy, not because he forgoes his narrative gift. He is bad because he fails to use language as an act of discovery, a door into that wood world whose secrets the pastoral poet unlocks. Dickey bangs dully, laboring more and more mightily, as if noise will overcome deafness, as in "For the Running of the New York City Marathon":

I am second

Wind and native muscle in the streets   my image lost and discovered

Among yours: lost and found in the endless panes
Of a many-gestured bald-headed woman, caught between
One set of clothes and tomorrow's: naked, pleading in her wax
For the right, silent words to praise
The herd-hammering pulse of our sneakers,
And the time gone by when we paced
River-sided, close-packed in our jostled beginning,
O my multitudes,

Whitman would, of course, would have smiled at this.

Even here, however, Dickey shines with the "right, silent words to praise." At his best when he resists pretension to social and cohesive opinion, when he celebrates the rural life dominant in the South until his generation, Dickey's interest lights up for the pre-rural, wild landscape, the Adamic scene of scars to our bodies and fears to our souls, marking him an American example of what Seamus Heaney has called a "venerator." His poems locate and report sites of energy like unploughed bottom lands our myths, legends, and souls regard as compelling and tutorial. More often an elegiac than an epic or dramatic writer, Dickey concentrates emotive power to evoke immediate, strong response. Necessarily pastoral, its attitude more backward facing than forward, the poem laments change that erodes the durable and good by which man has so long flourished; yet this attitude is less divorced from political and social engagement than might be suspected. To praise the past against a corrupted present is to lodge complaint against the causes and conditions of corruption. As the portrait moves toward articulated vision, a transcendent and improved, if mythical, scheme presses more vigorously into the receptive consciousness of the poet. The poem seeks to distill everything to essence beyond which no consciousness can go, the process undertaken by Dickey's poems after the mid-1970s. Two possibilities open for the poet: one in the formal structuring of poems, the other in scenic matter. There is nothing inherently southern in form (or forms), yet it is formal evolution, with great restlessness, that marks Dickey's poetry. Evolving a poetic sound, Dickey had the skills of the venerator but was driven by the imperatives of a republican voice, a divided duty. A retraining needed to address that dilemma results in the characteristic (and not very southern) sound of poetry Dickey has written in the 1980s and 1990s as collected in *Head-Deep in Strange Sounds: Free-Flight Improvisations from the unEnglish* (1979), *Puella* (1982), and *The Eagle's Mile* (1990).

Paul Ramsey, a southern poet who writes in the metric style, complains: "The metrical history of James Dickey can be put briefly and sadly: a great lyric rhythm found him; he varied it; loosened it; then left it, to try an inferior form." The rhythmic form Ramsey admired flashes in the twenty-five poems of "Summons," which opens *The Whole Motion: Collected Poems, 1945–1992.* Stanzas from "For Robert Bhain Campbell" illustrate:

> I like him; I love him,
> I shall soon sit cold in an office,
> Hearing the sea swing, the dead man step:
> The sun at sunset in the mind
> Never falls, never fails.
>
> There is Berryman's poem, where you were a bird.
> And I, an unsocial man,
> Live working for some kind of living
> In a job where there is no light. But
> I can summon, can summon,
> And your face in my mind is hid
> By a beard I read you once grew.

Wanting both intimate and statemental registers, the voice swings through uncertain feet that sound here poised, there about to collapse. But the last three lines display what Ramsey had in mind, an easy rhythm embodied in the line's assertion, its trimeter-making syllables falling delicately into the anapestic shape for which Dickey's poetry would become known. Still, I am unconvinced that Dickey ever composed by metric count; he seems to have worked in phrase parallels, a practice visible in so-called free lines in Whitman. Very shortly, one imagines, Dickey's sense of line might have led him to revise stanza one this way:

> In an office, hearing
> The sea swing, the dead man
> Step the sun at sunset
> In the mind, never failing.

Dickey's short line, faintly incantatory, has a talent for bodying drama *inside* the mind, a consciousness moving backward and forward in time. Aggressive, receptive, it rocks with a feel of speed but also with grip and distance. By 1962, in *Drowning with Others,* Dickey had learned subtleties inherent in this form, the lean, agile stanzas in five and six lines, clusters of perception that leaped from the real to the mystical, as in "Fog Envelops the Animals":

> Fog envelops the animals.
> Not one can be seen, and they live.
> At my knees, a cloud wears slowly
> Up out of the buried earth.
> In a white suit I stand waiting.

While four of the five lines make bold statement, a progression of tetrameter creates a background sense of reluctant movement at confronting the unknown. Each line proceeds as a consequence of the first fact line, though nothing else appears factual because of shimmery, slight, and oddly formal syntax which makes "and they live" a soft cry of discovery, also making the cloud out of the earth seem a spirit and inscribing the white suit of the speaker as the ritual dress of the about-to-be-changed. Dickey's anapests, although struggling against trochees, create the three-pace phrase which retards an energy threatening to bolt. Thus "and they live" holds back momentum and permits discovery, as "At my knees" sets it up.

By the mid-1960s Dickey mastered variations of anapestic rhythm. They were needed to avoid the inherent monotony of his stichic chant, a weakness especially troublesome for one of the two kinds of poems he wanted to write. Dickey had from the start a narrative talent for bringing life to a scene, coloring it, expanding it cinematically. The short line enabled immersion, the stress pushing ahead, the double drag of anapest retarding. The action of statement was realistic and external, right for direct moves. Dickey saw how to tap into moments of mythic reach. Here are two first stanzas that illustrate:

> When the rattlesnake bit, I lay
> In a dream of the country, and dreamed
> Day after day of the river
> > ("The Poisoned Man")

> Beginning to dangle beneath
> The wind that blows from the undermined wood,
> I feel the great pulley grind
> > ("In the Marble Quarry")

A penchant for blowing up ordinary scenes into posters of experience would force his work farther from the domestic arena and into such wilderness as may be left to an urbanized South, creating Dickey's need for a line form which resisted monotony and did not delay progression through time and space. He wanted lines capable of what he called, after Alfred North Whitehead, "presentational immediacy." The poems of *Buckdancer's Choice* (1965) appear restless in the irregular lines and stanzas (his gap space device appears) of "The Firebombing" and the long-line quintets of "Reincarnation," as do the sculpted quatrains of "The War Wound," giving way to the wall of words in "The Shark's Parlor" and "The Fiend." Dickey had worked himself into possession of multiple rhythms, none of which sufficed entirely for the tune he wanted to play, the evangelical ring of the undeniable. His hunt for that sound is shown by his draft worksheets held by Washington University. Here are the first eight lines of "May Day Sermon to the Women of Gilmer County, Georgia, by a Woman Preacher Leaving the Baptist Church," the first draft then called "Sears."

> The wide-open dance of motes.
> The swinging sand of the motes.
> The wide-open dance,
> The swinging sand of dust.
> That other glory shall pass.
> The stable wanders over the earth.
> And at night, in the animal's sleep,
> The stable wanders over the earth.

The initial lines fumble with the image of dust as if he can't find a way past tranquility to his violent tale of paternal and religious abuse, and indeed the struggle lies between potentially soporific iambs and anapests, all jarred by trochees. But by line six a stability seems to arrive as anapests set a dominant pace, one Dickey will couch in longer lines only in the very last draft before publication. Buried in the lines which seem cut out by a worshipper's intensifying in-breath and out-breath, the surge and drag of Dickey's old trimeter pattern sometimes counters an even older tetrameter whose sound is a composite of Anglo-Saxon beats and King James idiom. With this shift, and a bit of Milton's Satan thrown in, Dickey's invocation bespeaks a hybrid parable of joyful ascension:

Open   to show you the dark where the one pole of light is paid out
In spring by the loft, and in it the croker sacks sprawling and shuttling
Themselves into place as it comes   comes   through spiders dead
Drunk on their threads   the hog's fat bristling   the milk
Snake in the rafters unbending through gnats to touch the last place
Alive on the sun with his tongue   I shall be flickering from my mouth

Ramsey was certainly correct in observing that Dickey had "loosened" the rhythm. He did so to liberate the poem from its own success, the solid "click" of the trimeter lyric in, say, "The Heaven of Animals." Doubtless, the gain for Dickey was simply pleasure in stepping outside reader expectations, his own included. This will to change and change again seems, in retrospect, characteristic of Dickey's writing, as it was of Robert Penn Warren's. Having disguised and modulated his initial rhythm with the new spread of lines, other aspects of Dickey's treatment of language became manifest. In some respects language became his primary subject. He cultivated syntactic reversals, suspensions, word-fusions, print gimmicks, clausal ambiguities, and enjambments that left comprehension hovering mid-margin like annotation. "The Eye-Beaters," in fact, employed the poem's margins for authorial commentary. Dickey transformed verbs into nouns, nouns into adjectives, adjectives into phrases. He played loose with syllable counts; he truncated sentences to fragments; he made lines of single words. He often abandoned regular stanzas, allowing the words to determine rhythm visually by sometimes sprawling, sometimes marching, always defining their function in their management of the white space of the page.

The result of Dickey's improvisations was to move his brand of poem visibly away—as it had already removed itself thematically—from more conventional contemporary poems. In the *New York Times Book Review,* Hayden Carruth said he hoped that W. S. Merwin would explain what his mystical poems were trying to say, a chronic trouble for poems of that period and true of Dickey's poems that began to seem more hermetic than anyone's. In truth, Dickey's poems had never been all that accessible because an interiority he favored, a will to shift inner and outer forums, required truly attentive readers; but his poems became ever more oblique as he cut the reader's connectors and transitions, offered few clues to relationships, and often left a puzzle of wisps and grunts. Still, his tales spoke in the voice of what he had once called "the energized man," and nowhere more so than in *The Zodiac* (1976), as much about poetry and language as it is about anything. The energized man, to Ramsey and other formalists, was a howler. Could passion justify the willful obliquity of "Root-light, or the Lawyer's Daughter"?

> That any just to long for
> The rest of my life, would come, diving like a lifetime
> Explosion in the juices
> Of palmettoes flowing
> Red in the St. Mary's River as it sets in the east
> Georgia from Florida off, makes whatever child
> I was lie still, dividing . . .

Dickey hoped his form experiments would jam more intense life into the poem as enactment. Desiring to wed fiction, poetry, and film, he was moving farther from traditional predecessors in southern poetry. Only Warren evinced anything like the formal trials Dickey attempted, and Warren, to many readers, remained a fiction writer traveling in the netherland of poetry. Dickey, with the publication of *Deliverance, Alnilam,* and *To the White Sea* similarly aligned himself with the southern literature industry, but it is poetry and its motions which make him important as writer, and perhaps as southerner.

Dickey, to use Fred Hobson's word again, is *unburdened* by a sense of obligation. The pressure exerted upon his formal choices comes not from an antiquarian standard but from an attempt to accommodate present experience in a living language. Allen Tate said the problem for the modern was not that he had no form but that he had too many from which to choose. Dickey's problem has obliged him to know that any new form would have to avoid monotony that tended to sap his early and middle lyrics. At the same time, he wanted this form to make clear shifts away from narratives which undergirded his accomplishment and reputation.

The nature of what constitutes a southern narrative may best be known to the person who perceives it as such. If benchmarks of southern fiction are applied, then one supposes there must be violence, warfare, sexual encounters, pursuit of a wild creature in the wood or in the water, with an accompanying calibration of the spirit's experience. If the dominant subjects of the poems are family members, dysfunctional or otherwise, and if the stories invoke the memory that composes a compound of law and expectation for the family, then the definition for southern literature may qualify poems as southern narratives. But I see no reason why "In the Waiting Room," Eliza-beth Bishop's poem about a visit to the dentist, or Adrienne Rich's "Diving into the Wreck," an undersea divagation, might not be equally southern, ex-cepting, of course, neither poet identifies her landscape as southern and, in any regional sense, their landscapes do not function as actors of rhythm, voices of what James Applewhite has called, in "The Poet and Home and in the South," the southern proclivity for texture and a parallel inability to make direct statement that is the province of lyric.

With landscape as rhythm and a form evolving to minimize the narra-tive, squeezing it between the lines, Dickey's most recent poetry arrives at a new phase. I mean by rhythm, now, what Warren meant in *Democracy and Poetry* when he wrote that rhythm is "not mere meter, but all the pulse of movement, density, and shadings of intensity of feeling." Dickey's reason for the change, insofar as it may be a personal choice, cannot be known; we can see, though, that his interest in peopled dramas has lessened (though it is not entirely abandoned) in favor of an interest in states of being realized through intense, and, after *Puella,* drastically shorter clusters of language. *Puella* is an odd interstice, as I think is *The Zodiac,* for its poems attempt to speak in the voice of Dickey's second wife Deborah, hence as dramatic monologues, and they attempt the coherence of a *Bildungsroman* or a portrait much like an autobiography, a fictive self self-made.

These poems are unsuccessful heroic quests, narratives of a speaker whose goal must be an emergence from darkness into a treasure-hoard of bright knowledge. For all of Dickey's story skill, neither *Puella* nor *The Zo-diac* sustains a beginning-middle-end clarity and progress that we will pay to watch all the way through. I think neither voice is so credibly itself as it is Dickey's, pitched, squeaky, noddingly thrown. The life-plot in each poem is so subordinated to a massing of language appropriate to Dickey's interest in states of being that confusion results. Nor are we transported to revelation. Both poems are never "small," but they try too hard to be "big." In them may be seen the manner of his late poetry, its richness and its dross, a manner visibly the result of a shift meant to realign Dickey's formal strategies with his search for an inwardly intensified consciousness and an outwardly pres-surized rhythm.

Without study of his worksheets and drafts, no definite date can be as-signed for the emergence of the lyric sound characteristic of everything Dickey has published since 1976. It is evident, more and less, as a transitional character, then a central motif, and at last as a subject. These poems show a baffling, edged sense of incompleteness, arbitrariness, and rough-born form that some have regarded as proof of a failed talent. Although there is no doubt the late poems are tougher going, I think Dickey's last collections are not so opaque and lacking in an early, eerie clarity as some have argued. But there is a strange, new rhythmic pitch, visible early in *Puella:*

> With a fresh, gangling resonance
> Truing handsomely. I draw on left-handed space
> For a brave ballast shelving and bracing, and from it,
>
> > > then the light
> Prowling lift-off, the treble's strewn search and wide-angle
> > > glitter.

This passage from "From Time" buries statement ("I draw on left-handed space") in a haze of unpatterned syllables which make an appositional elaboration, a stretched and gliding sentence which features three suspensions or caesuric swirls. Dickey recognizes that his poem resists referential access, so he provides a subtitle ("Deborah for Years at the Piano"). The passage cited is, otherwise, unresolvably ambiguous—yet feels rhythmically persuasive as it works by accretion and momentum, prose principles, and alludes to carpentry, stress forces, and photographic effect all to reinforce a sense of "measuring" in the reader. The laid-in quality of language intense with intention but struggling to move explains the frequent verbals. To the extent that the lines comment on what it *feels like to play piano,* they are registers of inward awareness, slowed thought imitating act and look.

The registration of states of being, of conditions of feeling, as the enactment of poems appears to migrate toward a form which employs greater ellipsis, compression, and density, all provided for not through symbol so much as through the word-function shifts which Dickey favors, a truncated and often spatially isolated or dramatically enjambed statement for which the usual expectations are frustrated, subverted, and altered. He removes the scaffolding of dramatic circumstance and blurs the occasion of speech, leaving a language of emotive intensity, a sort of curriculum for the soul's epiphanies. *The Eagle's Mile* (1991) would pose, even for experienced readers, difficulty unmatched by any previous work, but close attention would have seen it coming.

Head-Deep in Strange Sounds: Free-Flight Improvisations from the Un-English (1979) is a baker's dozen poems, each carrying such handrails as "after

Alfred Jarry," "near Eugenio Montale," and "from the Hungarian of Attila Josef, head crushed between two boxcars." Are they translations? Imitations? Shared compositions? I think they are poems which seek a form-sound in the translation of European poets at the same time and in much the same way that James Wright and others did it. They break the chronological-anecdotal structure, the linear thought movement, seeking a dream-fusion of states of being, a braiding of voice in which the inhibitions of usual form and practice may be escaped. They are poems with a form that permits Dickey to speak of emotion as well as public experiences, about, as he says, "the evil / of just living"; or of the magic of the language of numbers "from the frozen, radiant center / Of that ravishing clarity you give."

Double-Tongue: Collaborations and Rewrites, the final section of *The Eagle's Mile,* contains nine poems very similar to those of *Head-Deep,* each displaying the phrase-making power that marks Dickey as a notably epigrammatic poet as well as an imagist with the skills of a jeweler. These skills are the heart of the brevity, spatial sculpting, and concentration in his later work. With compressive form, Dickey has vitalized landscapes as historical and evolutionary witnesses. In "Lakes of Värmland" he eulogizes Viking warriors "in water turned to brass" by old wars, his precursors, of whom he says "I wish to gather near them," a discourse as doomed and moving as that of the "The Seafarer," that Anglo-Saxon call to the death-tinged quest, poignant with late-life's hard wisdom. Landscapes in these poems are rife with danger, with cold, height, inhospitable trials, the blank mercilessness of rooms of air a man comes to—"No side protected, at home, play-penned / With holocaust." Dickey's late-season poetry has left him with chilling views, sometimes *vistas,* of mortal experience, which do not always offer consequence for the yearner. He uses his poems to evoke a sense of cyclical inevitability, a sort of master rhythm to which man must fit himself, and for which pastoral yearning has never been quite enough to satisfy him, despite his deep roots in agrarian and southern awareness of rhythmic elements. Landscapes contain now, it would seem, the full evocation of final ends. In the talky but, perhaps, undeniable "Farmers" he says:

> When love gives him back the rough red of his face he dares
>
> To true-up the seasons of life with the raggedness of earth,
>   With the underground stream as it turns its water
>   Into the free stand of the well: a language takes hold

His old habit of conducting big matters from the civic podium, one he lamented in Robinson Jeffers, permits Dickey to assert what he does not dramatize, the noble and exemplary synchronization of environment and manhood, deed and principle. The southerner knows this ordinary farmer, praised into mystical junction with his place, knows that language of pain and sacrifice; even knows this old tool in the program of heroes. But Dickey's landscape here has less poetry than the Burma Shave rhetoric somewhere behind it.

The new rhythm of landscape, an image strategy, antirational and associational, born of his interest in European modernist poetics, drives Dickey's reach for immediacy, a dream-like intensity of consciousness receiving unmediated impulses. Yet the "form" weakens under blunt statements lacking coloration, extension, appositional naming, relying on gimmicky spacing of lines as a volume control. "Gila Bend," a memory of pilot gunnery training in World War II, recalls the scene with "a cadaver / On foot," and it is really scene, not dilemma, which cranks the poem's energy, a desertscape of "small-stone heat / No man can cross; no man could . . . " survive to "rise face-out":

> Full-force from the grave, where the sun is down on him
>
> Alone, harder than resurrection
>
> Is up: down harder
>
> harder
>
> Much harder than that.

A slight comic bravado in the last line erodes the grim tone as the poet appears manipulative. The trochees, triply repeated as "harder," slide into lapel-shaking. The same intensity, however, leads in *The Eagle's Mile* to an unusual feel of colloquy with natural forces (often personified), and you feel strongly renewed energy in elemental and religious imagery such as that of birds, flight, and upward soaring. Poems praise yearning for heights. As Dickey says in "Eagles" about ambition, "The higher rock is / The more it lives." If suspension of disbelief falters before hierarchical ordering which Dickey loves, it is worth recalling that boasts once functioned in our tribal rituals (and literary heritage) to defend against self-defeat as well as to illuminate destiny. The stance of the aged warrior gazing at eternals, willing survival, reappears:

Where you take hold, I will take
That stand in my mind, rock bird alive with the spirit-
life of height

When the heroic imperative wanes and the pastoral waxes, Dickey lo-
cates himself once more at edges of change. "Circuit," "Daybreak," and "Two
Women" are all poems of beaches, apparently the Atlantic off South Caro-
lina. Dickey's beaches, sentient fractals, constantly remake themselves (as
the soul does) with "their minds on a perfect connection" which, when you
walk them, allow you to "meet yourself," even to make a kind of ultimate
prayer: "Stretch and tell me, Lord; / Let the place talk. / This may just be
it." The colloquial side-of-the-mouth tone of that last half-line has become
a staple finish for Dickey, used to cut against the statements of revelation
which he favors, statements typically designed as elegiac praise for places
he views as junctures of meaning and consequence. This aspect of Dickey's
poetry understands place to *have* historical consciousness; there he locates
rhythmic and final realities. There is a great sweetness he is adamant to ex-
press. It brings forth a gentler quality, a trimmed, efficient presentation as in
"Night Bird," the narcissistic "Daybreak," the playful "To the Butterflies," and
in "Two Women":

Early light: light less
Than other light. Sandal without power
To mark sand. Softly,
Her hair downward-burning, she walks here, her foot-touch

The place itself,

Like sand-grains, unintended,

Born infinite.

The liquid balance that sounds, with *l*s, the hieratic entry and image
power of this woman evokes Genesis, Eve, and Helen. Poe would have ap-
proved. With the poetry in *The Eagle's Mile* Dickey fuses image medallions
with narrative. The roaring rhythms of his mid-career lyrics slow to write
less and get more said. Always a page architect, Dickey's effects range from
list to epitaph. Even the civic witness works in "The Eagle's Mile," a poem
odelike in celebrating masculine, democratic virtues in Chief Justice William

Douglas, an outdoorsman and master of Hopkins's "cliffs of the mind." Dickey sees Douglas's spirit riding over the last wilds of north Georgia, making contact with Nature's sources of origin, if Tate and Ransom might have suspected an Adamic blindness:

> Catch into the hunted
> Horns of the buck, and thus into the deepest hearing—
> Nerveless, all bone, bone-tuned
> To leaves and twigs—with the grass drying wildly
> When you woke where you stood with all the blades rising
> Behind you, and stepped out
> > possessing the trail.

Beside this man-on-the-trail solitary, Dickey stacks a poetry of tenderness in "Daughter," a father's gladness at the delivery of his daughter becoming an exaltation of the guiding powers of life. It begins in the touch of a small finger:

> To him: not father of God, but assistant
> Father to this one. All forests are moving, all waves
> All lava and ice. I lean. I touch
>
> One finger. Real God, roll.
>
> Roll.

Dickey's poetry has turned autumnal, but it is not gloomy. He has lived as a warrior in spirit, a joy-seeker, a minister for whatever world he can act for and in. Richard Wilbur's phrase "the mood of manhood" describes what Dickey wants in poetry. He rejects the usual structures and visions of the contemporary poet; his pastoral depends on heroic enterprise, on out-of-shape Rocky-like runners ("The Olympian"), on a middle-aged man's fantasy of foiling a thief with his weapon ("Spring-Shock"), on a snowfall that may be someone's "very great winning hand" ("Snow Thickets"). He believes manliness connects to consequence, a way, a courage of behaving by which, as "Expanses" tells us, "a man comes; / It's true, he's alive." To know that is to frame acceptance, a submission to the rhythms of being, and finally

> Brother: boundless,
> Earthbound, trouble-free, and all you want—
>
> Joy like short grass.

The man at the heart of *The Eagle's Mile,* himself a fantasy, once forged a life from wilds we don't have much of now, one whose memory speaks the unspeakable, one whose destiny is not burdened consciousness, not sophistry. Dickey's motions are inseparable from his southern experience, experience that could have happened elsewhere, but did happen to him, in the South, with nuances that define a difference. In "The Little More," a catechism, he describes the quality of time between boyhood and maturity, an instant that cannot truly be said, but known as "Joy set in the bending void / Between the oars" of a rowed craft. Joy, he thinks, is the lure of living, the quest's end. It comes to the boy, he says, who evolves a capable self. "The Little More" is Dickey come out of the wood world, wise, offering the power to "carry" (here a football carrier) which is simultaneously metaphor and faith:

> Boy who will always be glanced-at
>   and then fixed
>
>   In warm gazes, already the past knows
>   It cannot invent you again,
>
>   For the glitter on top of the current
> Is not the current.
>   No, but what dances on it is
>   More beautiful than what takes its time
>   Beneath, running on a single unreleased
>   Eternal breath, rammed
>   With carry, its all-out dream and dread
>
>   Surging bull-breasted,
>
>   Head-down, unblocked.

Public cadence that exhorts, private cadence that knows are the regional markers in the poetry of James Dickey, as mysterious as destiny. Combining them, Dickey praises. What he wants is an "Eternal breath / rammed with carry," destiny, and more, a little more, as he says. He asks for consequence, order within all orders, and motions, which those who give their lives to poetry might leave on the page as the issue of life. Life's issue, as he might say, is everything. It is local rhythm. It is the many braided in one for which the poet hunts. It is.

II

Life in the Life of Poetry

Barbaric Yawps

LIFE IN THE LIFE OF POETRY

Walter Whitman, carpenter, journalist, temperance man, and opera buff, announced himself as the first modern American poet when he hurled "barbaric yawps" over the roofs of his unsuspecting countrymen. He intended to make the sounds of primal life in poetic form that contained it but scantily. No word describes what Whitman meant more than *appetite*. He wanted more of everything that was life inside his poems. His nineteenth-century critics, easily shocked, derided him as tasteless and ignorant of form. He sounded like what crude America was trying not to be. By the middle of the twentieth century, James Dickey would write that we were dying of the civilized. Between them T. S. Eliot argued, in 1932, that the true poet "must look into the cerebral cortex, the nervous system, and the digestive tracts." If that seems to call for an intimately personal poetry, Eliot would be more readily remembered for saying, "Poetry is not a turning loose of emotion, but an escape from emotion; it is not the expression of personality, but an escape from personality." American poetry early on posed itself the choice of a style as personal as the country still mostly frontier or a style as manicured as the graveled paths of estate gardens where they adored talk of tradition.

A primary context, and characteristic, of American poetry might be put simply. Following the immigration of various peoples into a wilderness abundant with potential, pursuing a great and hitherto unacted idea, the democratic invention of a country, there follows a long period in which people yearn for the wholeness of cultures they have left behind. These cultures appear, in retrospect, virtuous, cohesive, and religious in authority. The ordinary labor of culture, whether pursuing mere survival or glorious imperialism, selects and enacts parts of that culture as the vision of the people, their character. Other parts atrophy, rend, vanish only to reappear at some point as if summoned by another appetite. The natural action of life is change. An inevitable dialectic results between those whose imaginations turn to the past and those whose imaginations are drawn to the future.

This dialectic begins to be observable in American poetry just prior to the middle of the nineteenth century. Yet, providing we exclude oral poetries of native Indians and imported slaves, it is clear there is no American poetic identity before the Civil War. Ralph Waldo Emerson negotiates aloud for it in essays such as "The Poet," his evocation sometimes as palpable as the clouds of pigeons a man could shoot into with no fear of missing. Emerson wrote poetry, but it was not especially American. No American poet's work has been in print longer than Edgar Allan Poe's, or is more recognized as American, but Poe was, as Emerson said in recognizing the heritage of English poetry, our "jingle man." Herman Melville, great improviser of prose, wrote mostly old-fashioned verse, although in subject and tone it was near-contemporary. Longfellow, James Russell Lowell, Whittier, and many now unknown wrote poems little different and certainly no better. Until the middle of the nineteenth century, American poets remained essentially English imitators.

How could it be otherwise? Most Americans were displaced Englishmen, educated to look to the mother country for enlightenment and models of excellence. In all things cultural, London seemed avant garde. Architecture for colonial Americans up and down the Atlantic coast bore the grace of English manors and gardens carved from a wild landscape. American and English painters were interchangeable. Colonial verse promoted American accomplishment as it memorialized Anglican parentage. That is the action of both pastoral and elegy, dominant modes of English nineteen-century poetry. Our early poets applied these modes cautiously and in a manner more choral than personal. The sounds and form of English poetry are clear in stanzas by Emerson, Longfellow, and Melville:

> By the rude bridge that arched the flood,
> Their flag to April's breeze unfurled,
> Here once the embattled farmers stood
> And fired the shot heard round the world.
> ("Concord Hymn," 1837)

> But Ah! What once has been shall be no more!
> The groaning earth in travail and in pain

Brings forth its races, but does not restore,
>>And the dead nations never rise again.
>>("The Jewish Cemetery at Newport," 1852)

When ocean-clouds over inland hills
>>Sweep storming in late autumn brown,
And horror the sodden valley fills,
>>And the spire falls crashing in the town,
I muse upon my country's ills—
>>The tempest bursting from the waste of Time,
On the world's fairest hope linked with man's foulest crime.
>>("Misgivings," 1860)

An incipient nationalism struggling with formal habits forecasts the hunger for a story to carry forth the national identity Whitman would declaim. The stanzas are metrically conventional, syllabled in eights and tens, iambic and anapestic uncertainty prominent and, as Melville shows, overwhelmed by the need to make a pretty point. Rhymes and syntax are dutiful, unremarkable. If there is a surprising, discursive eighteenth-century edge, few readers now miss the shadow of revolutionary Romantic thought and its fretful step. Keats, Shelley, and Coleridge provided the music, each dying before Emerson, who praised them. Great Wordsworth lasted until 1850. These young visionaries charged American thinking and change, themselves energized by the world they knew in flux, one perhaps alterable for the better by what they wrote. But first was the duty to rebuff and redo the work done by old Pope and others. The voice of upheaval that was economic, political, social, and personal weaves the revolutionary manifesto of Wordsworth's "Preface" to the *Lyrical Ballads*. Storms of change leading to a nationalist poetry also led to the life-splintering, self-isolating, culture-shearing industrial age. Wordsworth's young colleague Charles Dickens dramatized the tale of the man who becomes something new in the orphan adrift upon the worst of times, dreaming the best of times. Edgar Allan Poe, three years Dickens's junior, wrote virtually the same tale in a blacker Gothic American poetry.

Even as industrial abuse of the American dream directly followed England's spoilage, American writers toiled in service of the idea that had brought them to exist. Our poets wooed a future sweetened by machinery and science. Benjamin Franklin, a tinkering genius, half-icon of our national character, lived so entirely as a pragmatist that he could dispense wisdom on both electricity and prostitutes. Franklin's spirit, had it written poetry, would have favored a stripped lyric, plain language, resistance to habit, decoration, dull convention; it would have been extroverted, full of facts, impatient, but also brash, vainglorious at times, a structure of fragments, shards of life, an optimistic soliloquy. Such a poem would want to be epic, but epic requires a fixed national identity. American had none. When Poe considered what this meant, he spoke as an orphan, and bitterly:

SONNET—TO SCIENCE

Science! true daughter of Old Time thou art!
  Who alterest all things with thy peering eyes.
Why preyest thou thus upon the poet's heart,
  Vulture, whose wings are dull realities?
How should he love thee? or how deem thee wise,
  Who wouldst not leave him in his wandering
To seek for treasure in the jewelled skies,
  Albeit he soared with undaunted wing?
Hast thou not dragged Diana from her car,
  And driven the Hamadryad from the wood
To seek a shelter in some happier star?
  Hast thou not torn the naid from her flood,
The Elfin from the green grass, and from me
The summer dream beneath the tamarind tree?

Poe's mother had died coughing blood as, apparently, he watched, age two, in 1811. In 1829, Frances Allan, his stepmother, died. Between them, Jane Stanard, a friend's mother upon whom he had a teenage crush, at age thirty-one fell to insanity and subsequent death. Poe's fiancée married another on the day he arrived for her. He was eighteen. Diana, violated in "Sonnet—To Science," is all the women in Poe's life, conflated by the sonnet's allegorizing. At the age of twenty, Poe composed this poem and abstracted the great felony of modern existence. Science had stolen individual life away from a larger community, and stolen, too, the sustenance of that larger definition.

Poe's sonnet would prove far too habitual in its bag of poetic tricks for a poet already stirring in New Jersey. In 1855 Whitman begins, "I celebrate myself, and sing myself, / And what I assume you shall assume," and the monumental "Song of Myself" tosses out most of what the English bards had floated across the Atlantic. Gone, in Whitman's scheme, are iambics, syllable-counted lines, rhymes, classical allusions, poetry's stage props; gone is personified nature, deities; gone the practice of hiding personal life inside a poem's artifice; gone a poem as old art (there would be plenty of arguments over whether Whitman mastered or only avoided art). Whitman cast off overt pastoral lamentation for worlds ravaged by modern ways; he resisted fear of mutation, coveted change, which T. S. Eliot would say meant "dissociation" from human sensibility. No longer Walter Whitman, now Walt, Kiwanis booster, the King of Positive Thinking, hailed the American epic of progress. The spirit's growth, he believed, was commensurate with business, with success in the democratic idea. His was a boomer country, not just more people, but more communities, myriads of opportunities, discoveries, jobs, health, wealth, all literally unfolding the new world. In his love of gizmos, trains, steamboats, telegraphs, of materials—"brick, lime, timber, paint, glass, and iron (so now you can build what you like)"—an endless catalog, Whitman was Franklin's man, too. He refused an old poetry of anachronistic myths, inkhorn lingoes, and prissy forms. Walt was the poet of men and women, here, now. The task was to open the poem to life in the new, democratic way.

Whitman appeared like a comet, as if no literary culture prepared for or conceived him. Emerson, however, had proposed the mystical spirit Whitman had to be; Franklin had brought the Yankee can-do temperament. Fused in Whitman's poetry, an American identity begins, one as internally contentious as the two-party political system that would evolve. In American poetry opinions about form and function mimic a grange meeting of farmers whose object is better production. But what that production is, voices of principle and of utility did not easily agree, hence the evolution of an early mimetic, discursive, function-directed style, the poem of civic discourse and prayer. Nineteenth-century English poets were, however, leveraging a variety of odes against that style. This appealed to a Romantic sensibility in America that would spread like southern kudzu. Jeffersonian thinking had set the will of the majority and the will of the individual into equality guaranteed by the Constitution and bled for by patriots. But this was political dialectic. The individual was, finally, more equal and this individual was a come-here country-maker and, thus, subject of the American epic of an expanded life, the poem Walt Whitman, in 1855, called *Leaves of Grass*.

When I was in graduate school, my professors, all New Critical thinkers, spoke of Whitman's voice as "the Universal I" of the poem. Perhaps those

Americans needed to do to Whitman what the movies did to Clark Kent, Clark Gable, all the Clarks from small-town USA, to homogenize him. Whitman's voice was not Shakespearean, not Miltonic, not even poetic to Anglican-tuned ears. Tennyson said, "Whitman is a great big something, I do not know what." This great gray woofer, an American original, to many of us wrote howlingly bad and mercilessly funny lines. Pound and Williams balked, but found Whitman was their kin, too. New Critical orthodoxy, following Eliot's argument for impersonal art in "Tradition and the Individual Talent," depersonalized Whitman until he became a cosmic "I." Teachers still speak, the aging ones, of Whitman with vague grunts over his rhetorically regulated lines, unconventional structure, aberrations, and stretches of rhetoric; they are yet baffled by his tapestry of improvisation and compensation. One of them, H. T. Kirby-Smith, in a brilliant study of the relationship between poetry and music, *The Celestial Twins: Poetry and Music Through the Ages* (1999), can only say that Whitman "is more of a phenomenon than a poet." I think Kirby-Smith is wrong.

Whitman invented a poetry whose object was to get one full American life, as it was lived, on the page, and he succeeded. He made poems of a literal place and time; he located reality by his senses. He believed the transcendent lay in the immediate, in the dignity and value of the ordinary democratic man and woman. Emerson heard this in Whitman and praised it, until the sexy Calamus poems overwhelmed him. Even Emerson, it turned out, had not been prepared for what his imagination had anticipated in bravura Walt's urgent form, its hybrid homemade solution to the puppetry of lingering Euro-identity. Whitman's boldness echoed what everywhere filled the street talk and penny papers, a new enthusiasm for ready-made potions, salves, chemistries, improvisations all. Whitman saw not as an orphaned changeling, not as the outsider, but as the democratized citizen the national idea had boomed forth. The Declaration of Independence had authorized him. He was the insider now, voice and audience. Whitman believed his appetite for spiritual destiny mirrored any American's. Thus, in letters, he gloated as real what he merely imagined, his "discovery" that deck hands working Brooklyn ferries kept copies of his book in their pants. Whitman's self-promotion, little different from Poe's anonymous self-advertisements in magazines, stands on one idea: the poet matters as entrepreneur of the spirit and must have a role in decisions. He acts. For Whitman, as for none before or after, the poem *is* destiny's voice for the American. That such a role raised questions few might ask or answer in the cob-rough new world, Whitman knew well enough. His prefaces stormed: who is the poet? Who is the audience? What is the poem? What is the poet's function? Blustering and hoorahing, he established a consistent, public argument which claimed the individual's life was the center of visionary reality. For every American poet to follow, there would be this examining of self and community, a dialectical relationship in the life of poetry.

While Whitman imagined his poems ferried everywhere, reclusive Emily Dickinson, alive and writing a few hundred miles from him, sewed hers into small, sealed packets which she hid in the rafters of her Amherst house. She may not have worried they would not be toted around in jeans, but she certainly left them to be discovered, and they were. If differences between big Walt and little Emily seem radical, they may deceive. Uncle Walt, voluble, garrulous huckster. Spinster Emily scurrying, seemingly shy, seemingly naïve. She said she would not dare to read the scandalous Whitman, though she would stand silent while her adulterous brother and a neighbor downstairs met scandalously. If Whitman was the poet of amplitude and she the poet of compression, both are imaginations marked by appetites for saying what the life was like then and there. Whitman, a Hoovering machine, embraces everything, taboos of the body, sex, language, religion, race, nature. Dickinson quietly tells us what violence feels like, inner or outer:

> I felt a Cleaving in my Mind
> As if my brain had split—
> I tried to match it, Seam by Seam,
> But could not make them fit.

It might be an advertisement for Prozac. Bluntly, she shows that modern life is different from what preceded it, and the difference is a consciousness of death. "It was a common night, / Except the dying; this to us / Made nature different." We are all dying, lost innocence complains. Yes, but personal pace makes all the difference, wit banters. For both Dickinson and Whitman the poem's value consists in how much life it can carry and make felt and, beyond that, repeatable. They have determined to speak in plain voices, though scarcely voices without distinction. They are tempered by democratic trust that any life matters equally, is holy, exemplary, redeemable, and has its inevitable identity of which idiom is signature, the mosaic of revealed histories and potential destiny.

This aggressive harvest of life is all the more remarkable before the fact that death, when one ages, looms increasingly as the ultimate, and only, reality. Death tends to make a personal poetry eccentric, its presumptions questionable, its authority to make statements about the world suspicious. Poe knew instinctively, one wants to say, what Nietzsche, famously, would declare to the nineteenth century, that God was dead. He knew this meant the death of Nature except as a suspect compensation. Whitman and Dickinson kept the faith. Always the optimist, Whitman believed in 5,000-year cycles of progressive amelioration of the human condition. Dickinson flirted with a transcendence she found as insubstantial as it was alluring. Both understood the terrible consequences of the industrializing world and, despite vigorous wills to live fully, they suffered in fear of separation from a transcendent unity: not the world according to God, but the world according to me. And if the democratic world made every individual's vision coequal, why was one poem better, or even different from another? Given minimal standards of quality, the answer had to be intensity, consciousness, awareness, even what the philosopher Alfred North Whitehead would call "presentational immediacy." In 1897, William James's *The Varieties of Religious Experience* praised what he termed "the felt fact," or a power of life which the self experienced as meaningful and expansive. It was exactly what the American poet wanted.

The task of the American poetic enterprise, reflecting lives altered by the nineteenth-century revolutions, loomed specifically in the balance of the self's drama of growth with the evolution of the democratic story. The poem must engage an impatient, unprepared, ill-educated audience; it must confront Franklin's wariness in all of us. The poem needed to absorb and use resources, accomplishments, visions newcomers brought to the American chance; it had to resist the dead past. Inevitably personal, American poems were ambitious for cosmological scope and wisdom that psychologist Carl Jung would call "the big dream." Life in the life of poetry, increasingly self-conscious poets saw, seemed an oscillation of personal and universal, of naturalism's dire feel and a mystical creator's presence few would altogether deny. Whitman, proselytizing, said a great poetry required a great audience, suggested a great audience required a great poetry, and implicitly recognized what the historian of ideas Lewis P. Simpson has characterized as the dialectic between "history and tradition." It has also become the dialectic between lyric, the personal form, and narrative, the collective form.

Poe's "Sonnet—To Science," emblem of this dialectic, yearns for stability in a wobbled world; we feel his complaint, but a part of us resists its verse configuration as untrue. We know this heart, but not its idiom. Writers, like painters, regard form as adaptive to function, for them content is the shape of the vessel. Those with little writing experience tend to regard poetic form, if it is thought of at all, as ordained traditional, content's only carrier, a done deal; arguments about form become, ipso facto, political and religious debates conducted in disguise. The unresolved dialectic is arguably either strength or problem in American poetry at the end of the twentieth century.

All sides agree poetry has little public presence and less consequence in our national life. A decade of American poets laureate treated as invisibles illuminates the marginal character of the bard where we are governed. The inclusion of a poet in presidential inaugurations of Democrats Carter and Clinton served, on the whole, to annoy television commentators. This can hardly surprise when eloquent critics, prestigious journals, juries and prize-bosses of our intellectual life display no concern for what poems actually have to tell us. Able only to equate poetry's difficulty with putative quality, critics help to isolate poetry, in the process devaluing its function as a life-voice. Able only to measure value in sales, publishers forfeit civic responsibility for quality and leadership. Able only to ingest the pablum of Jewel or Maya Angelou or this week's rock star, the ordinary reader isn't a reader at all. And able only, it often seems, to mumble in code, poets become the village idiots so wickedly satirized by Woody Allen's *Love and Death*. Poetry is in trouble.

For American poetry to walk among us, it would need crutches, wheeled help, a team of attendants. If poetry is not a morbid goner, it makes a good poster child for spiritual vacuity. Testimony about the patient's health is virulent and vitriolic. Critical studies are as much indictments as prognoses, among them Mary Kinzie's *The Cure of Poetry in an Age of Prose,* Jonathan Holden's *The Fate of American Poetry,* Vernon Shetley's *After the Death of Poetry,* and Dana Gioia's *Can Poetry Matter?* Stephen Yenser, in *The Southern Review,* diagnoses: "American poetry is in bad shape . . . By poets we mean a coterie of enervated academics who praise and in turn practice a mediocrity, shun political issues, and ignore the public at large, with the result that the public returns the favor in spades . . . [The poets] have got fat and lazy, thanks to sinecures at universities, honoraria for poetry readings, and grants . . .

Even worse, our lassitudinous, laconic poets have lost touch with the true formalist impulse and have turned *faute de mieux* to a paradoxically prolix 'confessional,' 'lyric' mode notable for its homogeneity." Joseph Epstein, then editor of the *American Scholar,* smoked the poetry world in the August 1988 issue of *Commentary* when he wrote that "poetry no longer seems in any way where the action is. It seems to belong to a sideline activity." Poetry, he thinks, is out of touch with our lives, is all the same, is boring, and who needs it. His reason? Lyric poetry cannot, he says, tell stories and thus refuses "to report on how people live and have lived, to struggle for those larger truths about life the discovery of which is the final justification for reading."

Epstein seems right that poets have refused a national report of who we are. He is wrong, however, about form. Lyric poems also tell stories. Even Aram Saroyan's wee one that goes "Wire air"—that's it, folks—hints at story. Without battling once more over turf-claims for lyric or narrative, a lyric poem is brief, its language is imagistic, its nature is symbolic, its speaker is recognizably an individual. Lyric wants to transcend realism; narration goes toward that. Story wants referential ground (the degree required has been responsible for notorious experiments with form among all twentieth-century authors); lyric wants to leap free of contingent facts and phenomena, or it wants to recompose that world through mosaic pieces that make up a book's collection, thus swapping Franklin's spirit for Whitman's.

While the poetry of Whitman and Dickinson affirmed the centrality of the self, Eliot's modernism found that self so intractable and chaotic, so untrustworthy, that he buried it in oblique structure. The small dreams of the personal life were "transmuted" to history's large dreams. Early modernism hid the self in a deconstructed form, as Poe said in "The Philosophy of Composition" that he had made a disguise of traditional form. Then, in the American 1950s, as Donald Hall argued in his anthology preface to *Contemporary American Poetry,* the swing of things hardened away from improvisation and toward a homogenized lyric style which could come to profound statements, as John Keats did in a poem on a piece of pottery ending in the tautology: "Beauty is truth, truth beauty," and Keats added, for good measure, a parental smack: "that is all / Ye know on earth, and all ye need to know." Tongue-and-groove artifice was the poem *bien fait*'s goal. Richard Wilbur's "Ceremony" set the American standard:

> Ho-hum. I am for wit and wakefulness,
> And love this feigning lady by Bazille.

What's lightly hid is deepest understood,
And when with social smile and formal dress
She teaches leaves to curtsey and quadrille,
I think there are most tigers in the wood.

Wilbur's iambic sextet prances nicely. Allusions to nineteenth-century French painting, a dance of leisurely royals, coded gestures and verbal puns, eye-winks of meaning, a concluding glance toward fairy tale—isn't this a thin life? It appealed powerfully to a nation under Eisenhower, out of the hurly-burly of issues, and especially to GIs back in school who, only five short years earlier, were marching through the horror of World War II. Wilbur was one of those who needed girls under apple trees and an old-fashioned poem. At its worst the poetry of the 1950s is escapist and elitist, even with good reason. The trouble isn't merely a blind eye to social problems, it's a retreat from ambitious vision, a running in place. This form ignored what Whitman called his "demonstrable," the evidence of the pulse; it filtered out what was before us and reimposed what was back there, over there. The poem becomes a fantasy of identity, not a life to be lived into. It lacked the power to bridge to a future looming up as "plastics," that baffling gift Mr. Robinson offered Dustin Hoffman's Benjamin Braddock in *The Graduate*. American poets seemed unable to accept what Whitman put into their mirrors. Pound learned rejection wouldn't work. Williams learned. Robert Penn Warren and Allen Tate, who were tutored by both Eliot's and Ransom's modernism and who would become influential men of letters, also in due course learned.

Warren and Tate taught Robert Lowell to write poems out of a fully, art-fully engaged life, not a life of gestures. It is almost that simple. Lowell, well-launched, heard what bard Bob Dylan would sing of the American heartland, that "the times they are a changin'." In 1959, Lowell published *Life Studies,* poems about what we now call family dysfunction. He included prose, mini-mized rhyme and metric, gave apparently scalding confessions, critiqued political events. He described socking his dad, a boob, for a remark about a girl's reputation. When Tate read the book, scandalized, he said it wasn't po-etry at all. It was, and few poems from that turbulent period in American life have the staying power of Lowell's. He put the true "demonstrable" in poems the way photographers take it from solutions of chemicals—with sudden im-mediacy—and, just as his late poem "Epilogue" says, he presented the "lurid, rapid, garish, grouped, / heightened from life, / yet paralyzed by fact." Lowell's American poem renders "each figure in the photograph / his living name."

The history of contemporary poetry after Lowell is a search for form capacious, flexible, and alive enough to lure back an audience that seemed to have left the building. It was, is statistically the largest audience in history, expanded by population, education, by newly enfranchised voices. Women, blacks, Hispanics, Asians, gays appear in anthologies, in new books, in public forums as never before. More than 150 books of poetry are published annually, many by brand-new presses, the small, regional, government-seeded "little" operations. One thousand literary magazines publish poems. No subject, no perspective, no author lacks for opportunity to be published. All the life one might desire fills somebody's poem publicly. Yet poetry's audience, it's said, flees with each season. Why? Is Joseph Epstein right about the wrong in poems? Another essayist and fiction writer, Philip Lopate, writing in the *New York Times Book Review* (September 8, 1996), says, "when I come upon a poem in a magazine, nine times out of ten it is disappointing." Yes, yes. Commonly, and quickly, we agree. Poetry is dull and petty. But Lopate adds, "atrophying of verbal eloquence has been going on for some time." Yes again, for in their time Milton, Wordsworth, Poe, Whitman, and Wilbur also complained about the poets' new words.

Poetry's distemper has increasingly been charged to the vastly expanded graduate writing programs. Both gay advocate Bruce Bawer and guru Donald Hall have made caustic complaint about a mediocre poetry they argue has failed to compete with the art's giants. Of course, the mediocrity they hate may be the vitally fresh another pair cannot do without. As a journal editor, I see a daily flood of submissions by poets apparently immune to what language can be made to do and not do. Worst, perhaps, is a competent mechanical ability that lacks sensitivity to nuance and to style. Doubtless, reasons complex and multiple say much about American character and education, and sigh for the hell in a hatbox we are headed to. Poetry's contending voices resemble tiny Pomeranian dogs fighting over tidbits, the noise horrifying only. The poetry blistered for being personal fades with the sun; the criticism is rarely more than learned habit and typing.

What, then, explains the sales of Maya Angelou, the followers of Robert Bly, the academic pandering for John Ashbery and Jorie Graham—work ranging from the transparent to the impenetrable? What supports the parallel reality movement hawked by self-declared Language poets, those once-upon-a-time renegades now legitimized by *Postmodern American Poetry,* an icebox of cold-cuts from W. W. Norton and Company? Poetry apparently sells enough to justify publication of an annual 150 books, to say nothing of burgeoning entrepreneurs of the online market. Perhaps W. C. Fields's remark to "never give a sucker an even break" better suits the democratization of poetry than John Milton's claim of "fit audience, though few." Who actually reads poetry? Students mostly; people under the age of thirty. The MTV generation is, itself, eroded by electronic media which does everything massively, commercially, instantly. Poetry can't compete well with movies, videos, computer interaction, talking novels geared to a voyeuristic spectatorship which may render page readers obsolete. Yet if electric technology has changed everything utterly, there remains what the late Larry Levis called "the geography of the psyche" that seems explorable only by a poetry which re-covers the self journeying through American imaginations from Poe to the present.

Following the Age of Lowell, two decades of dominantly image poets pressed life into a poem as girls once pressed flowers into books. The 1960s and 1970s poets tapped into translation and imitation, spurred by Asian presence from China to Japan to Vietnam, and an earlier interest in Spanish, French, and Italian surrealism reemerged. Bly and James Wright, the only Deep Imagists who matter, tried to stir the inner consciousness through Rorschach-like word pictures. Fresh in its touch of dream-quivery depths, abrupt as the venal world it so adeptly charted, this poetry grew as tiresome as any hunk of haiku. By the 1990s, the image tradition looked gimmicky, its poems interchangeable as counter merchandise. Bly's snowy revamp of Emerson led to wisdom poems, to self-help texts, and weird interactive mythchants in Robert Duncan and a host of his priests. Poetry made Iowa City its farm team site, dealing its products to every college and university that wanted players. Business was hot. Their style, what dissertations called Confessional, plodded in narration of personal tales that all too often sounded numbly the same, mannered and ordinary as the 1950s poetry had been.

The turn to stories of the self's adventures, exemplified by Louis Simpson's *The Adventures of the Letter I,* built on Lowell as an early model and evolved what Stanley Plumly called "the prose lyric." The prose lyric attempts to maintain intensity of language with orchestrations of image and sonic patterns that are idiomatic and variable within lines of a subterranean metric base. Such poems tended to be slightly longer than predecessors, with lines sometimes approaching prose, as in the poems of C. K. Williams, and prose opportunities for discourse, description, and meditation are routinely embraced, seeming especially to enhance a sense of unfolding time and space which gives individual life events its particular feel of force, seeming therefore to be a truth narrative. It is in fact an imitative or false narrative where chronology is subordinated to lyric imperatives. The prose lyric wants a charged language of "felt" facts arranged in narrative shape through which to pass to self-recognition and the meaning of historical experience.

Yet the most evocative and symbolic human stories, lacking memorable style and grace and the ordinary interest of the ear that knows poems, have left poetry indicted as too personal, one layer of the self's tawdry skin peeled away to another, and yet another, and no language that answers what all this has to do with me, which I think is the point upon which the poem gains or loses its reader. Oddly, the poem that is too personal may not contain, or reveal, too much life. Surface eccentricity is not necessarily that story of deep delight we covet. Some poets mistake journalistic report for power of the appropriately adduced detail. If the material of life doesn't yield a poem full of life, applied phenomena, aberrant textures, and pathology aren't likely to induce the reader to do the poet's work. Deliberate obscurity is simply bad writing, not new perspective. Hermeticism leads to the poem of mental tricks, verse crosswords. Until gravity changes liberate us from the earth, words remain referential, tools for communication; story stays meaning-construction. Lopate understands it is neither the self as exhibitionist nor the structure of narrative competing with lyric that dulls poems. He argues: "Paradoxical as it sounds, American poetry today suffers not from being too personal or confessional, but from being not personal or confessional enough. Often the poet pulls back from providing just those biographical specificities and idiosyncratic reactions that would bring him alive as an authentic individual."

When, just a moment ago, I alluded to Warren's phrase "a story of deep delight," I assumed, perhaps erroneously, readers would understand he means what we want from each poem: something like Jung's big dream and our own smaller individual dream speaking as one, a dangerous and impressionistic conflation. That story is always about freedom, the soul's liberation. All poems are about freedom. Freedom, of course, is a big dream, a dream that looks as different as blood to this Palestinian and that Israeli. Do universities still teach the value of dreams? Do poems affirm vision of a common code of principles, of manners? Who cares, when in the world's richest nation there are real fears about the gun in the dark, when life spoils for lack of health care, when children suffer our sins. And how hard, too, to believe a poem might salvage the secret life people die for lack of, as William Carlos Williams told us, a poet of the big dream. A voice of conscience and consciousness, the poem of "deep delight" rejects the optimism of simple answers to problems but celebrates the hunger for imperiled life. Language does not translate life; it is life. It has no need to speak obscurely but is desperate for clarity. We want that as we want a drink of bright water. Our poets need not reenact the encyclopedic sweep of Whitman, but as Whitman might say, what is needed is the exquisite tale of one man or woman, to show literally how the world feels, how life is to that mind, a democratic act.

One poet exemplary in this self-defining was the late Larry Levis, whose style resists labeling. Verbal style makes a writer distinctive and memorable, doubtless because it carries the writing personality's best shape, because it touches the reader's shape. Whitman tried to describe the idiosyncratic American character as having one element that, if it might be gotten into poetry, could be distinguishing. He said, "A wild strawberry, a wild grape has the very quality, the distinctive tang. Our poetry lacks 'race.' Most of it might have been written on England or on the Continent." Race, now a dirty word, meant something positive and essential to Whitman, essential individuality.

Larry Levis, like Walt Whitman, made an unlikely candidate for an American poet. He was raised on a grape-producing ranch in dry cowboy country outside Fresno, California, educated at the local university, and proved himself able to fail at the usual American stations of success. We know a good deal about him from his poetry: a dreamer, one found at rock concerts where sweet smoke blew, not given, finally, to many convictions but aware of himself as a citizen in a politically abused country. An intellectual who emerged from an agrarian background, he loved vineyard life for its pastoral character and for its community of struggle; he knew how to work hard, to hunt game, to read stars as he read desultorily several languages; he leaned toward the difficult art for art's sake of symbolist Europe; he lived a loneliness little compromised, one who never found himself at home in communities where he taught or in relationships that foundered. He was a father who loved his son, a teacher who took his students utterly seriously. He died prematurely, at the age of fifty, of a heart attack in 1997.

I first knew Larry Levis in 1973. We were young men, though I was older by five years and more, it may be, by personal trauma. From my perspective as a just-discharged sergeant in the Vietnam-era U.S. Air Force, he seemed to me an arrogant, hip, star-dazzled young Keats-to-be on the make. His poems reflected his age, and the age. *Wrecking Crew* (1972) won the University of Pittsburgh Press's prestigious International Poetry Forum Award. Its poems were the image-born lyrics of his teachers at Fresno, Syracuse, and the University of Iowa, notably Mark Strand and Donald Justice. He won prizes; they judged. He was in the right magazines. The handsome husband of beautiful Marcia Southwick, poet, he had an appealing vulnerability not easy to name.

There was an occasion that turned out badly between us, and I dismissed him as a lightweight pretender. By the late 1970s I had published some collections of poems. An unexpected letter arrived from him, saying he liked my poems, he thought we were more or less traveling the same road of elegiac tales. So of course, after his letter, I found that I had always admired him. Maybe I simply looked at his poems harder. His way was to wed a religious sensibility to memories informed by pastoral tranquility in those orchards, to say what human cost made them. Maybe I admired the understanding he felt for working people, migrant men and women especially and those with few dreams, and he seemed to have, though he would not have put it this way, a love for American ideals of ethical and moral fairness, our original charter. Maybe I liked a hawkish intelligence in poems that rarely missed an opportunity to look through events for that more permanent vision real talent seeks, and mediocrity avoids. He knew how to focus a street fight that scrapped over little nothings that mean everything. He could show injustice, not merely chant about it; he knew how to turn the look of a grape-cutting knife shockingly memorable. He had great tension that came of the contest between the part of him that adored beauty and the part that was, for lack of a better term, a pragmatist. He had been a farm boy, after all, and practical in severe ways. I think two things happened to make him write what James Wright called "the poetry of a grown man." Larry accepted himself, the life he had lived and had in him. Where, early on, he had easy-blame lyrics, he learned to follow finger-pointing inside to his own complex of hurts.

He got better with each book. His poems evolved a demanding, detailed, and cohesive view of what Americans were, and what they wanted to be. His poetry has both solidarity and complicity. He possessed the original, remarkable innocence which alone prevents any of us from being bullied into submission and, if we are poets, into mere imitation, an innocence that lay beneath Emily Dickinson's grit. Like her, he knew the world for what it is, and he knew the true poet cannot blink. It is possible his poems stay with

me, like those of Bill Matthews, because they were the first in my genera-
tion of poets to die, but I think it is because they have that quality Whitman
called "race" that makes poems remarkable.

Levis's penultimate collection, *The Selected Levis* (2000), displays a char-
acter rooted in life reaching for more knowledge, one equally determined to
know the intersection of individual and collective self-recognition. It was my
good luck, as editor of *The Southern Review,* to publish "Elegy with a Thim-
bleful of Water in the Cage," the best poem in his remarkable posthumous
collection, *Elegy* (1997). I heard him read this poem four times in public,
asked to publish it on each occasion, got his agreement and the poem that
last time, and lived with it enough to think Whitman would have admired
its fusion of poetry and a national consciousness.

"Elegy with a Thimbleful of Water in the Cage" manages more disparate
and multilayered stories than many novels, yet proceeds with delicate expres-
sion few poets accomplish. The poet tells us he sent a letter some years ago
to an unnamed and, now, listening recipient. What was in the letter, we are
not told; what effect it may have had, if any, we are not told. The mailing oc-
curred in New Hampshire, at a post office inside a rural store. We are given
additional sites for the poet's life events as narration veers forward through
its speaker's years, but we learn little more of allusions to stories in Piedra,
Paris, Piraeus, Athens, and San Francisco than of that post office. Still, a sort
of Conradian authority informs us these are significant stops in the geog-
raphy of a psyche whose growth, unfolding before us, proves instructively
American.

One story anchors the others. The myth of the Sibyl of Cumae, a Roman
tale, says that the Sibyl, a priestess, asked for eternal life, received her wish,
but because she forgot to ask for youth she was also given an eternity of
physical shrinking, a suffocating invisibility. Levis, however, doesn't begin
his poem with even this. Enigmatically, he says: "It's a list of what I cannot
touch" and only after he has worked through memories that contain dying
trees in Paris, flowers suggestive of innocence, and the postal counter with
its sleeping cat, does he arrive, as if he has peeled an onion, at the Sibyl who
was placed in a bird cage

> not to possess her,

> But to protect her from pedestrians, & the boys of Athens rattled
> The bars of her cage with sticks as they ran past yelling,

"Sibyl, Sibyl, what do you want?"—each generation having to
Listen more closely than the one before it to hear

The faintest whispered rasp from the small bitter seed
Of her tongue as she answered them with the same

Remark passing through time, "I want to die!" As time passed & she
Gradually grew invisible, the boys had to press

Their ears against the cage to hear her.

And then one day the voice became too faint, no one could hear it,
And after that they stopped telling

The story. And then it wasn't a story; it was only an empty cage.

The stage is one upon which Levis stands to unite his tale with hers, his
life with hers, as much as it is where she performed. For a farm boy from
Fresno to marry his life with that of an ancient spirit-poet and, moreover,
make a tale to speak for a national generation is no small task. Retelling
poetic tales (this one is Ovid's) marks a poet's knowledge; it connects, again,
tradition and the individual talent. That link is crucial to cultural learning.
Not surprisingly, Levis treats the poem as a moral tutor. He introduces the
Sibyl and chronicles her withering, withdrawing her until she exists as noth-
ing more than what seems a breeze rippling the surface of the water in her
thimble. And because a poem of psychic travel needs a Virgilian guide to
make sense of such enigmas as the Sibyl, Levis sidles into another story,
that of Stavros, a café keeper in an unnamed theater district (probably Levis
imagines all this in San Francisco). Stavros lectures in the manner of bards
and raconteurs; he tells stories and sings. He remembers the Sibyl was still
alive when Nazi officers arrived to violate the sanctity of his home, thus abro-
gating the narrative's chronological definition. For Stavros, all time is one; for
Levis, all time is one mind. The story the Sibyl tells, retold by Stavros, then
retold by Levis, and as we read retold by us, for all that it is the illuminated
soul of poetry endangered but stepping, must be and is rooted in the pastoral,
meaning of the natural body, in details of exact place and event. Nevertheless,

As the years passed, as even the sunlight began to seem
As if it was listening to him outside the windows

Of the Midi, he began to lose interest in stories, & to speak
Only in abstractions, to speak only of theories,

Never of things.

Then he began to come in less frequently, & when he did
He no longer spoke at all. And so,

Along the boulevards in the winter the bare limbs of the trees
One passed in the city became again

Only the bare limbs of trees, no girl stepped into them

and Stavros himself spirals off to chase Pentecostalists, investing himself in
glossolalia. How savage seems that indictment of speaking "Only in abstrac-
tions." And how self-scalding for a young poet in the years when Vietnam
seemed a noxious air we breathed, when every poem was a political argu-
ment against America. I do not think, either, that the de-sacralizing of Na-
ture, our source, can be more effectively put: without stories that are big
dreams, the matter of the world is only cellular.

In 1938 John Crowe Ransom's *The World's Body* gave voice to a terror of
fragmentation that underlay the New Criticism and the poems of the Van-
derbilt Fugitives. Ransom's anxiety over disappearing rural life, multiplied
nationally, would become the U.S. Environmental Protection Agency, and
Henny Penny must still fear the end of things. As early modernists felt the
bulldozing conflict between old and new, Levis felt the turbulence of the
1960s in waves of change that washed over California, which seemed then
America's most outraged heart. When San Francisco's good feeling turned
to predation, drugs, violence, commercialized and anonymous sex, infringe-
ment of freedoms, and the acid bath that Vietnam brought to all of us, what
was left but Whitman's democracy violated?

Poverty is what happens at the end of any story, including this one,
When there are too many stories.

When you can believe in all of them, & so believe in none;
When one condition is as good as any other.

Relativity sucks. Levis describes a condition of despair, a self without
definition, invisible as the Sibyl, unnatural in its state, sustained only by and
within the story that is, itself held only by relation to places, events, memories,
and narrators. Levis asks: "What do you do when nothing calls you anymore?"
Abstractions—religious, legislative, aesthetic—seem not to answer. Only the
list of "things I cannot touch" will answer, things in stories, particles floating,

so he begins with story, weaving the untouchable until it becomes palpable and useful, helping to sustain life that totters under its own weight, and the story becomes a sort of letter the spirit sends. To a girl, a lover, a muse? Well, to all of us. In it he compiles what matters, what can make one life better than another, and he finds the particulars, artfully fused, lead back to abstraction, and so the elegy praises acts of composition, expression, linkage, and memory as forces of vitality and civilization. Nothing could be more personal.

"Elegy with a Thimbleful of Water in the Cage," dependent on its apparent narrative of a traveler's memories, has, however, no narrative structure. It is made of overlapping circles, partially scored stories that touch at some point, a lyric of final and utter loss—because life can't go past that cage. Elegies praise the dead for their value, and Levis's poem praises all the poets and visionaries, but its greatest praise is offered, I think, for gesture rather than person. Its realism is as memorial as its mystical tale is enchanting. I do not hold that the poem or Larry Levis set out to establish an American identity, but anyone who lived through the 1960s and more in this country must feel this is a true and powerful portrait of who we were, of what happened to the innocents. "Elegy with a Thimbleful of Water in the Cage" is an emblem of my generation and, in the way of poetry, it is the tale of all who commit themselves to life under an idea. Levis affirms that even one good poet can keep alive in us what Americans came here to do, and to be, those who would know the country built of the spirit of courage, who would pass on the good news of our lives. Just as Whitman and Dickinson had done, he tells us the simplest and most personal thing at the end of his poem: "I pass the letter I wrote to you over the sleeping cat & beyond / the iron grillwork, into the irretrievable." What made Larry Levis both a poet and an American resides in that gesture, which is a witness to the unquashable cry for freedom, the work of poetry.

The Fat Man and the Dirty Bastards

REMEMBERING RICHARD HUGO

Richard Hugo's reputation is all but a dead issue. When remembered, he stands as a poet of the western United States where spaces are empty and readers are few. For him, it wasn't always so. I first read Hugo's poems in obscure literary magazines where I thought I might start to publish. I wanted to be a poet and imagined I could learn from magazines what was in, what was acceptable. Then, doing active duty service as a sergeant with the U.S. Air Force, I knew no poets. On the January 1969 night of Joe Namath's Super Bowl, I had entered boot camp in San Antonio, Texas. That night a boy from California two bunks away from me invoked the wrath of a drill sergeant because there was contraband in his foot locker, a copy of Hart Crane's poems. If you wrote or read poetry in the military, you learned to keep quiet about it. Hugo once told me it was the same in World War II when he'd been a bombardier. His war poems in *Good Luck in Cracked Italian* are among America's best, portraits of military harm that does not fade from memory.

Literary magazines, or journals if you like a prettier name, in the early 1970s were filled with wispy, cloud-heavy image poems that imitated Robert Bly and Mark Strand. The hot young poets were Terry Stokes, Albert Goldbarth, Larry Levis, Glover Davis, et al. I admired audacity and severity in such poetry and would have written it, published it, if choosing could have done it. I wanted to be with those I read in libraries near my base, but my mounting rejection slips confirmed only that I was in every respect not good enough.

Drafted in 1968, I'd enlisted because I thought I would never finish a graduate degree once I left school. The Air Force offered me delayed entry and a chance to avoid combat. Those were fatalistic days. Would I come back from Vietnam, if indeed I got there? I was twenty-six years old, maximum age for the draft. I sympathized with antiwar voices and longed to be afoot in my country with other young writers making their way. I was married, uncertain of my convictions, and just discovering what work life would offer me. Seeking to be a teacher of literature, I had fallen into the path of other students who knew and loved poetry. Whatever it was, and I was far from knowing, I wanted poetry in my life.

A poet I'd begun to read, his book won in a friendly wager, was James Dickey. As the 1970s taught us to say, I could relate. I trusted Dickey because his poems were not drawn from museum culture, books, psychoanalysis, the usual sites inhabited by poetry's networkers. Dickey's personal experience had been fields, family, women and sexual adventure, wild animals, contact sports, dangerous landscapes, combat, a life on the edge. I admired his World War II tales. He made poems of enthusiasm and appetite. It was and it wasn't my experience, for I was the child of suburbs beyond which field life was clearly visible and known—but not truly mine. I used to say Dickey's poems compelled me because we were fellow southerners. Something in his rhythms, in his feel for what matters, and why, spoke to me in words and lines I comprehended less than I tasted. Dickey introduced me to poetry as living, personal expression. With teeth, or something like that.

Richard Hugo wrote a different kind of poetry, though it has its parallels to Dickey. I might call it the voice of the soul squeezed by adverse circumstance, marginalized long before that word became tortured. I submitted to Hugo's early books, *A Run of Jacks* and *The Death of the Kapowsin Tavern*. They spoke to a listener I didn't know was in me, an ear I didn't yet know listened. Hugo's world did not smell like anything I knew; it wasn't southern; it did not celebrate manliness I admired. But it was a world a moody, apocalyptic boy might recognize. Anyone who had read Camus in college, who could call ordinary events *existential,* might hum to Hugo's tune about how relentlessly, hopelessly, and minimally everything ends. This, of course, is Eliot's gloom. Hugo had the sense to dramatize the self as victim of more or less whatever being alive brought. It risked self-pity, of course, so he made sure we knew there were more offended victims. He made himself as runner-up victim to Montana's Indians, all of whom seemed to possess wisdom that was natural and ultimate. Their names were palpable history to Hugo. He believed that "when you die you lose your name." There's a comic risk in that, too.

Hugo described scenes of loss in landscapes, usually Montana though occasionally Washington where he'd grown up. His place was littered with the testimony of failed farms, trashed towns, polluted waters. The burned-out

Kapowsin tavern on a high remote lake was, to him, a temple and a sanctuary. He wrote, "A church abandoned to the wind is portent." The Vanderbilt Fugitives had written the same poem with a different accent and, in England, responding to his own sense of the abandoned center, Philip Larkin wrote "Church Going." Yeats had proclaimed in 1919 that "things fall apart; the centre cannot hold." If Hugo had ever been able to find the center, he'd have agreed, and he looked in towns so small that, as he liked to joke, their names fell off the map.

Hugo's wild northwest seacoast attracted me. I found him interviewed in a small magazine called *December*. Glossier than most of its kind, thicker paper, more contributors—it bespoke authority and significance and conferred that on Hugo by giving him a stage of prominent visibility. The Richard Hugo I found was a man of simple origin, a democratic American, one who'd been to war unwillingly, without clear conviction. He had opinions but each came hesitant, with asides that deferred to all who had better opinions, better education, better lives. I wanted to know him. I especially admired the language of his poems.

I wrote a fan letter to Hugo, an unusual thing for me to do. What did I expect? Perhaps more than the silence of rejection slips, maybe a small glint of recognition. Hugo answered. I am hazy about whether it was a signed book, a poem, or a letter. I remember that he wrote, "for Dave Smith, who is one of my kind." His words to me were like the granting of a degree, a license. I believed he *knew;* he felt something in me, and his permission gave me confidence to write after daily tours at the air base. How, after that, could I be anything but partisan toward whatever he wrote?

Well, I have never had trouble mounting enthusiasm for Richard Hugo's poems. I respond to their webs of heavy Anglo-Saxon rhythms and scenes of exile, which are his as they are few others'. His sorrow is fundamental. I think it is the voice of love. I think Hugo's subject was love, though he hardly ever speaks of that directly. He wrote of love withheld, withdrawn, abused, yearned for, love as a thing that could be remembered but not kept. Inside every poem, nearly, there is the ache of loneliness for the girl, parent, house, and town that might have loved him but did not. He initiated poems with a scene, place, the context of painful memory, and it was always where love had been and was no longer.

This was close to my own life. We talked about it. I'd gone to college in the year after my father was killed in an automobile accident. No one in my family had gone to college. On my way home at Thanksgiving, I drank with friends in the car, drank too much, and arrived on my front porch in a state. I couldn't open the door, so I knocked. I remember wondering why my mother wasn't there to greet me. A man appeared in the screen door. Trying to be courteous, but confused, I slurred that I lived there. He was, I think, very calm. He said, No, you don't. He said he lived here. It was baffling. I repeated myself; he repeated himself. Then he seemed startled, and he said I know who you are. Your mother sold this house to me several months ago. And so she had. Only she had not told me. I drove, crazily, to my grandparents' house, an exact replica of the one I had just left, where I was told my mother had lacked the nerve to hurt me with bad news. She had fled to Florida with a new husband. In "Saying Goodbye to Mrs. Noraine," Richard Hugo replayed such a homecoming, defining how easily and unalterably we become orphans.

Hugo had been early abandoned by his mother. I don't know anything about a father. He was raised by grandparents who seem to have been harsh enough, though in fairness he may have remembered only the hurts and the pinches Depression-era families gave each other without willing to do so. Hugo had done poorly in college; he had been at best an indifferent combatant in World War II, the only survivor of his crashed bomber; he suffered a traumatic divorce; he felt himself incapable of success with women; he became an academic, taking Leslie Fiedler's place at the University of Montana. This, he said, convinced him he was an undiscovered fraud. He also could never convince himself he belonged with the poets. He bent under the weight of having been Theodore Roethke's student, with classmates James Wright and Carolyn Kizer. He looked like Roethke and Wright. Hugo called himself a "fat man at the margin" and said he was a wrong thing in a right place.

I did not then see how much of Hugo's pose was a deliberate composition. He played the role assumed by comedian Jackie Gleason in his Poor Slob skits. Speaking as the raw, wandering immigrant, his angle was verbal slapstick but with a poem's serious veneer. An American failure who managed to succeed, at least in poems, in ways he could not account for, he never stopped playing the victim, even as the clown whose bad days and grim hours might be redeemed by a love song. He opened himself to readers, claimed to be like them, no mysterious star to whom secrets were revealed; not mystic, not ascetic; no James Dean, no Mark Strand; no Thoreau-like Harvard-pedigreed Robert Bly. Hugo was a man in search of an American self, rejecting what he did not wish to be in the poem as laboratory. Crude and unfinished, he was a prototype.

At Western Michigan University in 1973, in my first college teaching position, I saw an announcement that Hugo would read at a community college in Flint. We'd exchanged a few letters then. I wrote to say I'd be there, eager to meet him. I had no idea how far Flint was from Kalamazoo. My wife and I found Hugo reading to a surprisingly large audience, students who had been forced to attend. On the sort of stage often seen in large urban high schools, wide and deep, with tall velvety curtains, the kind that leaves a speaker alone, Hugo appeared round and small at the podium. Yet he commanded with a voice gravelly and strong when it rang out lines. Some students came and went, but most listened. I listened. At the end of the reading, he said he would take questions. I had read his poems, his interviews, as much as I could find about his life.

The silence was heavy as early fall heat. At last a young woman stood, dramatically, in the center of the tiered seats, and asked what Hugo thought of his life. I said to my wife, he'll never answer that. An hour later, pacing the stage, mopping his bald brow, talking fast, he stopped. It was the only question he took. He revealed himself as shamelessly as he might have on a psychiatrist's couch. No one, to my knowledge, recorded a word of it. Dick would say anything, it seemed. It was a grand performance by a so-called worthless self among us.

When I made my way to him, he asked me to take him to his motel room. My young wife had no more idea what to expect of a poet than I did. We were delighted to squire what we thought was a man of extreme importance. It didn't occur to me his academic hosts had abandoned him. The motel was near. I don't recall that any of us said a word, though Dick must have directed us. It was a strip motel, a dark air-conditioned room; he entered and snapped on the television, plopping down immediately, heavily fixing his intensity on a World Series game between the New York Mets and a western team I can't now identify. When the Mets scored a run Hugo grunted, "those dirty bastards!" I didn't yet know that for Dick the East was the enemy, in all ways, in all events, always. His loyalties to the local team or town was unequivocally West Coast, which had orphaned him. It is the source of his most intense and beautiful poems.

When a commercial came, he looked at my wife. His face was glazed, not blank exactly, more puzzled and startled she stood there, as I stood, waiting to see what we should do. Dick barked at her: "Go get me a gallon of ice cream." She looked at me. She had no idea where we were or why she ought to obey this stranger, but she was out the door and gone before I thought to say a word. As the car pulled away Dick's face relaxed into weary suffering that seemed to me his most natural appearance. He said, "I can't get no women." I had, and gave, no answer. Dick was still playing the role, a pitiable victim who by actions inadvertent and unrecognized rendered himself sexually isolated and deprived. We had just watched him explain his poetry role to those students. Readers, I would discover, believed this was the real Richard Hugo, even the only Richard Hugo. It may have been a real Hugo, but it wasn't the only one, and it was an invented presence. In 1974 a small journal, the *New Salt Creek Reader,* published an interview with Dick where he spoke about himself and women:

> In Iowa in my cramped trailer house, drinking late into the night, the painful episodes of my past that I replayed were more immediate than [two childhood scenes of cruelty]. In those you'll notice in both instances I made a mistake and the result was a girl was lost. In one case, dead, in the other gone away. The success and popularity [which he had experienced at this point in this life] constituted an interruption of this dwelling which had become a psychic necessity and I deliberately set out to reestablish the pain. The pattern had to be the same: make a mistake and lose the girl. If the woman died or went away or rejected me, I'd be free again to wallow in those dirty images of self, other experiences where I was humiliated, rejected, degraded. The louder the acclaim, the stronger my urge to overcome the interruption. Of course, I only used women I liked for my dark purpose, since the rejection had to be painful. Sober, I didn't want those nice women or anyone else rejecting me.

Hugo's "dark purpose" and "use" of women is self-serving and melodramatic. He had an elaborate conception of what he needed to write, to make the poems come. His vision of women was a part of that artifice, a part sometimes offensive to female readers. His women can be hurtful shrews, often ghosts of his grandmother, but he more consistently depicts them as beauties, blameless, victimized, unreachable, ethereal spirits who, at any man's touch, are soiled beyond redemption. His treatment of my wife played that out. Poe, of course, treated women in precisely the same manner in his psychodramas. Dickey, in *Sorties,* does the same thing. There were, finally, no real women in the work, only the poet's life drama. Women are merely reflectors in the act of symbolizing states of pain the poems expressed. Hugo knew this better than any reader. He was not insensitive or unsympathetic. He tried, with poor results, to be "better" and in "To Women" he wrote, "You start it all. You are lovely. / We look at you and we flow." Limp and prosaic here, hardly the brassy urgent sound of his best work, his wimpy unconvincing lines about how to be a man in the new age are pitiful:

> In me today is less rage than ever, less hurt:
> When I imagine some good woman young
> I no longer imagine her cringing
> in cornstalks, cruel father four rows away
> beating corn leaves aside with a club.
> That is release you never expected
> from a past you never knew you had.
> My horse is not sure he can make it
> to the next star. You are free.

I next saw Dick after I took a one-year teaching position at a small girls' school in Missouri, a dismal experience. American poets were then reading his new book *The Lady in Kicking Horse Reservoir*, which appeared in 1973. His two previous books from small university presses were out of print, but this was breakthrough work, published by Norton, with a New York certificate of poetic success. It sold well. It was reviewed well. Poets wrote letters to praise it. People felt the loneliness, the rib-hugging ache for a good self not beaten away by the harsh Montana climate and social isolation. These poems reprised what had always held his attention: bars, lakes, rivers, Indian communities, ruins of ranches where people dreaming of a new American life had run out of luck, then out of breath. Nobody could evoke the gritty feel of that failure and despair better than Hugo. His poems were like daguerreotypes, stark lives that cleared before your eyes. The first stanza of "Montana Ranch Abandoned" still leaps at the reader like a father's tombstone:

> Cracks in eight log buildings, counting sheds
> and outhouse, widen and a ghost peeks out.
> Nothing, tree or mountain, weakens wind
> coming for the throat. Even wind must work
> when land gets old. The rotting wagon tongue
> makes fun of girls who begged to go to town.
> Broken brakerods dangle in the dirt.

In rural Missouri, I didn't have to go far to see a ruined place, but I knew the scene from southern Virginia. Along the interstate through the gorgeous Shenandoah Valley there were dead barns to see, failed lives to imagine. I think this is the effect of a "historic imagination," the only way I know how to explain why some of us are more susceptible than others to the emotional resonance of a place, something I shared with Hugo. Flat, irrevocable defeat was what Hugo saw in those ranch sites, that and madness it caused. Madness was a human mockery he had felt often enough that its wail never left him. With the Kicking Horse poems he became one of the elegiac voices of American poetry, but his elegy praised those who got no monument, no gain, no national celebration. He loved his country ruin by ruin with a tenderness matching Whitman's, but he sat on the other side of the bar from Whitman's optimism. Why not? He came from the end of the line, the bankruptcy of the country's promise, and he saw that more steadily than most do. He was a good rememberer.

I asked Dick to read for the young women upon whom I had been day after day pressing *The Lady in Kicking Horse Reservoir*. These were not Ivy stars, just junior college girls. They must have imagined he would be a kind of movie star because their teacher doted on him. What must they have thought of the shambling, fat, bald, sweating goof who blew a steady stream of cigarette smoke? He looked like a dying uncle as he told us he would recite, not read, his poems because Galway Kinnell—who was he?—did it, and all the hot poets did it. How unexpected then to see him strut out among the girls, speak off a poem directly into the eyes of this one, share a bit of conversation or laugh with that one. He was shrewd, practiced, an effective entertainer. This was a lesson, too. Poems were written by real people grappling with *our* world. They might sound like speech. They might not drone on, dull and portentous.

During the decade of the 1970s Richard Hugo's poems steadily gained admiration and audience. He campaigned hard inside that personal voice which scraped away at every hiding impediment to reveal his failures, his rage, his mental breakdowns, his drinking, his dream of the American good life gone rotten. He was the consequence of the Puritan juxtaposition of the dirty self and the pure Christ we ought to be. For a while everything he wrote brought felicity, approval, a public sign-off that he was right. We liked his brave cadences, his scenes of the American frontier, his sympathy for those who suffered. But as "To Women" showed, the result of issuing poetic bulls, he failed when he moved away from personal experience. He knew, because the American climate requires it, he needed change, something to push art farther than he had gone, or might ever go. He acknowledged that recognition and resisted it in the *New Salt Creek Reader* interview, where I thought he was treated rudely—until he told me he had written every word, each question and answer. He wrote:

> I know of cases other than mine where the poet's behavior has been adversely affected by "success." Yes I really am great and everything I put down is great so I don't have to work hard anymore. Yes, I am great and can treat fellow human beings any way I like. No, I am not great. I am unworthy of all this praise and once they see how outrageous I really am they'll leave me alone and I can go back to writing. I am great and will be a part of literature, therefore I must change my style to insure growth worthy of an artist of stature. In the last case of course, the writing itself is being affected and that's bad. If the poet has a choice between writing the same poem over and over, being monotonous and boring, and willing style changes so that every poem or every book is new and different, being novel and eclectic (styleless), he is far better being boring and monotonous. If the style is honest, it won't change any faster than the personality—not very fast at all.

Hugo is working each side of an anxiety that doubtless pinched him when he reflected on his old classmate and friend James Wright, whose self-proclaimed turnabout of style in *The Branch Will Not Break* (1963) vaulted Wright to the forefront of American poetry. Hugo also had read, like everyone else in 1973, Wright's confused further change in *Two Citizens,* a book Wright swore he would never reprint. To Hugo the problem was the gap between the artifice of his poems and the blunt record of any life he had, a strategic form problem. It was the old modernist trouble of too many options and none that fit his dilemma. If form was a self, and it was for Hugo, which self then? Hugo knew success would change any poet's life and, subsequently, the poems. In his late years he reverted to the hard drinking he had stopped as his self-discipline enabled him to write. Lionized campus after campus, he succumbed.

Hugo's success in the poetry world was and is the ambition of young writers, a thing vastly different from success in poems. Like others before him, he learned how far apart stood poems and accolades. What was that success? Public readings of his poems to enthusiastic, large audiences came easily, and paid a modest fee. Although he won no major prizes, he was offered prestigious teaching positions at large western universities. In literary journals he was interviewed, profiled, lauded by younger poets. Although no

American poet has the visible presence of any novelist, Hugo could feel the intellectual community had begun to notice him. Even so, his poems often were dismissed or ignored by eastern reviewers. He felt that as an old, deep grudge. Hugo would never have been named American Poet Laureate; he wasn't handsome like Strand, historic like Robert Penn Warren, venerable like Stanley Kunitz, ironic and chic like Louise Gluck. He knew what his life had cost him. In "Overlooking Yale" he wrote,

> With Yale below in gold light, I feel
> I should have read Milton, ought to be
> in the know about something, some key remark
> Dryden made about Donne. Not concerned
> with the way we talk to old cars;
> pat their hoods and murmur "sweet hero."

Hugo didn't need their bad opinions; he always had his own bad, and theirs confirmed his. Any success confused matters. It also permitted him his least effective poems, those collected in *31 Letters and 13 Dreams*. I remember driving him to a reading at the University of Utah when that book appeared in 1977. We were talking about baseball. He interrupted himself to ask if I thought the new book was a failure. My just-signed copy lay on the seat between us. I said not at all, felt immediately dishonest, and added that I hadn't warmed to it as much as his books that were by then a part of my inner life. "Yes," he said, looking at the Wasatch Mountains, "the dreams and letters are weak." He didn't say that he was trying to write a new, different poem, but that was clear. The work of Hugo's last decade wanders in structure and in sound. Poems lack that snap and step which earlier joined image by image in a sure propulsion through the landscapes of his bruised life.

When he won a Guggenheim Fellowship, he wrote to me about it, proclaiming this the salvation he needed. He had just got too happy and couldn't write anymore, he argued, what with his new wife Ripley and her love and his luck in the poetry stakes. And later on there would be another letter, this time from the Isle of Skye in the Scottish Hebrides. It exploded with excitement: he was miserable, he said, in that godawful land at the end of nowhere, living in a cottage not fit for a man's worst enemy, and now nearly done with a new book of poems. He had discovered the merciless Scots, their crofters scandals, bastards kicking down tenant farmers. Cold winds and bleak seas surged around him, swelling his poems.

For all his gloom, Hugo could also flash with the light and clarity of a Montana sky in country he loved. He combined scene and line for effective surprises. He kept things moving, the eye, the ear, the body's rhythm, with statements that yoked startling images in epigrams of what seemed irrefutable wisdom. He composed by the phrase, piling them up in sentences of momentum, hammering lines into stanzas that ordered the field of his attention. He seemed to some readers a poet too limited by one standard cadence and, in truth, he wrote almost entirely in the same jammed iambic pentameter, varying the grid only with unexpected doublings and triplings of stress and alliteration. But it is always the phrase that commands his best poems, with enjambment and juxtaposition subordinating line to the unitary strength of the stanza, as in the first lines of "Driving Montana," which also delivers that light-show he equated with rare happiness:

> The day is a woman who loves you. Open.
> Deer drink close to the road and magpies
> spray from your car. Miles from any town
> your radio comes in strong, unlikely
> Mozart from Belgrade, rock and roll
> from Butte.

In "Driving Montana" Hugo celebrated the thrill of going. He felt that American liberation from whatever wants to sit on you, one John Updike's Rabbit Angstrom loved in *Rabbit, Run*. We are a nation freed by cars, and free in our cars, and Hugo knew it. Like others he let the car take him to whatever epiphany waited. In his most anthologized poem, "Degrees of Gray in Philipsburg," he drives his Buick to a failed backwater town, eats lunch, watches a good-looking girl serve him. Its cadences step very nearly into the maudlin pity of those who never made it out of Philipsburg, for they declare everything the incontrovertible end of a determinism part naturalistic and part lack of nerve. But Hugo takes on the role of inquisitor or therapist and interrogates us, then turns us back on ourselves while we are still young, strong, prosperous enough to leave. When we go, and confidently, there is something low inside us. "Degrees of Gray in Philipsburg" implicitly attacks the national hypocrisy that Melville found so blistering. Philipsburg makes a bitter joke of the American paradise of our settler-fathers: "Don't empty houses ring?" But the steady-handed last stanza still offers self-redemption and the powerful deliverance of success, if not love:

Say no to yourself. The old man, twenty
when the jail was built, still laughs
although his lips collapse. Someday soon,
he says, I'll go to sleep and not wake up.
You tell him no. You're talking to yourself.
The car that brought you here still runs.
The money you buy lunch with,
no matter where it's mined, is silver
and the girl who serves your food
is slender and her red hair lights the wall.

Richard Hugo has been dead for more than a decade. New winners of prizes, writers of excellent poems, seldom recognize his name, just as he believed would happen. But he thought a poet's life was worth that chance, and he wanted it, its badges and gauds and shelf-life. He wanted, even more, poems with permanent and patient celebrations of what a plain man comes from, what he loves, what ordinary acts of telling the truth could mean against the swirl of mortal wind. Those are the reasons I admire his writing, but one of his poems I love for the most sentimental of reasons. He wrote to me that he admired my poem "Cumberland Station." He said it had drawn him out of a period when he was not writing, that it led him to an elegy about his childhood in Seattle, "White Center," for the town he had grown up in.

Reading "White Center" nearly twenty years after Hugo had read my poem, I see it has no narrative, no plot, is a recitation of unhealed hurts he had summoned into other poems over the years, poems on the whole better than this one. But it has his organization, his signature; his are the phrases, the leaps from image to image. His will moves a self down the page, past cruel neighbors, past the mean hours and the hopeless turn to repentance. It's a kitchen sink of a poem, and he liked it enough to make it the title of his 1980 collection. I knew what he felt when he wrote, "I am the man / you beat to perversion." I had written, "I am the man who stole it [a newspaper] and I wish you were here / to beat the hell out of me."

"White Center" is also an American funeral elegy, a reconciling song that walks us back through an old life's harms, hand in hand with Hugo's grandmother-ghost, one at the heart of his estrangement. She had the love he wanted. If he can recover her fully enough, he can reclaim all of them, everything, to enter the full blessing of a life without shame. A poem of memory becomes, then, a reprisal of self-forgiveness, a journey of wish-fulfillment.

Hugo wanted to go back to what nobody understands but cannot thrive without, our home, the place where they know our name, for him "White Center."

It is spooky, now I am middle-aged, to think of Hugo feeling that poem well inside him. A poet seeks a big and durable image of what life is. Hugo calls his collected poems *Making Certain It Goes On.* For him the will to make life work was the task of words, both redressing what was wrong and consecrating what was right. He told me once that during the many years he lived alone his habit was to tape typescripts of poems to his walls and to make changes as he passed, until they were completed and publishable. The act of revision, for Hugo, was to make language with life not as fantasy but as fact, and nobody put the names, the feel, the fact of the Northwest into poetry as he did. He agreed with Auden that poetry makes nothing happen. Except perhaps the electric recognitions in the reader, and that is enough. Poetry and memory keep alive those voices we should otherwise lose to death. As he stood alone at that wall in Missoula, Montana, muttering against "those dirty bastards," Hugo performed the only act we have any right to expect of poets. His words lodged an image of a life no longer orphaned, now part of a place and its public record, sweet and sour. An easterner Hugo felt obliged to hate, Casey Stengel, said you could look it up. You still can.

WHITE CENTER

Town or poem, I don't care how it looks. Old woman
take my hand and we'll walk one more time these streets
I believed marked me weak beneath catcalling clouds.
Long ago, the swamp behind the single row of stores
was filled and seeded. Roses today where Toughy Hassin
slapped my face to the grinning delight of his gang.
I didn't cry or run. Had I fought him
I'd have been beaten and come home bloody in tears
and you'd have told me I shouldn't be fighting.

Wasn't it all degrading, mean Mr. Kyte sweeping
the streets for no pay, believing what he'd learned
as a boy in England: 'This is your community'?
I taunted him to rage, then ran. Is this the day
we call bad mothers out of the taverns and point them
sobbing for home, or issue costumes to posturing clowns
in the streets, make fun of drunk barbers, and hope

someone who left and made it returns, vowed
to buy more neon and give these people some class?

The Dugans aren't worth a dime, dirty Irish, nor days
you offered a penny for every fly I killed.
You were blind to my cheating. I saw my future uncertain—
that drunk who lived across the street and fell
in our garden reaching for the hoe you dropped.
All he got was our laughter. I helped him often home
when you weren't looking. I loved some terrible way
he lived in his mind and tried to be decent to others.
I loved the way we loved him behind our disdain.

Clouds. What glorious floating. They always move on
like I should have early. But your odd love and a war
taught me the world's gone evil past the first check point
and that's First Avenue South. I fell asleep each night
safe in love with my murder. The neighbor girl
plotted to tease every tomorrow and watch me turn
again to the woods and games too young for my age.
We never could account for the python cousin Warren
found half starved in the basement of Safeway.

It all comes back but in bites. I am the man
you beat to perversion. That was the drugstore MacCameron
flipped out in early one morning, waltzing
on his soda fountain. The siren married his shrieking.
His wife said, "We'll try again, in Des Moines."
You drove a better man into himself where he found tunes
he had no need to share. It's all beginning to blur
as it forms. Men cracking up or retreating.
Resolute women deep in hard prayer.

And isn't it the same this time. I hoped forty years
I'd write and would not write this poem. This town would die
and your grave never reopen. Or mine. Because I'm married
and happy, and across the street a foster child
from a cruel past is safe and need no longer crawl
for his meals, I walk this past with you, ghost in any field
of good crops, certain I remember everything wrong.
If not, why is this road lined thick with fern
and why do I feel no shame kicking the loose gravel home?

The Talking Dick

STEPHEN DOBYNS'S POETRY

Some years back, when I left one publisher for another, I contracted for a new and selected poems. The editor who arranged this collection, a fiction editor by trade, asked if I thought of the book as a door from a completed experience to new experience. It's always important to please editors, so I thought of it that way. In turn, he directed me to compile a "largish" manuscript. After I had done so, he reversed course and determined we needed a "thin, hard" manuscript. So I pruned away. The "experience" was frustrating but salutary since the imperatives under which I elected or excluded a poem were different, in many cases, from what they been in the original books. One learns quickly about glaring personal deficiencies that have remained somehow hidden, decisions that were so patently wrong, good moves that have turned out so much gimmickry. Nevertheless, poets think of poems as if they are our children, and we are loathe to exclude any, and all fit *some* organizational scheme. I created and junked more architectures for that new and selected collection than I can now remember. Most criticism of poetry substitutes the critic's architecture for the poet's, although sometimes one voice actually concurs with another.

The "New and Selected" volume offers itself to career assessment and prods opinions which come with the gravity of a hanging judge. This probably explains why friends, when I announced my volume-to-be, often as not asked if I wasn't a little young for the event. That there was an unwritten but appropriate age to be reached before which one published such a volume puzzled me. I learned my friends meant only to warn against the impending noise, especially from young gun reviewers, made by those who assumed the state of the art was up to their capable selves for protection. I have in mind a type represented by Mary Kinzie and William Logan. They keep readied their powdery weapons to contest, as they see it, the almost certainly unwise and overweight books they must engage. Standing today in their shoes, I find to the contrary, a fat new book of poems, *Velocities: New and Selected Poems, 1966–1992,* by novelist-poet-critic Stephen Dobyns is a mostly welcome hold of two decades' work by a mind one cannot be uninterested in knowing.

The Pulitzer Prize in poetry has in recent years gone to the new-and-selected volumes of Charles Simic, James Tate, and Yusef Komunyakaa, members of the same generation as Stephen Dobyns, one whose birth is associated with the World War II years. Those voices belong less to America's northeastern elite, long associated with arts, than to the first children of working-class people whose opportunities for education, social ease, professional mobility, and enjoyment of the benefits of the great American Dream were always significantly restricted. As if to reflect the ironies of power and the powerless, often in the work of this generation there remains a consistent, ever-present faith in social progress, civic virtues, and art's supreme fictions. One might expect poets maturing in the caustic Vietnam years (though remarkably few of them actually did military service) and surviving the disabusing theologies and weirdnesses of the 1960s to count on a little less than a good Samaritan policy from fellow men, yet they trumpet a human cheer that, however compromised it sometimes seems, cannot be shaken. They believe poetry can and does make something happen. Their question, and it is pivotal in the poetry of this generation, is how to credibly integrate personal conviction and public experience.

Stephen Dobyns published *Concurring Beasts,* his first collection, in 1971, while American forces were still in Southeast Asia and the blood-spattered news was as daily to us as Cheerios. Richard Nixon, who as I write has been recently buried, had already become the emblem of our evil empire. Great anger and dissent lay upon the land. Dobyns was not one of those young men in uniform and harm's way, though by virtue of his then profession of journalism he was compelled to write the stories of hopelessness and outrage and moral failure and ravaged flesh that became the staple of our lives, stories, too, in poems which *Velocities,* a compendium of effort covering twenty-six years, composes. The world of 1971 seemed to Dobyns populated by the zombies of "Passing the Word":

> You open the door
> and there is the mannequin dressed in dark silks—

a jumble of arms and legs for you to assemble;
its face white except for the mouth, a red river
between the ears; and the eyes which are empty.

From his first work Dobyns was enticed toward a narrative strategy
which regarded stories as psychic emblems. But the fashionable poetries of
the 1970s exerted their muscle, and Dobyns wrote poems of inert allegorical
scenes and psycho-image medallions. He seems to have read, like so many
others, Strand and Bly and wilderness bard John Haines, admiring their pos-
tures of cool, their quasi-truths. Yet, as a journalist, he walked among the
world's actual horrors. Against a disembodied mysticism Dobyns employed
a tempering humor that ranged from wit to mockery to the soft surrealism
of cataloged body parts that like our national life could come to no spiri-
tual resolution: "He has refused absolution and moved piece by piece /
into silence. His tongue lies motionless, disconnected." Like many, Dobyns was
partial to apocalyptic pronouncement ("There is no sky today") which slid
easily to silliness ("A gray Pomeranian / wanders in, bored and hungry, /
looks once, then goes out again.") Poetry readings grooved on; ultimate
meaning could be had, man.

Griffon (1976), a second volume of juvenilia, indulged Dobyns's attrac-
tion to the fable of consequence embedded in the image. He must have gone
on to read W. S. Merwin, William Stafford, maybe Creeley and Levertov, but
Bly still hummed in his ear. He liked poems in a sequence, the confidence of
that form's obvious control appealing to a sensibility yet in its apprenticeship,
and he especially liked giving verbal body to abstractions such as the seven
deadly sins, or "Silence"—which was such a hot topic in those days it rivaled
any noun for prominence in book titles. One critic warned that if poets went
on yearning for silence, they would get it. Dobyns thought silence was "the
music you were born to." If that seems banal, it was Deep Image manifesto.
Though many of the poems in *Griffon* are as stiff as the school day pho-
tographs we recall with uncertainty that was really us, they show the poet
looking for a form he can flex, one which would become characteristic of
Velocities. What was not so easily observed was this poet's core convictions.
Stephen Dobyns is, was, and ever shall be a moralist. His four poetry books
published during the 1980s, *Heat Death* (1980), *The Balthus Poems* (1982),
Black Dog, Red Dog (1984), and *Cemetery Nights* (1987), manifest an emer-
gent narrative style that permitted him access to his writing gifts and helped

to stage his commentary on the baby boomer program. Dobyns has proven to be an elegiac social observer, best when he is astringent, angry, and satirical. He does not have the natural poet's ear; his lines are not continuously or even epigrammatically memorable; his power is not music, not even always tone. But he has the prose writer's ventriloquial talent for voice, for scenic composition, for sly and revealing action, and above all the moralist's outrage voiced comedically, no doubt the reason for his attraction to Bly. In "Pablo Neruda," Dobyns and his creative writing class happen on the poet who had become everybody's saint in the 1970s, and that largely due to translations by Bly and James Wright. Neruda stands on a street corner. Dobyns takes out his pocketknife, hacks off a piece of Neruda, and eats it.

> Glancing at the sky it now seems a deeper blue.
> My students see me smiling and licking my lips
> and they too take out Swiss Army knives and start
> cutting off small slices . . .

Once the students have joined in, it is only a matter of time until they have eaten the master entirely. In this delightful send-up (reminiscent of Strand's "Eating Poetry") of the way we were in our rushing hunger for the authentic art experience, Dobyns refuses to blink away the very real and violent flesh consumption going on across both distant and neighborhood battlefields. Dobyns, unlike many poets, is often wickedly funny.

Violence never wanes in Dobyns's poems but it is always washed *almost* clean by his comedic exuberance and prose cunning. Often he treats people like so many pettifogged Woody Allens who want a better life but can manage only adolescent jokes about whatever befuddling event surrounds them. As narrator, he takes the stance, though not the lingo, of the detective hardboiled by so much of the unfair, improper, extralegal horse manure he has seen, and yet, so tender of heart is he, there is never a chance he would behave in any way but according to a golden code.

If we only knew the rules, it would all work as we know it should: the pledge of the rogue cop and the private detective. It is a rigorously puritanic code, however hard-bitten and forgiving its accent. Voices in Dobyns's poems imitate the kibitzer whose jaded and grizzly knowledge debunks superficial aspiration while it clings to the heart's pure ambition. If Hemingway had written readable poetry it would have had this voice, and a mind which knows there is little in the world to count on, and nothing verifiable. The private dick's belief is that the end will mirror the horse races Dobyns loves: one temporary winner, a crowd of losing nags. But it wasn't, hope answers, always so. In "The Triangular Field" a man is left to "think of the morning he galloped the pink horse / between apple trees, and the world fitted together," although it would not prove to be the emergent world of "Birth Report." When the birthday of a child celebrated in that poem appeared, it fell on a day of protests, "people freezing to death," Russians in Cuba, racism, normal America:

> And everybody promised you
> your own place in the oven, your own meat hook,
> your own hole in the head, own hole in the ground,
> as they shut down their brains to the destruction
> and stultifying boredom and once more decided
> to keep their money on the big promise: the spirit
> of this country rising out of the east like a great
> red mouth—tearing and rending, devouring its children.

Into this voice pour echoes of fairy tales, folk songs (you almost hear Peter, Paul, and Mary), Sylvia Plath, and yet the ex-flatfoot, metaphorically commissioned, remains Dobyns's main prophet because he possesses a tested, and therefore reliable, generally incorruptible, knowledge. The stories carried by Dobyns's poems are the essential human dilemmas of betrayal, compromise, stalemate, and flawed choice which lead to extreme behavior of a sort rarely on the evening news but nevertheless comprehendible as a statistical case in a sociology text. That you can hear Dobyns asking behind the scene why so and so did such and such is as inevitable as a gumshoe's getup. Dobyns has published, it is worth noting, fifteen detective novels, twice as many of those books as of poetry, honing an ability to make things come out plotted and right. Along the way, he has taught himself to value poems with provocative, even outrageous, openings ("After the first astronauts reached heaven"), the subtle wink that promises great things ("A woman in my class wrote that she is sick of men / wanting her body"), the enhancement of image resonance toward a deft exposition, and the swelling and tucking that shapes vision from bald experience. He has developed a nearly Chaucerian band of pilgrims crossing up and down stage, some of whose tales rise to the frightening veracity of "Under the Green Ceiling." Here, reminiscent of serial killers, "Two men walk along the edge of a country road." One will kill the other in a progress designed to show the reader John Donne's argument about an island as always, is and isn't part of our loony lives:

> he's a fragment of a wall, part of a broken pot;
> he's like the quivering rodent under its
> protection of leaves, terrified when the chance
> rock crashes through its green ceiling, victim
> of a world that is endlessly random and violent.

Despite what all of us in this generation learned from our assigned reading of Camus, despite our nodding that Dobyns has got the daily regular world right in poem after poem, Dobyns is no Chaucer. Hell, who is? *Velocities* is flawed in two directions, I think. Milton's temptation to preach in "Lycidas" illustrates the first. The stance taken by a moralist historically forces the poet to execute his wishes—not the poem's—by trotting out stick figures who behave like existential stereotypes with bad marriages, tawdry, boiled ambitions—the things that turn parish priests to drunks in despair. Such poems, being content-ridden, employ words, ultimately, as statistics whose march down the page can lead only to the bottom line telephoned in. Robert Penn Warren, a superior narrative poet, thought the poem at its best operated as a laboratory in which the drama repeatedly tests human virtues and values upon which definitions of self and civilization have rested. There's always the real chance, in the real poet, the test may turn out different than we expect. If the test answer is not at risk, a rhetoric less artful than manipulative results. Damon Runyon's Sky Masterson must convince us, as well as the singing sister, that his heart has been changed.

The narrative poet has, perhaps, the inevitable tendency to let the horse of information take over on the hard road, foregoing poetry's poetry, the jazz of word-hammering that makes any verbal composition either compelling and memorable, or compellingly ordinary. Dobyns puzzles me on this count. Although I do not think he is an emphatically musical poet, he has a gift for the witty line, the piece of verbal grit lodged in the mind if not the ear. He writes epigrammatically and slyly, for example, "in death there are only acquaintances." Resonant language characterizes the poet's art to the extent that it *is* the poetry, and *it* makes the story. Otherwise, what we are told is merely a report from the news scene, just as surely as Thoreau long ago told us. Dobyns's poems are sometimes merely serviceable in this way. Weaker poems approximate poetry, with clusters of words constructed simply as scaffolding, naked and pressureless work by comparison to the more finished and edgy pieces in *Velocities.* "Song of the Wrong Response," "The Great Doubters of History," and "The Community," all from different stages of his career, suggest Dobyns writes fast, writes a lot, and perhaps too easily accepts for poetry a hypothetical contrivance.

But I have only said *Velocities: New and Selected Poems, 1966–1992* is uneven. Anyone who has written enough to matter to more than family readers, excepting those young gun purists and the purse mouths, might cut him a little slack on *that.* Dobyns permits readers to decide where the gold glitters and the false stuff doesn't. His book is a fat, wanderingly inquisitive kind of poetry, one in which you make mental notes about how many poems begin well, or develop well, or even end with a convincing resolution. There also are poems which do not satisfy because they fail a necessary unity of parts, admirable as this or that might be. I said wanderingly inquisitive because of the nature of speculation in both the very fine poems and the lesser ones. This poetry inclines toward something like a philosophical inquiry; it wants to release big ideas falsely accused and imprisoned in whatever holding-tank of circumstance. Few poems are funnier while challenging convictions than "Favorite Iraqi Soldier," in which one of Desert Storm's defeated warriors has doffed his uniform for a hastily assumed three-piece suit with which he "has tried to express by his general indifference / that he had stumbled into all this carnage." Bravery? Cowardice? Survival? Dobyns can make the very strange seem ordinary with language as magnifying as a Bausch and Lomb lens. The search for language has been the denominator of his form, which is sometimes skeletal and sometimes superstructure. He makes me understand why Allen Tate ended his essay on poet John Peale Bishop by saying, "Every road is long, and all roads lead to the problem of form."

Pursuit of form is the great quest for the contemporary poet. Dobyns has hunted along a line from image to narrative and in consequence his lyric interest has been subordinated in a pattern of vacillating enthusiasms. By *Cemetery Nights* he had developed a chorus of poems which set the invisible life of the dead into a sequence of relief moments of speculation, the "cemetery nights" which turn out not especially unlike any other nights. Dobyns wanted a time to "talk"—as prose more easily permits—and he moved toward the sort of stichic form Philip Levine made propitious, a narrative column rolling down the mid-page with language that seems to acquire human debris the way Velcro does. Yet Dobyns appears to have slowly come to lyric clusters, to thinned texture in the stretched lines, a plainer diction, serving a more personal and less staged tale. Interest in the efficacies and secrets of form is any poet's enthusiasm as nothing else is; only a few will be marked as masters of form. The difference is in how you spend your words. Mark Strand, Dobyns's early model, was miserly and gnomic to an extreme, revealing an existential distance from democratic life. Dobyns, inclined toward that austerity, possesses nevertheless an entirely different psychosocial makeup. He has spent as if he had infinite language. One detective show used to claim there were eight million stories in the naked city. Dobyns has written many of their confessions.

Despite those ascetic souls who claim they never face a television, even poets watch those televised dramas, just as Nabokov watched soap operas, out of passionate interest in seeing what happens to ourselves. Sometimes we are content with outer lives, but always most interested in inner lives played out intensely, arriving at moments where the world seems almost comprehensible and still all we want. Stephen Dobyns probably is the poet that Damon Runyan might have wished to be, one long on genuine respect for lives in the saddle of ordinary experience but with an idiom honed toward palpable eloquence. Among the memorable pieces in *Velocities* are "Oatmeal Deluxe," "Pablo Neruda," "The Guitar Lesson," "The White Skirt," "The Gun," "Funny," "Frenchie" (with Larkin echoes), "Kentucky Derby Day, Belfast, Maine," "Spiritual Chickens," "Short Rides," "Desire," "Freight Cars," "Noses," and "Confession" which nudges me with its brute start—"The Nazi within me thinks it's time to take charge." At his best in the later books Dobyns makes the inner webbing and shyness of the individual spirit loom through all that fogs what we are, speaking volumes better than the precious discourse of the MFA angel trainers whose books Henry James might yawn over.

Velocities, that is, carries large chunks of daily and fleshy experience into increasingly focused poems with the lives of people one might have found in John Updike's Maples stories, in Richard Hugo's bad towns, or in Anthony Hecht's iambic-fenced neighborhood. Often they are bruised women you might meet in upstate New York taprooms, or belabored men who laugh when you wonder how they are capable of it. They are the sexually burdened, for to Stephen Dobyns there is no failure and no joy like sex, sex in fact, sex in the glint of a breast, a thigh, a memory, a joke, a painting. Cézanne and Matisse make appearances in late poems, but it is the brawling, visual assault, the steamy Brueghelesque depth and Bosch-flair for erotic pageantry that finally makes Dobyns memorable, as he is in "Bowlers Anonymous":

> Here comes the woman who wears the plastic prick
> hooked to a string around her waist, the man who
> puts girls' panties like a beanie on his head,
> the chicken molester, the lady who likes Great Danes,
> the boy who likes sheep, the old fellow who likes
> to watch turkeys dance on the top of a hot stove,
> the bicycle-seat sniffer, grasshopper muncher,
> the bubbles-in-the-bath biter—they all meet
> each night at midnight and, oh lord, they bowl.

A fascination with skin dominates Dobyns. His seventh collection, in 1990, *Body Traffic,* chronicles the usual sorties of flesh as aggressive, though not especially oriented progress toward death. There is a stubborn naturalism prominent in poems that isolate and anthropomorphize body parts, functions, and contexts, yet it struggles with a *yearning* to know life as meaningful. This struggle finds a capsule form in the sonnet "Cézanne and Zola":

> At thirteen they were known as the inseparables.
> "Opposites by nature," wrote Zola, "we became
> united forever in the midst of the brutal gang
> of dreadful dunces who beat us." Inconsolable
> with Zola in Paris, Cézanne wrote, "I no longer
> recognize myself. I am heavy, stupid and slow."
> Despite many visits, their disagreements overthrew
> their intimacy and they grew apart. "A dreamer,"
> was how Zola described his friend, "a failure
> of genius." And in a novel he wrote how Cézanne
> "had lost his footing and drowned in the dazzling,
> folly of art." Cézanne replied with sixteen years
> of silence, yet when Zola died he fled to his room.
> "All day," a friend said, "we heard the sound of weeping."

Dobyns plays out a psychodrama in which he feels identity with both Zola the representer of the world of things and Cézanne the shaper of impressions, and it is a drama that asks, for the moralist, which is the right path we must walk in the world. That struggle informs the best work Dobyns has done and seems to have freed him to a more musical poetry than he had previously managed. In a loose sonnet, to be sure, the reportage on which the poem is built is wooed away from prose rhythm and toward a poise of iambs and anapests yeomanlike linked to unity in the end rhymes. An unresolved "ending" suggests not only the final grief all comes to, but also paralyzing inability to walk a right path. Still, Dobyns has matured enough to know the sweetness, the confidence that gives moments of acceptance when "briefly we're embraced by a joyful lightness, / as light as smoke rising, or a phrase of music, or butterfly wings, and then the darkness begins."

Among the strategies of architecture I alluded to early on, the builder of a new and selected volume gathers "new" poems which overtly define a departure in form or subject, or herald an exploration, which creates expectations in readers. Stephen Dobyns has, as his "Afterward" indicates, spent a good deal of time in Santiago, Chile, the home of his wife's family. It has encouraged in him a sensibility of tolerance and democratic affection for life's scenes that is Whitman's embrace. His new poems describe men playing soccer, pedestrians threatened by traffic, garbage men with chocolate cake—but his despair at the ludicrous and grotesque, his juxtaposition of the genital with the genial, his love of the vulgar shock have not changed: "What a dreadful world! The immortal / verse of Keats versus a dog's red dick on the concrete." For him there are always contests of lust in which men lose to themselves, and lose themselves, as in "Topless" (Dobyns's "community"), that makes possible, if temporarily, "life without the sharp parts, / thrills without regrets. . . ." What's different, for him, in that?

Well, the little that is everything. Dobyns includes only eighteen new poems in *Velocities,* but most have a personal engagement, an energy charge from the poet's fusion of experience and formal awareness that had been occasionally unconvincing. Now he treats as political people tortured by hurts, small and large, that eat our laughter and our ease. I like very much "Somewhere It Still Moves," a skewering of the events in Yugoslavia through a chatty reminiscence of a comic dinner whose shadows loom even as we laugh. "Pastel Dresses" delivers a portrait of that cruel moment when a boy has to ask a girl to dance for the first time. Its efficient quatrains chug and thump exactly like that frightened heart I well remember. And in the marketplace of "Santiago: Market Day in Winter," Dobyns turns pickpockets into Yeats's gay Chinamen, finding them in their concentration and skilled work worthy of a prayer that he might "sit among thieves and learn to steal."

Dobyns bites in the way of Jonathan Swift and Mark Twain to wittily show the despair and corrosive troubles we see and do not "see" attacking people. "Tenderly" offers a scene in a crowded restaurant with a man who "leaps onto his tabletop, / whips out his prick and begins sawing at it / with a butter knife." Flannery O'Connor said she used exaggeration because it worked with those who see badly. The grotesque, the sensational serve Dobyns, who has something urgent to show us. He is motivated by how "the world implants a picture / in our brains." He saws at art and life, the ways things are inextricably linked. I can't imagine where his tabletop dope is headed, but who, having seen that moment, would not feel for the man's end? Maybe crying out "The horror, the horror." If we have, as Dobyns does, faith in the capital of words and in acts for which words prepare, we might be the banker who "represents"

> the rest when he hopes against hope that the lunatic
> is parked on a topless foreign beach with a beauty
> clasped in his loving arms, breathing heavily, Oh,
> darling, touch me there, tenderly, one more time!

Dobyns, a good storyteller, knows a few simple things that compel attention and earn, if it comes, any success. The point is not merely to inform us that *they touched*. He wants to tell us what to touch and why, where to walk and with what result. While the poems of *Velocities* succeed most when they move toward *The Thin Man*'s wry humor and least when they tap dance like Mickey Spillane, Stephen Dobyns proves almost helplessly American in his willingness to believe all is not lost yet, even as you hear him humming, "Wouldn't it be pretty to think so." But wasn't that the role for the Lady who loved the man with no, ah, equipment for touching?

The Good Talk

Stephen Dunn, whose *New and Selected Poems, 1974–1994* has been recently published by Norton, is, I should say up front, one of my oldest friends in the world of poetry, and I will not begin to pretend impartiality to his poems. Dunn, born in 1939, is a native of New York City. He spent his formative years growing up and working in the "unreal city," as Baudelaire had called Paris, before he, Dunn, landed in an academic life in the wild highlands of Minnesota. It is true that upon arriving in the wintry fields of that northern land and asking his host what all that brown stuff leading to the horizon was, Dunn was told, simply, "Dirt!" His interest in the natural world and its relationships with the people who live upon it has keenly intensified since that point almost thirty years in the past and one might speculate that the shock he experienced in discovering that blank world led him to his prime subject, the domestic and erotic lives of families whose welfare is chronicled in and against the perilous contemporary landscapes all must pass through.

Because he possesses a gift for narrative and its resources, especially in the parables and anecdotes of domestic distress that is so latent with conflated and confused interior tales, Dunn might be imagined a fellow who makes poetry not terribly removed from the better moments of soap opera television. He is not, I think, to be so easily categorized, despite his ease and readiness with marvelously told stories of our ordinary experiences, whether of the scene-and-sequence ("Round Trip"), the slow-release emblematic personal anecdote ("The Routine Things Around the House"), or the nearly minimalist ("The Body Widens"). He doesn't hesitate to extend what he can do to the talent-testing catalog which is sparely narrated in that absolutely no events are chronicled but a progression of experience emerges in definition of a lyric personality. "Loves," for example, is a list of what Dunn has loved in his life, the pedestrian and the rare chronicled equally and by association. Country singer and poet Tom T. Hall might for a few million put such a list on the latest western digital-do, but Dunn has the language artist's ability to make feeling for each item increase because of the *way* it gets said rather than because it gets *said*. This is a lyric attribute. The reader may well feel a pressuring, shaping string of events behind each change of the speaker's attention and each shift of the poem's focus, but this is a change Dunn makes as chord progressions. Dunn is not a true narrative poet, and he couldn't care less about fidelity to the facts or even the causal, sometimes unmotivated nature of what happens. For Stephen Dunn everything is lyric style, or it ain't poetry. His style has evolved to meet a very specific set of psychic and social circumstances which are apparently characteristic of Dunn's life and many others' as well.

Although Dunn writes poems which provide glimpses of both the urban life in which he grew to maturity and the worlds, academic and suburban, in which he has lived as an adult, one scarcely has the sense of density or tangibility that identifies place. I mean something more than an allusion through a place name—say Maine or the Black Horse Pike—something like a sense of immersion in a context of place and life whose effect is the feel of a culture. I cannot, for example, imagine Seamus Heaney without summoning pastoral Ireland's Wicklow Hills and James Wright was virtually synonymous with the Ohio Valley. Even a scan of titles by Dunn yields the sensation of poems displaced, unlocated, a floating through experience significantly more cerebral than historical. Yet place, in Dunn's work especially, establishes a relationship to the sort of formal poet he has chosen to be.

If we ask what place is evoked by the 153 poems he has here collected, the answer, slowly, like a glass globe wherein the fake snow falls away, discovers to us suburban lawns, automobiles, the leafy shadowed place where American tranquility was planted in the great sigh for peace after World War II. Here the generations were to make their beds, their futures, their expectations: the shiny green and pink Formica, the bath and a half, the wind chimes in the lone tree that junior once could (he remembers) jump over. But generations went to factory jobs where dull repetitive work would leave them bored, sullen, spoiling, where for a joke they might piss in Coke bottles rattling the line ("Hard Work"), and we might, in weaker moments, cheer such a tawdry act because it was at least a little defiance of the machine grip that had us as surely as it had that bottle. As generations felt that grip, they moved away, if they could, for they would escape whatever caged the spirit. That life bred frustration, ignorance, belligerence, and impossible desire—because impossible of gratification, because each gratification upped the ante and more was wanted, needed, and never was enough enough. "Instead of You" suggests Dunn's view of earthly affairs:

> From the start all I wanted to explain
> was how things go wrong,
> how the heart's an empty place
> until it is filled,
> and how the darkness is forever waiting
> for its chance.

The saga of suburban experience, by now true for far more of us than any other saga (a word hardly recognizable as naming the struggles of the lives of quiet desperation, and yet, isn't it the right word?), leads inevitably to loneliness and to all the human acts thought capable of countering the miserable bone-ache of being alone. Infidelity is, of course, the most famous of such acts, and not only because its rending hurts the worst but also because we turn in such abject hope from one of us to another. It is only one of the behaviors we license that erode the heart and leave us unanswerable worthlessness and guilt. Against these daily and yearly and finally lifelong nicks, what does culture or community still provide to help us exist as anything but emotional outlaws? What can we set as guardians but small gestures, the smallest efforts to love and to understand? Suburbs are only the outer pale of lost community, not a true or even a dependable society at all, only a scene of houses, an open-air Japanese hotel. In all that yard-by-yard of fenced isolation what is lost is the pressure of how to conduct oneself and what to care about and why—which provides us with virtually the one infallible system of meaning we are likely to have in a life without religion. Stephen Dunn's poems are messages from the suburban void, the same as Louis Simpson's. The difference is that Simpson, a true narrative poet whose imperative for the shape of each book is a fictive model, wants defiantly to show, not tell. Dunn wants to peel away every surface, as if it was a bad paint job, and explain.

Calmed and calming, the interior action of intelligence moving toward consciousness is so characteristic of Stephen Dunn's poetry that to read his early work in *Looking for Holes in the Ceiling* (1974) is to recognize this is a poet who has made a great and deliberate effort to arrive at necessary form.

It must have seemed for a long time to be an effort to know what his necessary subject might be. One of the generation of poets who are now plus or minus fifty, Dunn began to learn his poetic lessons during the reign of Bly, Hall, Simpson, and Pack. Arriving in the wake of the so-called New Critics, who favored (can we agree on this, at least?) a poetry of rational expression, of clear relationships, of part and whole tending toward unified composition and dignified result, Bly-Hall-Simpson-Pack represented the first wave of war-tutored, upward to college and outward to the suburbs poets. They naturally rejected those who held the high ground of poetics (not to mention the launching pads of journals, awards, and books). They clamored for a poetry of direct experience, unmediated life and spontaneous artifice (if they contradicted, very well etc.), a direct and headlights-on forward motion.

The workshops and journals of the early 1970s were flush with the ideas B, H, S, & P had promulgated in the 1960s. These tutors and their visions were abetted in determining what was hot by the last wave of hardened Vietnam Veterans and whatever was left of the drug-zapped academic stock—collegians and faculties in residence. Any poet wanted to publish in *Ironwood, Kayak, The Seventies,* wherever there was Merwin, James Wright, early Gregory Orr, and the deepest image you could swim up to the surface. It was not thought cool, particularly, to speak up in verse as did Howard Nemerov, James Merrill, Mona Van Duyn, and Marilyn Hacker. Can we be surprised that some poets vacillated, attracted to the new game as well as to the solidarity of heritage? Look up the early books of Stanley Plumly, Louise Gluck, Charles Wright, and you find story, sharp and hacked, maybe in the waistcoat of verse, but there as step-child. You will not find discourse of a sort common now in Jorie Graham and Robert Hass. That narrative is there may only admit that no poem succeeds very long unless it tells us what we want to know, who and why and how. Story's presence was in part due to what at the time were outsider poems by Stephen Dobyns, Larry Levis, Ellen Bryant Voigt, and others. Forms of lyric which agree to speak of ideas and abstractions but resist the conformities of verse and shards of image were a contribution of Stephen Dunn.

The last thing our teachers told us we could want was the mind talking and the tale being mounted. During the first half of the period Stephen Dunn's poetry covers, the orthodox opinion (its fathers all have since taken up Dunn's form, a variant of what Stanley Plumly identified as a "prose lyric narrative") held a fierce opposition to a poetics marked by story as well as personal experience, a structure whose charms continued to have its advocates. Not the least practitioner was the critical bête noir of Hall and Bly, Robert Penn Warren, whose long poem, in lyric segments, *Audubon: A Vision* (1969) ends with Warren pleading, "Tell me a story of deep delight." That intense yearning for the missing element of the tale, the speech, the poem with large information marked all of Warren's late poetry as if he believed it would, should it be discovered, reveal *destiny* and a condition of joy. Warren wanted to understand moral and ethical behavior, and he was not reluctant to speak openly about the elements of his quest, abstractions which language brought to visibility. For this, Warren was reputed a philosophical poet. Stephen Dunn can sound surprisingly like Warren, as in "New Mouth": "Somewhere in the world / is the secret name / for God, many-lettered, unpronounceable."

It was not always so. In *Looking for Holes in the Ceiling*, Dunn did not know whether his power lay in lives observed at a distance or in his own life bared through densely imaged anecdotes. He had to discover his comfort lay with a style, what he called "the good talk." It would be a poem that cultivated charm, repartee, witty information, the sort of material you hoped you handled well on a blind date, only lifted to the level of resonant wisdom: "I want to find the cool, precise language / for how passion gives rise to passion." Such style may have a short shelf-life. Dunn's poems wobbled with what was too obvious to say, wielding bon mots with the profundity of a freshman discovering the deliciousness of being smart. During those years we were urged endlessly to make the inner life step out, our teachers having got enough Freud, Jung, Neruda, and Rilke to convince them poetry's future was in raising psychic flash cards. I recall Joyce Carol Oates telling a hushed Michigan crowd that "no one ever dies" and the crowd ooohed in agreement. In "What," Dunn advised, "there are no endings," and then he said:

> people die between birthdays and go on for years;
> what stops things for a moment
> are the words you've found for the last bit of light
> you think there is.

The poem, like us, had no end because the words, fickle and slavish lovers, refused it. How provocative he must have hoped that last half-line, slumping like a lissome Marilyn, would be. Yet Dunn knew well enough the world was fouled and violent, as "Teacher Answering Young Radicals" suggests, but he hadn't, we hadn't—most of us—either actual experience of public events or poetic skills to render with subtlety our emotional confusions. "Biography in the First Person" alludes to an identity problem in the outer life:

> This is not the way I am.
> Really, I am much taller in person . . .
> . . . .
> My poems are approximately true.
> . . . .
> I would like to make you believe in me.

Tennis phenom Andre Agassi bubbled on TV that "image is everything." The contemporary poet's problem seemed as simple as figuring out who looked back from his mirrors. Dunn's solution, at first, relied on an American comic sensibility audible in "How to Be Happy: Another Memo to Myself":

> Remember, finally, there are few pleasures
> that aren't as local as your fingertips.
> Never go to Europe for a cathedral.
> In large groups, create a corner
> in the middle of a room.

Dunn was trying to give himself permission to find delight, joy. He has Whitman's optimism at his base, but what to do about the rules, the histories, the gruesome facts? While Donald Justice had been his teacher at Syracuse University, Dunn did not find Justice's verse agenda, Anglican and southern (Justice had done his master's thesis on John Crowe Ransom's poetry), compelling. Although he early on imitated surrealists and might have inclined to Ashbery, the goof-and-rapture of Ashbery was, like Stevens, too baroque, lacking humble idiom. Berryman was gridlock. Lowell and Ginsberg didn't dance. Frost, Hugo, and Roethke, each of whom had visible value to Dunn, stayed in the flowers too long for a city sensibility; they could make you snore. Maybe some O'Hara. Some Stafford, Ignatow, Kinnell. Their presences show in his lines. But the rhythmic citizen he could not deny was William Carlos Williams.

Williams appealed to Dunn's preference for plainly colloquial diction. He loved those hieratic New Jersey locales and the doctor's secession from English form. What if Williams did not speak so directly to an audience's lapels as Dunn, a boy resettled from Queens to the New Jersey shore, a poet who wished and was hardly ever funny? What Dunn had to tell was himself and the intuited experiences everyone had had. In the early 1970s, narrative form that might accommodate Dunn's need was less prominent than the quirky associational poem loosely called the "surreal." James Wright said Americans didn't get the point of surrealism, that it was meant to be funny. Dunn got the point: be interior, be funny, be image-built. Others, like James Tate, made painterly, cinematic cuts a strategy and made a poetry oblique, angular, juxtapositional as well-timed jokes. Dunn, although he leans in that direction, for two reasons chose otherwise. Such poems necessarily are short; they do not permit amplitude or exploration of manners, both of which drew Dunn magnetically.

Moreover, the comedy of the surreal, of even linear dream-imitation, is singular, one might say selfish, and inhibits the intimate low-key conversation of a bon vivant who offers every expression as a doorway into grace, for himself or his semblable, the reader. Dunn has kept only ten poems of his first collection where "How to Be Happy: Another Memo to Myself" shows the slack prose lineation, the postures of rhetoric and scrutiny which were then marks of first books seeking a way between the counseled inner and the actual outer life.

> When you get together
> you must feel everyone has brought
> his fierce privacy with him
> and is ready to share it. Prepare
> yourself though to keep something back;
> there's a center in you
> you are simply a comedian
> without. Beyond this, it's advisable
> to have a skill. Learn how to make something:
> food, a shoe box, a good day.

Nothing goes on; there is nothing to see in this poem. It is perilously close to psychobabble by which we might be emotionally "centered." Many of us wrote words without connection to a community, a lived force, because we had pushed out into suburban deserts where we made nothing and knew little but talk. Still, in those final advisory lines, Dunn heard the call of craft, a craft that would permit him a convincing poetry of wisdom and delight, and perhaps the greater richness of responsibility and community.

Full of Lust and Good Usage (1976) and *A Circus of Needs* (1978) develop poems remarkable for one thing, a coloration in the speaking voice that does more than convey what the voice feels about its situation. It has the capacity to change register and volume, but ordinarily it expresses a coolness, a deliberate, reticent personality that few inventories of experience disturb. Eventually it acquires the sharpness and trust we give to a confidant, but in "Truck Stop: Minnesota" what we hear is less, a flippant, insular self-awareness: "The waitress looks at my face / as if it were a small tip." In a line Richard Hugo would have loved, self-depreciation and mockery are comic tools the poet engaged to locate identities in the unmapped terrain of the outer life, but relationships are what he is already trying to talk about. With the discovery by his second and third collections that his ostensible subject will be "the sweet combat of love," bodies and emotions, all the awkwardness and fear and possibility of sexual wars, Dunn claims his proper stage. He achieves a confidence he approaches with no other subject.

> I sense the aromas of sex,
> the delicate, stale drift
>
> of arguments and spite
> no amount of cleaning will solve . . .

he says in "In the House." He has new strength because he simultaneously finds the tonal power of the man who thinks, who by dint of thought, or perception, controls circumstance. If this man admits weakness, it is a strength. Confusion is sorted. Anger, bitterness, despair, all are restrained, harnessed. Language leads to mystery. Dunn's tone is dispassionate, slightly sorrow-tinged, a voice that has "a firm seat in the balcony / of ideas while music plays."

The central drama for his subject is that poem about meeting, loving, leaving, missing, remembering, meditating on, and memorializing women. Here is the last union in community, where the inner life and the outer life connect. That love's drama is as dangerous as random violence or natural mortality, "A Primer for Swimming at Black Point" reveals, nodding at what his future holds:

> The bottom drops off quickly
> and you're in over your head
> among the crosscurrents,
> the floating sea plants.
> This is where to swim, though.

The feel of his authority seemed to intensify with each poem as Dunn found his form for good talk, his poise. He typically favors the short line, a cadence for speculation that Williams recognized as an equally enabled carrier of things in the moralized landscape. And he likes the plain diction that, as with Williams, is less plain than a deft dialect. Dunn is a sifter, a holder, the poem acting like a mouth to swirl for taste and aroma. He is interested in the fable, parable, and mystery tale, usually composed with the cast of elegy: a man not named but emblematic encounters unusual, burdensome, and ponderable experience ("The Man Who Never Loses His Balance" and "Danse Manhattanique") that leads to some revelation of the end of things. Dunn has learned the tone of *knowing* that permits him to speak intimately and credibly, as thinking, ultimately rational man:

> I am tired of hearing the insane
>   lauded for their clear
>   thinking. If they do
>
> get to the reddest heart of things
>   it's because they can't see
>   the world of appearances,
>
> where you are, struggling to separate
>   the difficult jewel from the
>   chalcedony that surrounds it.

These triads from "Essay on Sanity," show what becomes a dominant form in Dunn's poetry and announce the clash of rational and irrational that underwrites his "love" and its ruptures. The startling, unusual stone in this stream, "chalcedony," makes Dunn add "And I love the world" to reaffirm ordinariness, the quality most coveted by a man intent on speaking honestly. This ordinary man covets love, believes in love, but its wreckage is, Plath-like, intense, everywhere, and violent ("Split: 1962" and "Instead of You"). There are two primary kinds of poems, then, for Dunn: the autobiographical lyric and its discursive, speculative counterpart. The coupling of these poems feels something like inner and outer voice, and it seems to bespeak a necessary choosing of one or the other. In fact they are masks which permit the poet to make formal choices, to arrange an ongoing contest between the Whitman and the Williams in him. Dunn has certain complaints to record. The worst he can imagine of man's situation, and it bears reminding this is measured against the war horrors and racial horrors and other malfeasances of humanity that so blighted the 1970s, is the inability, literally, to speak, the fear of and the life of non-speech, which as Tillie Olsen and others had said, was a death in life, a radical aloneness. What difference would it make to commit the finest interiorized poems if they remained unreceived, unheard? For Stephen Dunn speech constitutes the permit to understanding, consciousness, love, and grace. By 1981, in *Work and Love*, he knew he was writing about life "where philosophy lives with despair," and about that "nothing can be done." This last echoes the chilling recognition of the little darkness that life is, the darkness Larkin reminded us was waiting just outside every high window.

Yet the second complaint, terrible as well and recurrent through all of Dunn's poetry, distrusts grand speech and its maker's designs as merely artificial. Life, said Berryman, is boring. For Dunn the missing element is "that relentless buzz, more / than mere desire, less than misery." He chafes not at the unexamined life but at the unlived, unrisked life. "A Good Life" notes his blessings and says, anyway, he knew:

> his true life lay elsewhere, it must,
> so much acceptable pleasure here
> yet so much yearning. He was home,
> some muted pinprick of unease
> prodding him, dully, from afar.

Dunn so often, so variously, bemoans the entrapments of the suburbanite who covets his wine, his jazz, his films, his love affairs, that we might well cry hold, enough. He wants, though, what we all want: "to lean into life, / catch the faintest perfume." Workers home from the Coke plant, people tangled in their alibis and desires, our gestures are like airplanes that end up skywriting off "little essays to the wind." Yet his life, or yours, is as emblematic and mysterious as any saint's, he thinks. We listen to him because he evokes our joys and hungers with delicate, avuncular gestures like those of "As It Moves":

> Look, nothing's simple.
> It was almost dusk. I was thinking
> the seagull is a comic, filthy bird
> magnificent as it moves
> upward in imperfect air.

When he started, Stephen Dunn hadn't access to the felicitous rightness of that tone, that cadence, or how he might balance "magnificent" with "imperfect" and illustrate his thesis. He had to learn the accent of patience and wearied acceptance that is his brand of paternal love. *Not Dancing* (1984), *Local Time* (1989), which won the National Poetry Series Award, and *Between Angels* (1989) are insistently focused on the domestic history and rhythm of love. Dunn has a growing and sometimes indulged appetite for the philosophical statement, the position paper as poem, but he has no philosophy, in fact, if by that term we mean a systematic and extended program of thought. Dunn likes to describe a domestic scene and therein stage a revelation of the meaning of experience. He knows that his Scylla and Charybdis are sentimentality and soapbox rhetoric. Against those bad angels he deploys his poetry, the weave of which permits moments of perception that arrive and pass like slides in a carousel. "After the Argument" details the psychic hostilities of married life and its rules—we know *them* don't we? Dunn's view, crisp and objective, details what goes wrong:

> Whoever spoke first would lose something,
>   that was the stupid
>   unspoken rule.
> . . . .
> The trick was to speak as if you hadn't
>   spoken a comment
>   so incidental . . .

the whole matter would become "Yalta, always / on some level the future. . . ." Ever since Sylvia Plath the note of high dudgeon, the shriek of fury has belonged to the ladies, but Dunn stakes a real claim to domestic poison—not so readily to the Armageddons of noise as to the lockdown of silence and sullenness. There are few poets better at achieving the feel of that paralyzing, bitter knot of lovers in the rhythmic struggle of destruction and self-repair, men and women on their own without gods, communities, or, perhaps, selves. Because he struggles to accept the flawed nature of the individual soul, Dunn claims interest in what he calls "the messiness of the erotic," the energy dynamics and finally violent overloads that go on mocking us, like city substations, below the surface of appearances. He is among the most comforting and seductive of poets. His eye is always on the contest between delight we seek and cost we pay:

> In my heatless room I've been thinking
> that the duty-before-pleasure people
> balance the books for those of us
> dutiful about our pleasures . . .
> ("A Petty Thing")

It is possible, I imagine, for the evidence has been reported that way, that our fore-kin were generally content in their lives, or at least accepted what could not be changed, and felt the affirmations of a culture which, stripped away, made the twentieth century that well-known waste land. But Madame Bovary and Hester Prynne, to say nothing of Faulkner's Joe and Hemingway's Jake, knew something about yearning for a bit more life than they were getting. The most frequent names in Dunn's poetry for what they wanted, what he wants, are pleasure, love, and grace. Its names telegraph absence, boredom, detachment, inconsequence: "all the dead / unforgivably correct afternoons" inhabited by people who performed "the speaking parts from the life we were in / then drove to the party." But those acts of intimacy, in this poet's style, are less autobiographical recoveries than metaphor's representations of the huge hunger for hope, for an understanding life-frame that relieves littleness:

> If there isn't a God
> maybe there's just a sense we're not
> sufficiently large.
> Maybe only through irreverence can we find
> our true size.
> ("Honesty")

Dunn's struggle is for the fulfilled life, and a life outside the community strictures which have made us lonely, insular, freighted, and uncertain. Maybe good moments, old habits tell us, are enough: "Now and again I feel the astonishment / of being alive like this, and in this body." Most of us think that silently from time to time. Dunn thinks it out loud.

Dunn feels pulled through the wear and tear of unhappy days slogged out, as so many do, but poetry permits him not simply therapeutic self-escape but the temporary lagoon where it's possible to live in faith that families can muddle ahead, civilization can exist. It may be a certain justice inheres in thinking of Dunn, in this light, as a philosophical poet, for his insistent examinations of the tiniest nuances of personal relationships, of motivation, of act, and of consequence, are compelled not by act and consequence but as set-ups for meaning he covets. By dint of this dramatization, Dunn creates the tension and unresolved feel of life that is art, not melodrama, not soap opera, not preacherly program. He focuses on the pulse of what happens, however small; he tasks himself to follow the link between the always-foundering outer lives and the sustenance of an inner life of awareness. He enacts a conversation about the complicit acts of a self who loves and will be responsible for what he is, but who refuses to be ridden by culture shibboleths. The shape of his mature work has been to know the relationship of a conscious and conscientious soul in the most intimate nuances of his life.

The price for that local looking is a certain bourgeois, commuter, pat quality, the poem-as-commentary; it is, admittedly, sometimes tedious. Billy Graham's life interests us less than Jimmy Swaggart's, though which of them we might trust is never in doubt. Dunn has tried, with some good results, to broaden his sweep in the newest poems while retaining that precisely honest voice. As he says, "The cricket reminds me of Eastern Europe, / some bewildered communist holding on." In his poems one encounters Bosnia, Foucault, Joan Sutherland, Colorado's Snow Mass ski resort, dogs (Dunn is a very tender poet on pets), and wine. But his poetry happens most acutely, as we might expect, on the domestic island of family experience. "At the Smithville Methodist Church," its Americana echoed by its title, shows us one of the squeezes of love that is not erotic but parental, communal. The subteen daughter is invited to attend with neighboring children a summer Bible school activity:

> It was supposed to be Arts & Crafts for a week,
> but when she came home
> with the "Jesus Saves" button, we knew what art
> was up, what ancient craft.

Parents all over America have smiled at each other in the recognition of that smug evangelism that means to divide and cash in, that craft. Your child asks, you say sure, for what harm could it do? I like the tang of a poem that corners the parents' wish to embrace the best for a child. The child, of course, comes home happily singing about standing up for Jesus, which Dunn wants to give in to (though ironically Stephen Dunn is the son of a Jew), and he might, if he and the wife weren't whizzing daughter home in the family Subaru, take on that car-filling passion for the Christian martyr. Instead, all they can do is think of Jesus as a friend from the past, a memory, at best a delusion.

> It had been so long since we believed, so long
> since we needed Jesus
> as our nemesis and friend, that we thought he was
> sufficiently dead . . .

and who needs fairy tales? Dunn's appetite for a cohesive and progressive scheme of existence is nowhere more evident, but he is a voice of social realism, not transcendental witness. Pinched between daughter's innocent belief and his own lack of immersion in what can't be verified, imagination's biggest dreams, Dunn's comedy charms but the point is sharp enough.

> Evolution is magical but devoid of heroes.
> You can't say to your child
> "Evolution loves you." The story stinks
> of extinction and nothing . . .

To this dilemma there seems only one end and Dunn has it cold, the match of words and event, yielding to the daughter who sings all the way home: "There was nothing to do / but drive, ride it out, sing along / in silence."

Because that's what poetry is, that speaking (which may or may not be singing) in a language right for the occasion, Stephen Dunn has to find the good talk for what he feels compelled to say. He is not oblivious to the idiosyncrasy of his personal catechisms that place such a burden on style, tone of voice, and that subdued, if not wholly bland, subject, the 'burbs. He has chosen to foreground our most intimate lives and seems to have no illusions about the causes of our injuries: "It's a sexual song, isn't it / that crickets sing? They do it to be heard." That is not to say problems are only glitches of reproductive biology, but Dunn does argue a sort of mechanical snafu which, with the right amount of speech at the right time and place, could be reordered, even corrected. A romantic at heart, his working conviction, good man that he is, trusts in the goodness of people to preserve selves by making enlightened choices, to refind through acts of awareness the community that lives. He refuses to cede only to columnists and therapists the right to talk grandly, abstractly. Dunn's poetry has been, to an unusual but not unique extent, the evolution of a man who wanted to speak, just that at first, then to find expression for complex desire and loneliness, that which makes us act and react, and last to be able to tell, with such exactness as only poetry permits, what happened to us, and why. Poetry, he believes, comes to those readied with grace, style, and power, and it ought to be no surprise that his poems are a vestibule of echoes from writers he has studied. When poetry comes, he has learned, true poets have the means to speak as simply as forces of Nature, though smooth effect be entire artifice. Dunn means to speak reverentially, with effect, of how it has been with his generation, in the upheavals and turbulence of post-Vietnam America. Despite recent faint-hearted willingness to dance off in corners with the latest airhead, poetry always has done that. In Dunn's *Landscape at the End of the Century* and in sixteen new poems of *New and Selected Poems, 1974–1994,* he has acquired the obliging, rare, welcome poise that makes us feel that this is how it is supposed to sound, how the opera can actually go when talent and discipline and passion and luck play poker together.

Stephen Dunn stands comfortably in the ranks of poets who accept the right of the "delight and instruct" in poetry's ancient marching orders, as well as the praiseworthy left. Dunn is one of those poets who powerfully remind us that poems may be charming lessons, not always as repulsive as castor oil nobody much anymore swallows, as we once did. He likes a poem that, even when pleasant, lingers with the memorable taste of metal in the mouth. In some ways his closest likeness is Robert Pinsky or, earlier, the methodic save-the-woods poems of David Wagoner, neither of which quite has Dunn's capacity for entertaining while the barb lodges under the skin. Dunn's wisdom, and it cannot be delivered too frequently to poets inclined to tolerate a little fuzziness, says language is everything, honesty is everything, and yet everything is negotiable. Or, as another poet has told us, it don't mean a thing if it ain't got that swing. How like Stephen Dunn to have written a poem whose witty title turns out to have been the lesson in most of what we need to know about a real poem:

DECORUM

She wrote, "They were making love
up against the gymnasium wall,"
and another young woman in class,
serious enough to smile, said

"No, that's fucking, they must
have been fucking," to which many
agreed, pleased to have the proper fit
of word with act.

But an older woman, a wife, a mother,
famous in the class for confusing grace
with decorum and carriage,
said the F-word would distract

the reader, sensationalize the poem.
"Why can't what they were doing
just as easily be called making love?"
It was an intelligent complaint,

and the class proceeded to debate
what's fucking, what's making love,
and the importance of context, tact,
the *bon mot*. I leaned toward those

who favored fucking: they were funnier
and seemed to have more experience
with the happy varieties of their subject.
But then a young man said, now believing

he had permission: "What's the difference,
you fuck 'em and you call it making love;
you tell 'em what they want to hear."
The class jeered, and another man said

"You're the kind of guy who gives fucking
a bad name," and I remembered how fuck
gets dirty as it moves reptilian
out of certain minds, certain mouths.

The young woman whose poem it was,
small-boned and small-voiced,
said she had no objection to fucking,
but these people were making love, it was

her poem and she herself up against
that gymnasium wall, and it felt like love,
and the hell with all of us.
There was silence. The class turned

to me, their teacher, who they hoped
could clarify, perhaps ease things.
I told them I disliked the word fucking
in a poem, but that fucking

might be right in this instance, yet
I was unsure now, I couldn't decide.
A tear formed and moved down
the poet's cheek. I said I was sure

only of "gymnasium," sure it was
the wrong choice, making the act seem
too public, more vulgar than she wished.
How about "boat house?" I said.

Playing for Grace

WILLIAM MATTHEWS

He was thirty-eight days older than I am, born November 11, 1942, during the second year of a war we were then losing. I always thought he looked as old as my father, slumped as if he were chronically fatigued. In the jacket photograph of his posthumous collection of poems, *After All: Last Poems* (1998), he looks better, healthier, more charming than I remember. I cannot say he looks "younger" because I can't recall a time when that word might actually have fit him. Not that he wasn't possessed of a remarkable zest for everything that appeals to a man of passion and intellect, but rather that he seemed always to be sapped by indulgence, to the point that he looked, as the country song said, as if life had been a little bit hard on him.

Matthews's poems acknowledge but resist temptations to elegize pain and suffering, which made him different from his generation of poets. His middle name was Proctor, linking him to the business of fortune and consequence in American life. He was born upper-crust in Cincinnati, Ohio, as T. S. Eliot had been born to the crust in St. Louis, Missouri. Both left home and stayed gone. Yale University and a first-class education welcomed him. In graduate school at the University of North Carolina his friends included the distinguished novelist Russell Banks and the poet Robert Morgan (now an Oprah-certified novelist himself). They founded together and edited an influential literary magazine called *Lillabulero.* His initial two collections of poetry, *Ruining the New Road* and *Sleek for the Long Flight,* appeared from Random House before he was thirty, before even the end of the Vietnam War, which he did not serve in. No poet in his time had a more auspicious start.

As with so many of his generation, an abundance of Robert Bly, William Stafford, Mark Strand, and Hayden Carruth shows up in his early poems, with a dollop of A. R. Ammons, his colleague when he taught at Cornell University. Matthews's poems are all over the landscape of the 1970s in search of something said simply. He wants to say it about big subjects: love, death, war, psychic instability, music, and writing. If he was the most political of men, and he was, he was not a political poet, just one in need of ideas. This was the tail end of the Zeitgeist of the 1960s; ideas were like loaves of bread, you could get them anywhere, they went with anything, they cost almost nothing, and they soon were as thin as our hair. The poets he admired trafficked in them, even his home-state mentor James Wright. The sound in a Matthews poem, especially early, is quick, terse, barbed, an off-the-tongue remark with the sting of wit that, maybe, he hopes, can carry wisdom's heavy weight. It's American rhythm and vocabulary, plain image, delivered the way Mohammed Ali flicked a jab, who could float like a butterfly and sting like a bee, as he said and said and said. "Suddenly" brings Matthews back to my ear, apocalyptic in little bursts, tweaky humor, a sighing piece:

> The truth is out, and nothing
> is the same. You are
> the last surprise, I am
> an elk come too far south,
> puzzled by villages.
> Too late, too late, I run
> through snowy fields
> on melting legs.

The poem gives so many eerie hints of notes he both struck and abandoned in his later, mature poems that it is hard to remember how playful and self-depreciating the poet is. Bly talks through him, and maybe it is Richard Hugo who entices him to say he is "an elk come too far south," a ludicrous notion for a poet Teflon-protected against self-pity, a young man who wore Armani silk and was Euro-slick before most of us knew there was another world over there. A silly image, running "on melting legs" (which would prove a bitter irony by his early fifties), was the cat's meow to the young comers like Larry Levis; it tried to give body to ennui, to claim suffering where none, really, existed. Matthews would lose it.

In his earliest poems Matthews deflected the risk of sentimentality with a rare humor whose range was pun, satire, irony, and always self-mockery. He turned a metaphor brusquely rather than extend a conceit. The cost was often enough gimmickry, novelty, something seen through. He might unconvincingly yoke an ordinary present with a discordant past, as in

> The 727 trembles
> on the runway
> like Cortez just come
> over the rise, gorging . . .
> ("Leaving Mexico City")

or with jauntiness he might describe the family car as "the invalid Volvo / flying its pennant of blue fumes" or, at his worst, submit to the precious, a delicate and impossible image of contradictory touch: "Always put your gloves / of ashes on before you knock." But many of us loved what he brought to the table, and I am surely not alone in remembering how the first read through *Ruining the New Road* produced a little gasp of admiration, a little conclusion that this might be genius, effortless, slippery, airy, a poetry that seemed like our synapses talking. Nothing was more true, even obvious, than that we thought our lives were just what he said in "Help": "We hunt with animals' bones / and learn love from each other." Unless, of course, you read the lines when you are sixty-two, not twenty-two. With distance, those poems, like many from first books in the 1970s, seem to slide off the page, a callow glibness surfaces, the enemy of poetry just as James Wright said it was.

I met William Matthews in Norfolk, Virginia, in the fall of 1970 or the spring of 1971, I think. I was then on active duty with the U.S. Air Force at Langley AFB, a young sergeant with ambitions for a poetry I didn't understand and with the same appetite to scoop up whatever might work that marked his new book. He was to read poems, probably at Virginia Wesleyan College, and his host poet, Bruce Guernsey, invited me to come over for the day. A game of pick-up basketball ensued. On the court, Matthews was smooth, clever, but not especially quick. He made a nice white forward. Probably he was a decent shot, for he would have practiced that. Probably he had once had a deft fingertip touch. His poetry argues that he would have that. I don't remember. He was slightly taller than I am, but I was stronger and a better jumper. We guarded each other and in consequence I made a discovery about him that I would never have reason to dismiss. He was an intense competitor who valued grace and style above everything. Except winning. Bill had no intention of permitting me to outjump or outmaneuver him. When the ball went up, his elbows came out, and they were bony and sharp. I don't mean he was a dirty player or malicious. I mean he understood limits, and he meant to use whatever was possible to enhance his opportunity to win. No quarter offered. Young poets could learn a lot from Bill, I thought. I did. I still think that. Maybe I should say that his intensity and sly moves made competition extraordinary fun.

By the publication of *Sleek for the Long Flight* in 1972, the last year of Vietnam and the year I was discharged to return to graduate school, Bill had become a handsome, charming incarnation of the good young man of America who was also devilishly smart, and widely known to be a star. He liked the role. He had written poems against the war, against politicians, against the ills of bad marriage, bad sex, bad karma. Mostly, now, he was writing against loneliness, even sometimes in favor of loneliness, with a distinctive, smoky, bluesy quality trying to nudge into his poems. He wrestled with an urge toward statements of wisdom that made him seem, in poetry readings and conversation, so much older, more vivid, solid, and wiser than the rest of us. By then he was a professor at Cornell. His name was among the first sounded as a leader of new generation poets, the first to be anthologized. He was up to writing prose poems, catalog poems, even one-line poems like "The Invention of Astronomy" which told us "The eyelids fall, the star-charts." There seemed little he wouldn't, or couldn't, do. The heavy-lidded undergraduate girls wanted to be close to him, and would be.

The truth is that he still didn't have a subject in his grasp. He made a new turn to the world of Nature but it wasn't very convincing. Ammons, his Cornell neighbor, felt the weight, metaphysical and back-bending, of snow. Bill used it as decoration, the way he had used Bly's landscape. Matthews was a poet of the salon, the saloon, the inner rooms, the play of people in domestic arenas, and the Nature world was, well, out there. In "Stone," dedicated to Charles Simic, then pioneering his fabular blend of world that means and says more than most notice, Bill couldn't resist the pun and the wisdom statement as all he needed:

> The creek has made its bed
> and wants to lie in it.
> That's why spring is terrifying.
> Water rises like the bloated drowned
> against the ice. In the churn
> stones are born stunned.

Those stones would make a whole book for poet Gregory Orr and fill pages of the mystical journal *Field*. Matthews assumes the trope of cause-effect with his pun and extends it to account for the Eliotic observation that fecund spring is cruel. But there is no reason for the poem to say what it says, no occasion to jumpstart even leaping logic; the follow-on image of water resembling the bloated dead is inert and sentimental. The problem is the poet's hurry to get an effect, and that propelled by wanting to give voice to profundity more an idea than it is a felt reality to the poet. We know this moment is stage prop. Here, nothing is happening. Matthews asserts, and never mind useful footstones over the stream are missing. He is determined to scare us into believing "Evolution makes us sleek / for the long flight."

"Stone" revealed, especially in that metaphor of chosen flight in Nature's parts, what would become clearer with each of Matthews's subsequent books, a pervasive and abiding fear of death. He was always a poet looking for consolation against an end he knew to be inevitably bad and unredressable by anything in which we could take pleasure. He described that naked fear early on in "How to Die":

> You aren't surprised.
> You take in water, you lie in the sun.
>
> As warped as an old plank,
> you split along the grain.

It wouldn't be painful, then. No big deal. Just what Nature did. He was telling himself to be cool, find grace, that Hemingway grin in the face of it all. He was also telling himself that the only answer was pleasures, of the body, of sex, of touch, of intimacy and intensity, of the flesh that he knew would unravel, as flesh does. He hadn't quite got to music yet. His poems turned to falling in and out of love, portraits of family, often enough what we now call the dysfunctional thing in so many betrayals and divorces. It was always loneliness he studied. In *Flood* (1982) he wrote, "Our true subject is loneliness. / We've been divorced 1.5s time per heart." With Bill, if you had asked who that royal "we" was the answer would have been equally smart and funny.

By the early 1980s he was into his best work, the poems celebrating music, jazz at the heart of everything, the slick delights of wine, travel, good company, a lovely, frothy mix that seemed more than a game yet played, somehow, with his skills against time and mortality and boredom and the ever-present absent significance. His game was evidently poetry, and he loved it, its self-consumption, varieties, nuances, its emblematic work. He understood better than most that writing is not often living, but it always proposes living. In poetry you tame and examine and purge and discipline suffering; you transform it to grace. If it exists in words, it must be there for a purpose, and the purpose is to give the distraction of pleasure. He wrote, "A light burns / where a man is writing." The poem meant a light "to fool burglars," but he knew the thieves, pain and suffering, would not be put off forever, at least not the kind inside the family for which there is no balm, no alternative. Because he liked a game of comparing poets to glamorous stars, I thought of him as the sardonic, witty William Powell of poetry. No one seemed as "laid back" as Bill.

Matthews slowly became a poet of philosophical and meditational style, his poems wry trials of grace. He wanted to say profound things he felt were beyond sensations; he wanted to say sensations released him to larger ripplings of awareness. This was the poet who once defined Boulder, Colorado, as "the capitol of the spiritual-growth-without-pain world," a city where he lived and taught and knew himself as the other in disguise, for he was never one of the drug-sucking shoddy irrepressibles who didn't care. He cared. He still had those elbows, could be tough, hard, unblinking, while humor ruled, a grin, a drink, a joke. In *A Happy Childhood* (1985), he took on abstractions, the very thing the poets of the 1960s image kingdom had driven away. He wrote poems called "Bad," "Tardy," "Loyal," "Right," and "Wrong" among others. His structure became more anecdotal, then more narrative, blending events from his childhood with allusions that made popular culture, as it had been for T. S. Eliot, his own personal kit resource. He may have learned this from David Wagoner, his colleague at the University of Washington where he had begun to teach. Wagoner perfected what can be called the "how to do it" poem in which acute observations about the way an activity is or might be conducted, say swimming or logging, configures the poem as instruction. Whatever the activity, Bill knew, it was about poetry, too. One of his sweetest poems is "Masterful," an elegy for the batting prowess of the great baseballer Ted Williams. It is not accidental the poem is an expression of Bill's faith in style and grace, now becoming increasingly slippery, that marries the ever-decaying body to ultimate pleasure, something that lasts:

> They say you can't think and hit at the same time,
> but they're wrong: you think with your body, and the whole

wave of impact surges patiently through you
into your wrists, into your bat, and meets the ball

as if this exact and violent tryst had been a fevered
secret for a week. The wrists "break," as the batting

coaches like to say, but what they do is give away
their power, spend themselves, and the ball benefits.

When Ted Williams took—we should say "gave"—
batting practice, he'd stand in and chant to himself

"My name is Ted Fucking Ballgame and I'm the best
fucking hitter in baseball," and he was, jubilantly

grim, lining them out pitch after pitch, crouching
and uncoiling from the sweet ferocity of excellence.

Here, enjambment breaks like the curve ball pitchers call a hook and is
almost, in Matthews's deftness, equal to a hitter's timing. Bill knew when ev-
erything else was gone, or gone shabby and soft, you still had to aspire to and
hold out for *excellence,* and if you had it, then it couldn't be taken back by
time or fashion, and the evidence of possession was style he could inscribe
like an aura. In his late poems excellence is in a light touch he conferred
upon verse, permitting a near-conversational, ever-speculating voice that
goes on talking long after everyone has left the building, a voice as familiar
as a piano or saxophone just overheard.

Anyone who got near him on the basketball court, or faced him across
the tennis net where he might swat it at you, understood why Bill admired
Ted Williams and understood, too, what Bill meant in this sonnet that posed
mastery in two apparently contradictory actions. The poem's premise is
baldly stated, that juxtaposition of giving and taking, the wrist image as syn-
ecdoche, and it depicts a model of greatness whose effect is as accomplished
as effort. Bill praises the star who had to talk himself into poise, being "ju-
bilantly / grim," maintaining a vulgar force and a self-creating discipline he
could see through if the public could not. This diction is plain but not collo-
quial exactly, clinical as an instructional video, a commentary on the duplic-
ity of language, with the hitter made transparent emblem of art and its labor.
These couplets are masterful units of observation, full little cups of shim-
mer that spill over enough for propulsion and suspense. The poem's timing
rhymes the hitter's so we know both the great ambitious swing and the solid

thunk that flies the ball outward; we experience, without feeling our arms twisted, movement from abstraction to abstraction, a tidy illustration of an idea: excellence exists, it can be demonstrated, it has function that makes life valuable. I think Bill might even have said that excellence is life's value for it is, as Robert Penn Warren once wrote, "beautiful as a law of physics."

In the early 1980s I spoke with Bill on the telephone several times monthly. We served together on the board of the Associated Writing Programs. When memory recalls him for me, he leans against a kitchen wall in a hotel suite, or he hovers at a bar; his head is swathed in cigarette smoke, his eyes are blear and red, his skin looks as if he experiences a heavier gravity than the rest of us. He's just poured a glass of ordinary chardonnay which he sips as if it had come from Donald Trump's best stock. It won't be long until he will laugh, snorting first, then his head tilted back, mouth open to grin, looking down with what appears a frank happiness to be with you, so that you feel he isn't waiting for someone else, he's really interested in what *you* think. Bill liked people; he conveyed pleasure, he cultivated it, and it was magnetic. I remember funny things he said as much, finally, as I remember the poems.

In 1978, I think that was the year, there was a bizarre poets' tennis tournament at the Wickenburg Inn somewhere in rural Arizona. Stephen Dunn, Galway Kinnell, Marvin Bell, Coleman Barks, Bill, Ross Talarico, and I were hired to read poems each evening for a week while paying customers did whatever they do at such a ranch. In return we received lavish free accommodations, terrific food, as much tennis as we could play, and candy kisses on our pillows. Only no customers ever showed up. I remember thinking how stunningly strange it was to be, in a horse-drawn wagon, taken on a hayride with the seven other poets singing western ditties to the empty night. Late in that week, an interviewer tracked us down, certain there was an exposé to be had, harassing Bill especially. Finally the man shrieked at the doubles court, "Tell me what the winner gets!" Our only prize was being there. Exasperated, Bill snarled back, "Fifteen minutes in a phone booth with America's hottest female poet." Soon we howled as Bill huffed off to cajole agreement that remark would never see print.

He wasn't always a funny man. The father of two sons, William Jr. and Sebastian, Bill frequently talked to me about teenagers. Having them in the full blossom of their rebellions, we both felt afflicted. He seemed steeped in obligation to them, raising them alone, proud and attentive. He loved his sons as if they were small copies of what he had been, and he forgave them everything. Sebastian's memoir, *In My Father's Footsteps* (2004), could hardly have been more startling to me in its portrait of the ways Bill had been an inept, hurtful father, absent more than present, self-protected rather than protecting. Sebastian's description of life with Bill sounds, maybe, the way I thought life was with them:

> All through high school I slept under my father's study. Every night I'd drift off to the faint pounding of his Selectric typewriter, to the flowing bass of a jazz record. On nights when I couldn't sleep, home late and tanked on espresso, I'd make my way up the carpeted stairs and take my seat by the bookshelf in the corner. While Dad composed and revised his poems, I would listen to his records, read books off the shelf, try out my own awkward poems on his trademark yellow typing paper. We had a terrific view of downtown Seattle from our third-floor perch—of the Space Needle, of Puget Sound, the Cascades off in the distance. Below us, rows of houses gave way to the neon lights of Broadway Avenue. Dad would open a bottle of wine, turn up the heat, flip the disc, and we'd settle in.

There's more local details, more place, in this paragraph than in all of *Search Party,* maybe because Bill never lived anywhere but in that room of the mind. It could be a ghastly place. Sebastian, eerily like his father in appearance and angular intellect, though gentler altogether and a very fine prose writer, was a junior in high school then. He describes what it might be like when Bill hit the poetry circuit. Bill about to leave calls Sebastian into a meeting of his graduate poetry workshop there in the living room. Sebastian recalls: "My father took me aside and told me I could choose whomever I wanted. I was not entirely sure what he meant by this. They'd all agree to stay, he was sure, so it was my choice. I caught on." The mouth drops open, doesn't it? William Matthews, for Christ's sake, pimping for his son, the graduate student doing her thing as elected house-sitter and more, the son trying to know how even to speak about this, a thing as far from grace as ever bubbled from sewer gas. Bill didn't speak about that, or job moves, women moves, and much else lodged safely beyond the poems.

Still, the poems of *Search Party,* are aptly named because they pursue the guilty, the runner who may be guilty. "I'm all of my voices. Creeps, I said, and Creeps, / I sang, but I'm one of you . . . I bet you're full of good stories," he wrote. He had always been somebody not quite visible, and this was the man who, Sebastian writes, had kept near his typewriter the sardonic lines:

"Laughter is the best medicine. Unless you're really sick. Then you should call 911." For many of us, Bill had been the equivalent of 911. He was readily available to help, phone calls, letters, friendly words, listening. He didn't want the loneliness that he lived with, and he certainly gave every appearance of having few problems with it. Unless. Unless you read the poems. Unless you were one of the very few people he had let inside the dark room he was. He would have approved, I think, this lovely, hurt, delicate, respectful portrait by his son, *In My Father's Footsteps,* as much Sebastian's story as Bill's and a model of the character Bill coveted in words, and very often had.

He wasn't always funny. He could be sweet and extremely generous, as poets have often remarked. At a party in the house he loved in Seattle, he found me off alone admiring his books. Writers always scan the shelves in another writer's house. It's one carpenter admiring another's tools. He knew that I collected Robert Penn Warren's books. I happened to be holding a hardback first edition of Warren's *The Legacy of the Civil War,* a book whose used copies are so rare it is almost never for sale. I mentioned I didn't own that one, replaced it, and went off for a drink. Bill typically discharged his guests at the door, a matter of manners, and when my exit moment came, I found him grinning. Then he handed the Warren book to me, now signed "from Bill," saying he knew I would enjoy it more than he did. I wasn't then aware that Warren had been his poetry teacher at Yale. Bill's good heart, his generosity, his serious respect for the work of writing and its students may have been something he got from Warren. I don't know. I do know he gave all that to students and friends. In the 1980s something changed. I suppose that's a way to put it. I didn't see him and knew of him only through gossip.

The rumors that reached the East Coast were fragmented and ugly. It was said Bill had been charged with sexual harassment at the University of Washington. It was said that he was the subject of a class-action suit, that six women had charged him with something that sounded, with each individual case, like a lover's betrayal. Probably somebody I knew must have known, and even now does know, the whole truth. I don't. It seemed like a joke he would have made, some rube poet caught with his pants down, legends building with each mouth that bespoke it. I thought it odd, even amusing, that six women would publicly admit to being promised something they couldn't get and would hold him legally responsible for its absence. I'd have felt different, maybe, if one had been my daughter. In any case, rumors only bully us if we permit them to do so. Sebastian has written of this scandal that "any student who had ever slept with my father decided to speak out against him. And there seemed to be a lot of them." No doubt the campuses of America were filled with anxious poets in the days afterward, their mating habits being what they are. Matthews resigned at Washington, moved briefly to teach at Houston, moved again to New York, took a position at CCNY, and transformed what he could of his life. New York fit him as no other city had or could. He wrote better than he ever had. He let the culture of the city absorb him; he became president of that old folks' home, the Poetry Society of America; he throve. Sebastian and Stanley Plumly, Bill's lifelong friend, have edited the posthumous *Search Party: The Collected Poems,* wherein Plumly, introducing the poems, says Bill "never lost his sense of humor about himself nor forgot where he came from." I think that's partly correct. I think Bill had nowhere to be from, only that room of the self, that blank Midwest voice all radio stations employ for commercials. He'd use the poems to get to the other place where he could belong. Wasn't that what musicians and poets had always done?

In the summer of 1995, at the Mt. Holyoke Writers' Conference, Bill came to read. I saw him as I walked over the lawn. He was by himself, sitting in a chair on the porch. Though it had been nearly ten years since we had spoken, I went brassily to him and took his hand and said, "How about some tennis this afternoon?" He looked at me as if I had drooled. Bill Matthews always appeared weathered, even haggard, but what was on him now was well beyond those words. He said he didn't play tennis anymore; in fact, he could hardly walk. I thought he was joking. I waited for him to pop up and do the shuffle-away as he always did. But those baggy eyes so like a basset hound's only rolled a little. He said he had congenitally bad hips and would soon need joint replacement surgery. But, and here he grinned a little, they only last twenty-five years, so I am holding off as long as possible. Then there was the familiar snort, the laugh of lower wattage now, but still *that* one. It was so sad I could not go on talking and, after a bit of evasion and fill-in about family, I left him. I had looked forward to telling him how stupid the silence between us had been, how much his friendship had always meant to me, how I hadn't understood whatever grievance had come between us. But it hadn't come up.

That evening it was my turn to read, as the staff at conferences do, and Bill, it turned out, had asked to introduce me, a loving gesture. Stan Plumly had showed up by then, and I could easily summon that good feeling when once again we had played basketball years back in Ohio. Nothing explains, I suppose, what one keeps or loses in memory of a person. Why do I remember Bill's elbows on the basketball court? They weren't especially grievous, only efficient. He knew how to be effective when he wanted and was the most naturally diplomatic, tactful man I ever encountered. As an arts advocate, he could lay his hand exactly where the money was and come away with it. He could talk to anyone with dignity and equality and make their anxieties, at least temporarily, his own, but he could go beyond that, too. I remember how he stood in that small, hot room at Mt. Holyoke, where Emily Dickinson had once studied, wobbling on his painful hips, praising me for what he had done much better, and me thinking nobody alive could schmooze as he could. Then I read. Then I hugged him with thanks and affection, which I was glad to give him again, and we talked about wives, children, hips, poems, and staying in touch.

But we didn't do that, really. He sent me a handful of poems for *The Southern Review,* which I was then editing, but I was going on sabbatical leave, had accepted all I needed for some time ahead, and to tell the truth I didn't read them all that closely. I sent them back with a lame demurral. Although I urged him to send more, I knew they wouldn't come. I just didn't know why. Then one day Julie Kane, the poet, then a doctoral student at Louisiana State University, came in to say she had heard he was dead. He had taught her at Cornell. I called friends. It was true. It turned out he had had a difficult operation for something not at all related to what killed him, a worn-out heart. Age fifty-five. No one expected this because he had been, they said, healthier of late, looked better, stopped smoking, damped the drinking, was happier than anyone recalled. He had been dressed for the opera. His date found him waiting in a chair. I don't know what others may think, but I fancy Bill would have liked that ending: tuxed, elegant, jazz playing, wine near, a woman he loved hurrying to him. Was he reading a book of poems? I like that notion. That's how it must have been. Maybe reading them aloud, that marvelous, graveled voice I expect to hear every time my wife says Bill's on the phone.

After All: Last Poems and *Search Party: Collected Poems,* both posthumous and aptly titled, stand with the books I love by my generation of poets, among them Jim Applewhite, Norman Dubie, Stephen Dunn, Louise Gluck, Ellen Bryant Voigt, Henry Taylor, Yusef Komunyakaa, C. K. Williams, and the late Larry Levis. There have been critics who argue our poetry is at best dull, maybe dead, and certainly abandoned by an American readership. Philip Lopate wrote in 1996 that "when I come upon a poem in a magazine, nine times out of ten it is disappointing," and often, he thinks, the poem has tried too hard. It inclines to "the fallacious expectation that poetry should dispense wisdom. Wisdom being scarce, we get platitudes." The very reach of a poem for visionary statement which Lopate dislikes is, he says, only an attempt to make an audience sigh for a post-verbal epiphany. That, he argues, "is one of the factors that gives American poetry today an anti-intellectual cast."

Lopate, for a smart and articulate man, is surprisingly obtuse here. That same reach for visionary realization is what William Matthews brought to poetry along with humor to balance its weight. The progress of this generation has been to escape the snow fields and dark enigmas of Bly and Strand, to find a vehicle for personal life with vision, to touch expanded significance and complexities. The need has been for form that renovates mere memory, that mythologizes as it retells the same stories of the individual life and place, a form willing to resist the relativity of each truth which diminishes all truths. Something has to matter or poetry is, actually, more pernicious than dead. Matthews understood that language treated with respect and care and expectation is what any trumpeter or saxophonist musters for each note, and is a personality, as Lopate adds, of "quirky, uniquely voiced individuals." Trouble is, who's to say what's just quirky? Art that is only eccentricity doesn't last, is what Language poets do. It's what comic mugging comes to, poems without gravity. Poetry's gift, which you have to labor for, comes with no surety of favor, only the transparent topography of wisdom. It is what we all want as the fruition of a life's work.

Had Matthews been a painter, we might say he learned to brighten colors, crisp lines, evoke depths. Were he one of the jazz musicians he loved, we would say his notes became leaner, more glanced off, more fluid and natural too, his reaches outward and dances back more intricate and fragile. Were he a court man, we might praise his vision of the whole floor, his navigation for the open and potential place, and use of all he had available to exert what he called grace. Grace meant, for him, not manly or gentlemanly conduct (though manners count) but the use of words with weight and heft inside their lovely dance, a way of conveying harmony, integration, belonging. In "Spent Light" Matthews wrote, "'Let there be light,' God famously implored, / and the dark released a few hostages." His pivot on *few* conveys the shiver of far more than it says. Matthews cannot diminish the grim world, but he can love it and even be playful in words that become, despite frustration and discontent, something more than fustian, a kind of encouraging song. "Inspiration," from *After All: Last Poems,* maybe reminiscent of Philip Levine, could grumble about the pitiful little our labor comes to, especially a poet's bad day, even while deflating art's angst:

> Rumpled, torpid, bored, too tasteful to rhyme
> "lethargy" with "laundry," or too lazy,
> I'll not spend my afternoons at the desk
> cunningly weaving subjunctives and lithe
> skeins of barbed colloquial wire. Today
>
> I loathe poetry. I hate the clotted,
> dicty poems of the great modernists,
> disdainful of their truant audience,
> and I hate also proletarian
> poetry, with its dreadful rancors
>
> and sing-along certainties. I hate
> poetry readings and the dreaded verb
> "to share." Let me share this knife with your throat,
> suggested Mack. Today I'm a gnarl, a knot,
> a burl. I'm furled in on myself and won't
>
> be opened. I'm the bad mood if you try
> to cheer me out of I'll smack you. Impasse
> is where I come to escape from. It takes
> a deep belief in one's own ignorance;
> it takes, I tell you, desperate measures.

If W. C. Fields had written poetry, it might have sounded like this. Language that bends and echoes, double entendres, sentences twisted, ugly sounds, an emotional intensity that depends on timing and momentum as it skids to a stop, a harnessing of tones that settles into the band's balance with the falling susurrus of "desperate measures." Matthews knew that if he placed too much weight there he would slide into half-witted lounge wisdom; if he placed too little he would become bombast's unwitting clown. Balance tells the reader the writer knows, has control, has let the horses go just enough. Is it great poetry? No, simply good. He wasn't always that good, even when he was appealing, as he was in his version of TV's "Cheers," his view of how we are all living in the same language, sort of:

THE PLACE ON THE CORNER

> No mirror behind this bar: tiers of garish
> fish drift back and forth. They too have routines.
> The TV's on but not the sound. Dion
> and the Belmonts ("I'm a Wanderer") gush
> from the box. None here thinks a pink slip
> ("You're fired," with boilerplate apologies)
> is underwear. None here says "lingerie"
> or "as it were." We speak Demotic
> because we're disguised as ordinary
> folks. A shared culture offers camouflage
> behind which we can tend the covert fires
> we feed our shames to, those things we most fear
> to say, our burled, unspoken, common language—
> the only one, and we are many.

It's way too tempting to say you had to know him to see all the puns and plays. He was a wanderer, absolutely, and far from that enjambed "ordinary," and isn't that little underwear joke nifty. I wouldn't do it. Few of us would, or did. It was his pleasure, and it didn't always work out. The last five lines became clotted mud on his Bally loafers, oh dear, oh dear. Bill was as far from an obscure experimenter as possible, but I don't think he was "demotic." His poems cultivate quick clarity, visible, recognizable moments from which he riffs, his raids on the inarticulate made to seem stream froth, natural, but with the fullness of dark current visible too. He knew how hard and unforgiving writing was, especially writing well, and did his best to ease intimidation by jokes, but he would blink:

> "Tears, idle tears," the poet wrote, but they've
> got their work cut out for them, the way
> a river might imagine a canyon.
> ("Bucket's Got a Hole in It")

Search Party shows Bill thought about, prodded, wrote over, debunked, belittled, giggled at, disassembled, rebuilt, and enjoyed poetry as voraciously as anyone could. He wanted to write love songs as if they answered formlessness and loneliness, but love never seemed to last. I think that's why Plumly ends the collected book with "Care"—because it tells us love, "in thanks / for tending it, will do its very / best not to consume us." He wanted a way to talk

that was serious but not runic, as it had once been for him, and not oper-
atic, as his middle poems threatened to become, something that if scratched
would respond. Those poets, language or otherwise, who think they need to
educate the rest about the slipperiness of language might study the layers he
commands, the surge and shine of words communicating like good pistons
at work. But what good is language if it has no urgent purpose? Writers like
Philip Lopate mistake the impersonality of lyric form for lack of passion
when it is one of the seductive ways of lying to corner an objective truth.
But nothing works very well, or very long. As in "Frazzle" where Bill says "
'I cannot tell a lie,' he said, which was a lie / but not the kind for which the
bill comes after all. The French word is *l'addition*." A soft way to hand you
the hard reality, even in an epithalamium, and maybe the best of Bill's ways:

THE BAR AT THE ANDOVER INN
May 28, 1995

> The bride, groom (my son), and their friends gathered
> somewhere else to siphon the wedding's last
> drops from their tired elders. Over a glass
> of chardonnay, I ignored my tattered,
> companionable glooms (this took some will:
> I've ended three marriages by divorce
> as a man shoots his broken-legged horse)
> and wished my two sons and their families
> something I couldn't have, or keep, myself.
> The rueful pluck we take with us to bars
> or church, the morbid fellowship of woe—
> I've had my fill of it. I wouldn't mope
> through my son's happiness or further fear
> my own. Well, what instead? Well, something else.

He always seemed, as I have said, wiser. Perhaps it was only the quality of
courage that wants to know, must know, how things actually are, if only to
laugh in the face of the worst. Taken all in all, he was a poet who knew how
to play all the games that mattered. In "Manners" Bill was literally the young
man Martha Mitchell, wife of Nixon's attorney general, sent for a drink, out
of his league at the Washington cocktail party for the sharks who broke our
world into Vietnam's bloody little pieces and then ate them like snacks on the
water. What hopes we had. What music we had. What poets we had. William

Matthews, who had almost believed he, and we, could achieve grace, saw
through even that. It hurt him to say so.

> A well-fed scholar, I sought out and brought
> back a tall bubbin for the nice lady.
> Yes, there's a cure for youth, but it's fatal.
> And a cure for grace: you say what you mean,
> but of course you have to know what that is.

Johnny Dominguez, a Letter

LARRY LEVIS

Sometime in the late 1970s, when I was teaching at the University of Utah, a rumpled letter arrived, handwritten, on lined yellow school paper, looking as if it had been done on impulse, shoved into an envelope upon which my departmental address had been scrawled with gray pencil. The letter's hand-writing leaned and flowed casually as if it mirrored the thought of a man not to be hurried by an act of circumstance. That letter, it seems now, might have been composed on an afternoon in a faculty office where a student conferee has failed to appear and an empty hour remains before the next obligation. No letter could more fully give the character, even the appearance, of the Larry Levis I came to know.

Levis seemed always distracted, a little, only partly engaged with any task or person, unless it was writing a poem, a man whose movements in time and space were less swift, somehow less deliberate than those of other men. He was big enough to have been a high school forward on a basket-ball team—had he ever played anything?—but as he entered middle age his frame began to look a little bent, as if by a past labor his prodigious memory might be troubled to recall. Anyone might think him sleepy, perhaps hung over, when first he loomed into view, for the gaze he offered came from a face cocked slightly, a questioning though not really puzzled aspect in his features. It was a welcoming face, one playful with humor like that of the late Ernie Kovacs. He could seem wickedly handsome, like Omar Sharif. Come-dian Flip Wilson used to say "What you see is what you get," as he clowned in a drag costume that made his words deliciously transparent. But with Larry, the face was not even a mirror; it was what he was.

He favored a style of clothing appropriate for the worn creature. He wore his clothes with such an easy indifference that you could assume the baggy, unpressed look bespoke a need to dress in a hurry. He looked at times like a silent movie star, one to whom clothes were an irrelevant necessity. When he spoke, it was through a penumbra of cigarette smoke, his movements heavy and slow to create that toiled-over, used-hard weariness that gave everything he said a weight no listener could ignore. He and William Matthews often appeared to have survived the same party. In my mind's eye, he is a man in his forties. I knew him first in 1973 but can't recall what he looked like then. It is easy to doubt he was ever really young, so intense and burdened and eccentric and even mature he had become. His letter, if it could be produced, would display exactly his poise and charm and experienced, even avuncular, manliness so rare in most men. Most especially in men who are poets, and Larry was above all things a poet.

It would be a gross mistake to presume that Levis was only what he appeared, for he was neither a casual nor an unserious man. He certainly was not old. He was never inattentive. At his death by heart attack in 1997 he was not yet fifty. He is always remembered by those who knew him well as devoted to much good laughter, carrier of a buoyant sense of life's abundant oddness, possessed of an optimism that buffered like courage. But because he was complex, his appearance could deceive. I once misjudged him quite badly, in part because he was not what I thought he was and in part because I was not what I thought I was. I would discover over the years of an intermittent friendship that he was a master-builder of intricate poems, keenly conscious of what he was about, a diligent and studious caretaker of what interested him. What he didn't like after a bit just didn't exist.

His letter, fuzzed now in memory two decades old, said he had read the poems I published in the late 1970s and he saw them as unlike what was then "typical." He made specific comments about virtues and vices in the poems, but those opinions are long lost. His interest lay in the kind of form he saw my poems seeking, a story told lyrically, orchestrated by recurrent images and motifs that, in fact, made the story that mattered. He thought poets on this road meant to wed narratives of remembered incidents to an idiosyncratic speech, thereby making a poetry from colloquialized expression. He described what I had failed to articulate over many hundreds of journal pages. He read my poems as if he had written them himself.

Who was he? Levis had grown up among the farmers and Hispanic migrant workers who harvested his father's grape crops outside of Fresno, California. This was not the hip wine and cheese land but the artificially watered desert bottoms that melt pretension and ambition, one of the places where dustbowl immigrants wound up and hung on, country singer Merle Haggard's place. You could grow up the boss's son and still love your father. Levis wanted to write the stories of people he knew were hard up against matters there; he had a feel for his place and its characters. He understood the danger of making them over into sentimental heroes or tin villains, but distortion was something he had to remind himself about:

PHOTOGRAPH: MIGRANT WORKER, PARLIER, CALIFORNIA, 1967

I'm going to put Johnny Dominguez right here
In front of you on this page so that
You won't mistake him for something else,
An idea, for example, of how oppressed
He was, rising with his pan of Thompson Seedless
Grapes, from a row of vines. The band
On his white straw hat darkened by sweat, is,
He would remind you, just a hatband.
His hatband. He would remind you of that.
As for the other use, this unforeseen
Labor you have subjected him to, the little
Snacks & white wine of the opening he must
Bear witness to, he would remind you
That he was not put on this earth
To be an example of something else,
Johnny Dominguez, he would hasten to
Remind you, in his chaste way of saying things,
Is not to be used as an example of anything
At all, not even, he would add after
A second or so, that greatest of all
Impossibilities, that unfinishable agenda
Of the stars, that fact, Johnny Dominguez.

James Wright said the great danger to the contemporary poet is glibness. What is the opposite of glibness? Johnny Dominguez. There is little glibness left in the poet who wrote this poem, one whose books show how he faced the primal danger that failing to tell the truth of his own life and his father's would be a fundamental dehumanization. In such matters, Levis was incapable from the start of lying, but that is not the same thing as knowing how to tell the truth, a thing good poets have to learn.

Levis would come to feel his life, and Johnny Dominguez, hadn't got into American poems. Maybe in rough moments in the poems of Robinson Jeffers. And in John Steinbeck's stories, of course. Having no local models, Levis would have to claim what he wanted. He was fortunate in teachers. His first was Philip Levine, whose poetry had its roots in sympathy for the work men and women do, and the lives that work carves upon them. No one could have been better equipped to teach Levis to trust personal experience, to follow his own nose, than the anarchist poet who'd been chanting the unrealized life of the Detroit dream. Levine gave Levis an appetite for poetry of unreachable purity, but it would not be odes to hothouse flowers. Levis learned from Levine the great poem was historical, a life story. Levine has said he had learned something about narrative construction from Robert Penn Warren; it resides in everything Levine has written. Warren, in "Pure and Impure Poetry" (1943), had said that the will toward a pure poetry does not easily tolerate the world we live in, a world of messy, impure prose. That world, Warren held, is nevertheless a prime reason for poetry, and the source for it, too. Levis loved the world as Levine did. He wanted a pure, democratic poetry to memorialize a bruised community in his head, but he didn't have the skills early on. Few do. Too, the world in there was not the one he thought the poems should give us. He had to labor for an awareness of what was his to do in words and what way of poetry would work for him.

Wrecking Crew, Levis's first collection, was published in 1972, the winner of the University of Pittsburgh Press's International Poetry Forum Award. The poet, then twenty-six, became overnight a serious contender. If his origins did not propose, as Emerson says of Whitman's first *Leaves of Grass* in 1855, "a long foreground," Levis had prepared well by studying with Donald Justice, Mark Strand, W. D. Snodgrass, Philip Booth, Marvin Bell, and Stanley Plumly, in addition to Levine, five of them Pulitzer Prize winners. Great race horses have had less fastidious breeding and grooming. And in 1972, the last year of Richard Nixon and Vietnam, the poet began work on a doctorate in literature at the University of Iowa. He brought with him from Syracuse University a fondness for the European *poète maudit* that the poems of *Wrecking Crew* were about, insofar as they were cohesively about anything. His was an inner life troubled by everyone's problems and social concerns; his narrating character would be sensitive, tender, cool; words would be his axe for breaking through the iced-over Kafkaesque interior. Others were assuming the same role, usually playing it better than they wrote.

Today the poems of *Wrecking Crew* seem tedious, mawkish, and callow. Levis was at first a poet of rhetoric whose poems have little life and much learned gesture. They reach for a voiced intensity the poets in that glibly political time accepted in place of life fronted, as Thoreau said. Life was more complex than many poets were ready, or able, to say. That substitution is the weakness of academic poetry. It was often the result of little talent and modest labor. The 1960s had been ripe for radical change; what came was quickly passed on via the acolyte system of graduate schools, institutionalized in journals where one published and worked up the ranks of status, a process repeated in books put out by new university presses competing with the Ivies. Prizes were competition medals. The end was a tone, merely. Levis could have been the poster boy. In the poem circa 1970, all conclusions are geared to a final surprise, itself a knot of attitudes. Here is the young Levis writing in Mark Strand's voice about the ennui and corruption he will feel when he has turned forty:

AIRPLANES

I get a gun and go
shoot an airplane full of holes,
and stare at the thing on the runway
until it's covered with rust.
        This takes years.
I turn forty somewhere, waiting
for the jet underneath me to
clear its throat of burned
starlings.

To be in your twenties in that year meant a fearful awareness of guns and jets because Vietnam and a good chance of death waited for you, or someone near you. *Wrecking Crew* has poems about bombings and Vietnam, Cambodia, Thailand, all wholly predictable, few not forgettable. "Airplanes" loves the scorched starlings—but who didn't? Levis was not writing as himself about the desert birds he knew where he had grown up hunting quail, but as Mark Strand, as Robert Bly's *The Sixties* and *The Seventies* magazine said he ought to write. Bly, guru of the good consciousness whom Philip Dacey once called "the Reverend Robert Bly, Lutheran Minister," criss-crossed the Rand-McNally teaching young Americans that imagery like scorched starlings was the true blood-poetry in a nation of old academic whiners. Levis feared becoming a fortyish ghost worse than he feared combat, the poem's real threat. He had at least had a taste of the military, unlike most of those on campus, having, as one of his very funny essays reveals, screwed up so badly in basic training his unit asked him to take a graceful early departure. He was lucky enough to avoid combat, not so lucky with age.

Levis learned to look hard at life, to accept it, and to dramatize it differently than Bly. Writing criticism which drove the docile versifiers of the 1950s off the stage, Bly harangued America like a kind of Emerson, advocating minimalism his own poems used for reductive image prints. Levis wrote an expanding poetry after he learned to face and to engage what couldn't be changed, to love what was complicated, dark, bitter, and worth praise. But he first blew Bly's pipe for a parabolic, awe-filled image supposed to leave you sucking a breath:

DRIVING EAST

For miles,
the snow is on all sides of me,
waiting.

I feel like
a lot of empty cattle yards,
my hinges swing open to the winds.

That he caused an intelligent young man to imagine he actually feels like empty cattle yards ought to dog Mr. Bly into whatever eternity may be granted him.

But Levis wasn't faithful entirely to the Minnesota hymn. Other prominent talents resound in his chorus. Galway Kinnell appears in "Hunger"; Charles Wright speaks inside "Untitled"; W. S. Merwin informs "Unfinished Poem"; and James Wright works in "Poem." Wright was the permanent mentoring voice after Levine, but it would be the Wright of the late, more narrative poems. The imitations Levis mounted nearly drown out his own mature sound, but his most characteristic poetry, the voice in *Winter Stars* and *The Widening Spell of the Leaves,* is also present. It's less mystical, more exact, grittier in "For the Country":

One of them undid your blouse, then
used a pocketknife to
cut away your shirt

> like he'd take
> fur off some limp thing.
> Or slice up the belly of a fish.

Here is restrained anger that is the empowering fuel for Levis's elegiac art, an anger different from the one he could not wholly lift from Philip Levine. Levine is angered by what you do to him as much as what you do to others, Levis almost entirely by what you do to someone else. But he needs the provocation of something he has actually experienced, unlike, say, Cambodian bombing. In "Fish" he wrote:

> The cop holds me up like a fish;
> he feels the huge bones
> surrounding my eyes,
> and he runs a thumb under them.

It's an imitation realism engendered by James Wright, a manner many younger poets adopted, and, as with any manner's derivative, it lacked tension, credibility, and finally interest.

If he couldn't take Levine's anger, Bly's religious pastoralism, Wright's toughness and comic surrealism, or Justice's meter (the least likely effect for the Fresno Kid), Levis had to find a way to get the ragged and, to him, American character of his place into poems. He found that way in the confidence of his own idiom which he released through the storyteller's arrangement of carefully orchestrated details and the circularity of verse working through and against event, always working the phrase in plain diction toward unexpected eloquence. His is a vocabulary of elemental movements and clean language that resists precious assertion and cliché gesture. If he was, as he certainly was, a product of schooling, he would become one of its successful rebels by insisting on identity with a community of people who had plenty of brutal experience. To make their stories live was his mission.

It is odd and a little unnerving to think you are doing a thing more or less entirely your own way only to discover others have taken the same road. America is, of course, a big country, with lots of space to be lost in. A poet can imagine he is out of sight of any orthodoxy, but its outposts and sentries loom everywhere. Few American poets are long unknown to other poets if they compete in the serious publishing markets. In the middle 1970s, in Utah, I imagined myself out of range of poetry's campaigns and, conversely,

I believed Levis was one of those leading the style. He was the system prod-
uct. It was the age of the Deep Image, the terse and surreal lyric. I, if poet
at all, hoped to write something more emphatically narrative. In 1972, that
sea-change year, awaiting discharge from the U.S. Air Force, I was denied
admission to the Iowa writing program by Norman Dubie, who has told
me he, then, made the selections. Dubie's poems, often in the *New Yorker*
and *American Poetry Review* seemed synonymous with achievement. These
narratives, whose control and manipulation of language deranged usual ex-
pectations for poems with disoriented syntax and fragmented plot, seemed
to me to have roots in the same sources as Levis, to be as "in" as Levis, a
testimony to the blinding power of conspiracy fears.

Norman Dubie also wrote to me in the 1970s, admiring a poem of mine
he had read. That initiated a long friendship. But his letter had less weight
for me than Larry Levis's had, for we had a personal history. When I was
discharged from military service, I enrolled in doctoral study but left during
that first year to take a short-term teaching position, which I then left for an
assistant professorship at Cottey College, in Nevada, Missouri. An enormous
chip on my shoulder testified to my resentment at having been drafted into
giving away four years of my life while others were permitted to safely write
against world evils from poetry's bower. Daily, as a payroll clerk, I, Bartleby,
envied their fortune, their community of poets, not seeing how a person may
be eaten up by ambition trained on the wrong ends of things.

To teach at a small school for women, I must have thought, would of-
fer pastoral meadows and the tangy breaths of muse-like creatures who
could engender subjects, energy, an appetite for poetry. I could teach *there!*
It turned out the young women cared but marginally more for poetry than
the four faculty in English, all of whom were composition experts. I was
lost. Maybe I wasn't a very good teacher. Maybe I thought poets had to be
Poe-like and weird even in the rural Missouri town, home of Firp & Bob's
restaurant, a landscape which could not have been surpassed for gentle quiet.
I knew it was trouble for me the first day I drove down Main Street and I told
myself I'd be leaving very soon. Still, I was raised to do the job given to me. I
meant to bring poetry to campus. It didn't take long to become desperate for
a writing pal. It was said that Larry Levis was teaching at the University of
Missouri in Columbia, a short drive north. What did it matter that *Wrecking
Crew* wasn't my kind of book? It was, he was, a prize-winner. My students,
increasingly excited by poems, deserved to see a poet. The college offered

fifty dollars, the letter of invitation went forth, and the poet was soon in town, girlfriend in tow.

Levis seems now, in my mind, to have been blond, tall, sort of rakish, Californian. He was in fact dark and slumped. Before the reading, we drank bourbon; we talked. He seemed to know everyone; I envied him. After the reading, at my house, he stepped outside to smoke weed every so often. We joked, japed, and laughed at much in the poetry world. What that much was I couldn't have told anyone the next day. I have no doubt that I was scalding as I released pent-up complaints and resentments. Little, by me, would have been said in favor of marching students and righteous faculty poets saved from the draft that snagged me when I was twenty-six. At dawn the phone rang. Larry announced he would not come over for the breakfast we had arranged. In fact, he said, he hadn't slept well in the motel and so had got up and driven in the dark toward Kansas City. He wanted, he said, no more communication with me because offensive things had been said about people he admired, my friend and teacher Stan Plumly among them. The check for his reading, he said, was already in the mail to me.

As it happened, I admired those marchers and poets more than he could have imagined and was more than a little convinced it was braver to refuse military service than not. Perhaps I said as much in apologies for offense unintentionally given. At any rate, I wrote immediately to Stan, described this bizarre event, asked his forgiveness for whatever I may have said, and received a funny, warm letter in return and a bear-hug of friendship when we next met. If Mr. Plumly has any warts, a lack of loyalty and a dearth of understanding are not among them.

Nothing could change the shame Levis conferred upon me—because, as I have said, he had been confirmed as the real thing, whereas I was, well, something less, and worse. My shame fueled a deep anger, and I had spoken bitterly to him before that phone call ended. Why didn't I see how difficult the matter was for him? It is no easy thing to call your host on his behavior; no easy thing to reject a check for work done, however small it may be; and no easy thing to demand satisfaction because you have been morally offended. For the next four or five years, that shame quietly stung.

Larry's letter made no mention whatsoever of this incident. That meant, apparently, he had forgiven me. It was as if poetry had forgiven me. When I finished reading his words, I felt a lightness in my body, a happiness still memorable. His tone was that of an old friend who has put off writing so long it has become, in his mind, a grief, and one for whom he asks understanding. He allowed me the grace to forgive myself. After that our paths crossed enough to say we grew to be friends, though perhaps not intimates. He was, it is clear, a good man, maybe one born to the purpose of carrying innocence from that California farm, a true bearer of democratic promise whose voice, like Whitman's, would become poetry. He also stood recipient of his parents' compact: an agreement to give and to suffer the exact and real pains a farm life requires. Levis had to learn a way to express the idealism of his innocence and the rottenness of mortality in a single poetic structure. Few have done such work so well.

Levis imprints his life and those lives he has been part of into mature poems that make clear that writing poetry was his way of hating and loving— hating the immoral viciousness we are capable of bringing to each other and loving the beauty in each life as it is. He owned an unusually large capacity for forgiveness, for charity of spirit, and he possessed a rare goodness of soul. No one claims he was saintly or pure or that he exceeded anyone in decent behavior. Mostly, I don't know very much about how he behaved or who he was in his daily acts. He had personal demons but he was thoughtful enough that he grew to understand his limitations and gifts better than most of us do. He understood how to use himself tactfully and effectively in his poetry, and perhaps in his life. And because he had that, he could accept us as we were. This is wisdom of a high order and he could be seen to practice it in the presence of, and on the books of, many kinds of poets. He must have always had something of this, to judge from the love people have felt for him, but it was a skill he developed until it meant a method by which he could lodge himself against tides of elimination and negation that threaten everywhere. There is joy in him that glows through the sad doom he cannot and will not evade. In "Family Romance" he describes the delight of driving his brother's car to his own wedding, a delight made sharper by knowing how heavy the world's weight would be, joy or no joy:

> He was selling soap in Lodi, California.
> Later, in his car, & dressed
> To die, or live again, forever,
> I drove to my own first wedding.
> I smelled the stale boutonniere in my lapel,

A deceased young flower
I wondered how my brother's Buick
Could go so fast, &
Still questioning, or catching, a last time,
An old chill from childhood,
I thought: why me, why her, & knew it wouldn't last.

I used to wonder why Larry Levis wrote to me. There had been nothing to recall between us; he had nothing to ask of me; he did not complain of any slight, the usual motivations for correspondence between poets. That he was simply generous and curious makes a poor but true explanation. He had read my poems and liked them. He knew how hard it is to write a poem, even a bad one, and, if he found something that pleased him, he wanted to say that. It was a part of a courage that his students have known because he gave it freely. But perhaps he needed to affirm, as we all do, something that he was alone in, that arriving at what you imagine is a new thing and all yours; he needed to register the leap he had been making in poems that were no longer imitations. His leap, because it was rooted in so much powerful instruction, and rejected much of it, was farther and more frightening than most. He created an incremental but immediate experience whose tone is astonishment and also sorrow, also a recognition of how plain it all is—how remarkably vivid life is because it is doomed, and he is still alive, the story goes on. Just as James Wright said in *Two Citizens,* a book that scared Wright so much he said he would never reprint it. Levis's journey led him away from the authorized and into what was individual for him. He says it in "Crescendo":

It is all like the doomed singers, Cooke & Redding,
Who raised their voices against the horns'
Implacable decrescendos & knew exactly what they
Were doing, & what they were doing was dangerous.

The poetry of Larry Levis is the autobiography of a mind, what a man has come through, what he has understood, what he has sloughed off, what he hopes for, what he loves. But it is also the carriage for innocence, a gentle spirit. When James Wright's poem speaks of how his body "would break / into blossom," Levis hears him, for he learns from one of the great American lyric poets about self-transformation and how you say it. In "Sleeping Lioness," his closest poem to a self-portrait, he says, "Anything is enough if you know how poor you are. / You could step out now in wonder." Levis was feeling rapture, a love of the world. But he had seen, and remembered, suffering among the California migrants. If he ever allowed himself to be blinded by rancor and envy, he had learned he had to work past that, and he had done it. His early poems had appeared to be little more than socially agreeable tone, but later collections engaged large, unresolvable dilemmas of conscience.

There is, of course, a danger in suggesting the value of a poem lies in the subject chosen, in its wattage or importance. And yet good subjects make good poems, to paraphrase Mr. Frost. While Levis would not have denied the value of what the tale has to say, he would have insisted that poetry consists in the language as window, and as valuable in the extent to which it admits life stories. One can see in the early poems his magnetic drift to the subject of poetry and language as human definers; he was a poet through and through. Because he identified poetry as incarnation of a divine spirit, albeit a divine spirit reduced to something like Ransom's "Captain Carpenter," Levis follows the same drift in his later poems. Whatever he talks about, he talks about poetry, alludes to it, threads it as image or metaphor, and it is always the central mystery, the inexplicable good that exists, finally, only in the words a poem enacts. For Levis the essential poem is the narrative of awareness, its quality measurable, like a tree, by the rings of its layered resonance. "The Perfection of Solitude: A Sequence" is a drama about—among other things—how to listen, how to see. A meditation on Caravaggio's self-portrait, which is to say art and self, leaps nimbly from the grotesque saint of light to the "patina of sunset glinting in the high, dark windows" of the center of hippie life, San Francisco's Fillmore Auditorium, where Jerry Garcia plays Chuck Berry's "Johnny B. Goode," a banging joyful anthem that evokes the buoyant, infectious feeling of righteousness people had in those days, days that would end as abruptly as the joy that soared until, perhaps offhandedly, you heard a high school buddy had "strolled / three yards / Off a path & stepped on a land mine." If art offered the glorious and endless Italian dreamlight of tranquility, it also showed the only thing that doesn't end is Time. Against forces that diminish us the poet takes a ministerial and necessary view, adjusts perspective, details, composition, recalibrates possibility, fits the parts of the story into a place that the memorial stones tell so that

> You see, you must descend; it is one of the styles
> Of Hell. And it takes a while to find the name you might be looking for;
> it is

Meant to take a while. You can touch the names, if you want to.
You can kiss them.

You can try to tease out some final meaning with your lips.

Levis has become in *The Widening Spell of the Leaves* not merely an ele-
giac poet but an American regionalist whose turf includes something more
temporal and global. His lines grow longer, they surge widely, embracingly;
they retreat and collect their thought with the somber pacing of clerical
poise; they have the weight of wisdom. His effect is achieved less through
direct narrative of this and then that, than through the circular patterning
of under-image that shows subtlety. This is the art of the jazz musician sus-
pending notes in patterns that risk dispersal, each note nearly lost as it hangs
out there apparently alone, and yet in the right collocation the poet reclaims
it, re-cites one after another, and thereby extends the pattern, renews the
old image, retells the important story of life. Perhaps it is also the ceremony
of the Mass, that rhythm, action floating in, sustained by the continuity of
something we can dip into and rise from but cannot render except as a local,
palpable thing just as holy as it is itself. Johnny Dominguez.

By the pages of *Elegy* (1997), his posthumous collection, Levis's poetic
voice has become a priestly speech, immediate, urgent, its way an interrogat-
ing, catechizing, guiding tone, a sifting of the mind that believes it can sort
through the wash-over of dimmed perception. It can, this mind presumes,
win through to shapely order, a civil world with enough submission to the
pain of experience. This voice coils out to touch all things with the spell of a
final recognition, a looking and naming, deific and brave, which he describes
in "The Widening Spell of the Leaves" as the unique experience of poetic art.
He says "That was the trouble; it couldn't be / *Compared* to anything else,"
and it has no need to forgive or resent anything, or to fully understand any-
thing because it accepts. Declarative, spiral-climbing forward through cla-
sual suspensions, each modified by the next, Levis's late poems build rhythm
to a sacred tenor which turns, ultimately, to a litany that praises what is. He
recognized this style in "At the Grave of My Guardian Angel: St. Louis Ceme-
tery, New Orleans," from *The Widening Spell of the Leaves:*

But it's all or nothing in this life; it's smallpox,
    Quicklime, & fire.
It's the extinct whistling of an infantry; it is all the faded
    rosettes of blood

Turning into this amnesia of billboards & the ceaseless *hunh?*
  Of traffic.
It goes on & I go on with it; it spreads into the sun & air &
  Throws out a fast shade
That will never sleep, and I go with it: it breaks Lincoln &
  Poe into small drops of oil spreading
Into endless swirls on the water, & I recognize the
  pattern.

There it is, one wants to say, that "and I go with it," which is what Conrad meant in *The Heart of Darkness* when he said the way is to immerse oneself.

Elegy, Levis's best work, begins in lyric voice with a contemplative poem about his name in Latin and abruptly turns to "In 1967," which remembers, "Some called it the Summer of Love," and ends, "When riot police waited beyond the doors of perception, / And the best thing one could do was get arrested." That was the time of Chicago's Mayor Daley, death in the South, and real violence in the land. Everything one reads in Levis marks him as a man devoted to perceiving and telling truth. Early on that "goodness" seemed about as assumed as the rainbow costumes of the 1960s—we wear them in photographs we have all kept in the deep drawer—but in retrospect one sees that an appetite for the ethical character of the sacred pushed Levis to poetry. Indeed, his poetry is religious, his faith the energy that binds together his intricate assemblages, mosaics, braidings, everyone in the crowd a Caravaggio might have painted, among them Levis himself, ruefully grinning out at us. But if *Elegy* is that crowd all at once, the memorable moments are Levis alone thinking, ruminating, trying to see the pattern of things he has remembered. "Elegy with a Bridle in Its Hand" is a poem about horses and has much in common with James Wright's memorial "A Blessing," although for Levis, the horses are individuals, not symbolic players in a real life. Levis remembers two old horses from his father's farm, "one of which would stumble & wheeze when it broke / Into a trot" and the other "creaked / Underneath me like a rocking chair of dry, frail wood," and these form a marvelous catalog of horses from that boyhood ground:

The palomino was called Misfit & the bay was named Querido Flacco,
And the name of some of the other shapes had been Rockabye
And Ojo Pendejo & Cue Ball & Back Door Peter & Frenchfry & Sandman

And Rolling Ghost & Anastasia.

Where had they gone? "I began to think that the world // Rested on a limit-less ossuary of horses where their bones & skulls stretched," Levis writes, Caravaggio-like, his poem painterly in leading our attention not through chronological tale but through an image-orchestrated list of what denominated the horses, who they were, what their fate is, and the last spiral of perception leading to denials of heaven, the Christian end of forgiveness and redemption: "Heaven was neither the light nor was it the air, & if it took a physical form / It was splintered lumber no one could build anything with. / Heaven was a weight behind the eyes & one would have to stare right through it," and, moreover, "the idea of heaven & of life everlasting / Was so much blown straw or momentary confetti / At the unhappy wedding of a sister." He yearned for the place where the good were supposed to go, but it didn't exist evidently. And yet in Levis the more steely the denial, the stronger the yearning for redemption and joy and, for such occasions, his narrative touch reaches its most delicate ironies. His horses, he decides, could have been the sleek ones before the crowds at California race tracks, Santa Anita or Del Mar, where, at the last instant he, a kind of shepherd-rider, might be called:

> And if the voice of a broken king were to come in the dusk & whisper
> To the world, that grandstand with its thousands of empty seats,
>
> *Who among the numberless you have become desires this moment*
>
> *Which comprehends nothing more than loss & fragility & the fleeing of flesh?*
> He would have to look up at quickening dark & say: *Me. I do. It's mine.*

That, as the Beatles said, was a ticket to ride. And it is what Larry Levis's poems offer with the only bet that ever matters, that the world may be good, whatever else it is.

I suppose I think of Larry still in this world, at some point appearing for another friendly talk about a poet we've been reading, excited as if no one else has heard about him or her. There will be the arrival, somewhere, of that tacky, battered car he drove—Volvo?—its make abused into anonymity, and he will step from it with that impious, welcoming grin which barely precedes some delicious gossip, some silly joke, some eccentric oddment of the world's tale that he has been carrying about, it seems, precisely for me. I know he has already forgiven himself the telling for any small offense it might echo. Even now I feel his presence so strongly that I take out my notebook and restart the letter I have been wanting to write in which I tell him what gratitude I have for his letter of more than twenty years back. I would add what admiration I have for poems he has written, the paths taken in the way many of us might go after his example. I would tell this last thing I remember of him, too. Seated in the dining hall during lunch at the Warren Wilson College writers' gathering, I watched him shuffle with his tray across the room, stopping to chat briefly with this famous writer and that one, having a laugh at each station. Then he stops where I sit alone and asks, with the humility of a monk, if I would mind if he ate his lunch with me. Larry, I said, nothing, not even your poems could delight me more.

III

Hunting Men

Hunting Men

My father, the first man I saw hunt anything, stood ten yards from me, his shotgun crooked in his arm, the barrel pointing at a knot of briars. He talked to a friend whose arm swung in a graceful arc to indicate where the beagle was off beagling the rabbit they knew would soon circle to the spot where we waited. I wanted to call to my father but could not. It was as if I had lockjaw. Instead I lowered my Red Ryder BB-gun and tried to point just toward the end of my father's barrel. For there, panting, its shiny brown eyes barely visible in the thorned vines, the rabbit hunched. Watching me. I tried to take aim with my little weapon but each time I did so, copper BBs rolled out of the loading tube I had accidentally left open. Although the prey was small, my shame was large when that rabbit bolted free.

If ever either of us shot that day, I don't recall. No other man held my father's shotgun again until the day, long after his death, when I crossed a fallen oak over a creek, slipped, fell hard, and heard it discharge in my hands. Maybe that cheap J. C. Higgins still rusts in an eastern Virginia swamp. I wish I owned it now. All I have is a memory of the one hunting sortie my father and I made together. In that I am frozen with and apart from hunting men, those with whom I feel the resonance of fathers and brothers and home ground.

Before I was ten I began to hunt with my grandfather, Harry M. Cornwell. Fridays after school in Churchland, Virginia, I caught a Greyhound bus, usually packed with Norfolk's sailors bound inland on shore leave, and I was ferried over bridges across the Nansemond and James Rivers, thirty miles through swamps, farms, and woods until I got off at Newport News. It seemed an epic journey to me then, meeting the bus by myself, offering my silver change, never speaking to strangers, as I had been warned, and dismounting at the bus station where so many people swirled about. Newport News was in the postwar flush of many commercial successes, dominated by the coal export piers on the east and the Newport News Shipbuilding dry docks on the west. In between the little city thrived with shops, like the small Montgomery Ward with the creaky wooden floors I still recall. I loved to be picked up in my grandfather's car and trundled down Jefferson Avenue near where, as he once told me, Pearl Bailey grew up. I had no idea who she was.

It was always a holiday for me at my grandparents' house. No homework, no rules. My grandmother, it seemed to me, had very little to do but wait for us, and nobody could have been more excited to see me. As soon as we walked in, supper appeared on the table. Then, following supper, ice cream, and the inevitable late radio shows, then the large bed at my grandmother's bungalow, only three blocks from where the Merrimac dueled with the Monitor. My grandfather barked me awake at 5:00 A.M.

The windows sometimes gleamed with ice, but the smell of eggs and bacon always filled that small house and I'd dress quickly by the huffing furnace, swaddled in layers that often included an ancestor's too-big wool shirt. Soon we were gone out into the lingering night's darkness. An automobile accident in which he had killed a child left my grandfather with a nervous habit of hunching his body like a boxer's before the plastic steering wheel. He was never completely still and his canvas hunting coat rustled constantly, but his Hudson was as quiet as a big comforting room. My hands can even now remember its smooth dash, the prickly upholstery, the wheezy heat blown over us. When I'd hear a moist sucking at his Camel cigarette, I'd look for the ash glowing like a tiny sun. He talked little. In compensation, I believe, I talked much. I asked questions about everything, but mostly about hunting men. I wanted to know who they were and what you did to become one.

Having crossed a black five miles of the James River where World War II's mothball fleet silhouetted its far ships, where the moonlight looked so cold you shivered, we took to hardwoods near Smithfield, the same country William Styron, who was from the Hilton Village section of Newport News, would write about in *The Confessions of Nat Turner*. We passed the farmer's kitchen light glowing down upon him at his breakfast. My grandfather seemed to have in mind a particular tall tree in a woods where every tree looked exactly alike to me, and when we came to its ghostly trunk, we cleared with our boot heels a small loamy space below the leaves. There he smoked his Camels. Soon we emptied ourselves of urine in different directions and, done, we sat. On his knees the long, heavy Winchester Model 12 pump with two brass-capped shells in the holding chamber and one in the barrel. He had been given this gun by his Great Uncle Dickey, who taught him to hunt. It would be given to me, he said, when I had learned to be a hunting man. It waits, now, in my closet for a grandson.

Nodding, dreaming, warmed by his body, I feel it: blam! Then blam! blam! The morning explodes. My grandfather is up, standing, wordless, shooting, and it happens again and again, the squirrel's body drifting out like a far diver from the tree's crown, tail puffed, ruddering in no wind, and the quick flat thud at the leaf-padded earth, and the blood-flecked eye and the mouth-drying stillness that followed. Until, sometimes with the sun not high enough yet to graze the hollow's other side, we rode in the Hudson back to the city. The radio played a catchy tune about dogs in windows, Patti Page asking how much they were.

In the last century we owned land, a people my sister calls *we*, of whom I have not bothered to learn much. It was a place called, she says, "the Silk Farm," in Lynchburg, Virginia. Like others, we fell on hard times by the coming of the Civil War, though how isn't given, becoming drifters who scattered in the Appalachian hills, becoming in time railroaders, laborers, men with good hands, laconic watchers called Cornwells in western Maryland, then in eastern Virginia, people ever on the move. Some of my ancestors hunted the shale ledges and fed their families on game. In them, maybe, there was yet a little edge of the wild that shines from a man's eyes when he is pushed more than he likes. A few, my grandfather said, could hunt like good dogs. Some of their sons, my kin, lit out for new places, remembering how to run rabbit and outsit squirrel.

My grandfather came alone to Virginia when the Depression released its grip enough to cast a rumor of jobs down South. He had two children, a sick wife, and nothing else. People without land need jobs. Men hunt for other men, becoming service providers. Because he had a head for drawing things, he made himself into a naval engineer and then an aeronautical engineer, studying in night schools run by Johns Hopkins University and MIT. It was what he did, not what he was. Nor was Virginia the mountains of Maryland where he had grown into the society of his fathers. He never lost the loneliness of a man in a place not his.

The hunting woods became my grandfather's country, but only on weekends because he was otherwise an employee. In the woods, his constitution was pragmatic. He taught me utility and self-reliance. We did not hunt with other hunters or dogs. Especially dogs. We went in before daylight. We sat, silent, until driven out by bad weather, or we got our legal limit, or noon arrived.

We offered all game we killed to the landowner, or we ate it. We left no trash; we crossed no posted land; we cleaned the guns twice. I never asked why we were hunters, but I knew it wasn't for love of the awful smothered squirrel. It makes me grin to think how he would have glared at anyone fool enough to call him a sportsman.

He had led the family, like many others in the postwar 1950s, away from its people and its old ways in the old place, and to the jobs in the new place that advertised and offered change. In time my father left his family back in Maryland, married my mother, served in the navy, and took a job under my grandfather who determined to teach him how to be an engineer. Eastern Virginia still had fields, fishing villages, codes and rituals outsiders found hard to see, let alone penetrate, but outsiders and developers were changing it all. Our subdivision was Sterling Point. My father took up suits and brown shoes. Near the Elizabeth River in what was then the village of Churchland in what was then Norfolk County, neither of which now exists, he built our house, a brick rancher with pink and aqua tile in the bathroom. We could still see soybeans and pig fields. Lawns rolled because they had been the farm rows where vegetables had got trucked to boats for Washington and Baltimore. I was one of the first graduates in the new, suburban Churchland High School, one of the "Truckers." Or I was one of the last of the rural kind. Something was disappearing around us, but we did not see it, being too busy with lives we hadn't yet lived. New neighbors polished second-hand Cadillacs and mowed inside new chain-link fences. Some had the new nerve problems. My mother bought antiques from people who seemed to have no further use for them. My father bought cars, azaleas, and golf balls.

By junior high school I seceded from my grandfather's nation of hunting men after squirrels on weekends. A photograph shows this group of my buddies in the Churchland Junior High seventh-grade class—Paul Smith, Billy Smith, me (Dave Smith), and John Woofin Speers, known as "Buddy" like so many southern boys. Henry Willet, our teacher just out of the army, stands beside us as fresh as pennies in his loafers. He would become Dr. Willet, president of Longwood College, and I would hear rumors about him from time to time, but in Virginia you didn't ask what behavior was in one's elders, unless it was unavoidable. I wanted to be like him because he was our teacher, Mr. Willet, and he loved the boys in that photograph: Billy, the meekest of us, turned out a U.S. Air Force Top Gun, a much-bemedaled colonel. Paul, who had a lovely twin sister Mary, did what? I think he did not graduate. I became a poet. Buddy Speers made and lost a million. Before this he was my best friend. He lived in a compound of houses on a tidal creek with his father Big Bruce and brother Little Bruce and uncle Big Grady and cousin Little Grady and Uncle Edward. They kept a pen of bird dogs, mostly drops of setters and rail-thin pointers, maybe half a dozen. Sometime during high school they took me in as a hunting companion, one of four or five who went with the dogs after quail along the edges and ditches of the Everwine farm or the swamps of the Nansemond River. This was my connection to the fathers and to the land I didn't even know I belonged to.

Most of that land had always been owned by a few families, among them the Bruces. The Speerses were, I think, the last Bruces. They had been, as the name suggests, in the Scottish migrations leaving their kin up and down the South. These were from Georgia originally. Their once sprawling farm was, by 1960, less than a hundred acres. You took winding Bruce Road to get there and crossed C&O tracks by bean fields to reach the oval of wooden houses where pickups and old Fords waited more or less stopped rather than parked. They had sisters and wives, too, but you didn't much see them. By outboard on the river, we lived no more than five minutes apart. Half an hour by road. They always raised some vegetables and had enough peach trees to claim they tended an orchard, but mostly they toiled with trotting horses, the kind that pull a dangerous little cart called a sulky, the kind that seldom won the races they often went away to. On weekends, more or less. Like my grandfather, all the adult males had had to take government jobs, except, of course, Uncle Edward who was in the navy.

Nothing was more different than my home and Buddy's. His house felt warm as a barn and smelled of steady use. Creaky wooden floors sloped to the river you could see through a crack in the plasterboard of Buddy's upstairs bedroom. No door shut entirely. People seemed to appear and leave at will, stopping those cars where they came to rest. If you were tempted to say that the Speerses hadn't a pot to piss in, you'd also have to say that family couldn't be wedged apart with a jaws-of-life tool. They were poor, if they once had everything, but with them you were immersed in a spontaneous and joyous life. It was nowhere more evident than in the hunting of quail. Fathers and brothers, weekends, holidays, after work—gone hunting!

The dog pen was in the front yard where the dogs endlessly barked, depending on who was hunting and which dogs were loaned out and which were pregnant. I remember especially the 1950 Ford, Old Blue they called it, no back seat and much dented, hence perfect for Freckles and Lady, the best dogs, who waited there. It *carried* us as we would have said, to ground owned by Carneys, Johnsons, Blanchards, Everwines, most of them kin to the Speerses, though how I could not say, though I am certain it was given to me like a catechism. Sometimes Old Blue took us to farms we'd just visit and ask to hunt. Nobody ever said no, but there might be a few squints to ask, one way and another, who are your people? Where do you come from? I have almost no memory of growing up where I am without the presence of Buddy Speers, but if anyone asked me where I most imagine him, it is at the dog pen. Uncountable but not unrememberable days. They come easily as moments in a poem, disconnected and out of sequence, latent with meaning not known.

With my father, who did not hunt, communication had mostly ceased by my fifteenth year. My solitary grandfather was increasingly a distant presence. Their places and pasts were not mine. Hunting with Buddy Speers, I adopted his family and wove what I had of a past with what I would take of his. They had, through a braid of time and place, an unquestioned sense of belonging, and with significance. I felt that significance and I wanted it to be mine. Maybe I keep whatever it was in the way of words. Words were everything to Buddy and me.

We were neither of us bookish in the usual sense. I don't recall any books he read, or told me about, except the Bible, over which we argued because he was the better preacher and took its tales more literally than I did. He had, by then, more literal experience in what the book called sins, so could relate, as we would learn to say. I have known a lot of southern writers and most of them put in time being, or intending to be, the sort of word man that anchors a pulpit. I inclined that way for a while but was, finally, too shy, and so I consumed such weirdnesses, or so he thought, as biographies of people like Simon Bólivar and novels by Englishmen like Thomas Hardy. We had, as we walked behind the dogs, rambling discussions of music, boats, girls, guns, dogs, and ultimate mysteries. Quail and God and Jesus and the punishments for sin were enormously real to us, and we hunted for one as much as the other. We were hardly philosophical, but the talk was a sort of attempt at ideas. Neither thought the other's ambition was odd. I wanted to live in books. He wanted to go to the Yale Divinity School. We were rough but liked to think of ourselves as civilized.

That's what he said quail hunting was. Civilized. I thought it meant you didn't have to go to the woods before daylight, you didn't have to drink off the slicing winds in a duck blind, and you didn't have to shiver in a tree stand until deer happened by. Hunting as you chatted and strolled like gentlemen through bean fields just harvested, where coveys, like southern families, more or less hung out together, wasn't that civilized? We thought, I suppose, that we were up-to-date, modern young men, able to change things, even immune to change in things we loved. If we had been asked, we might have said we were the New South's new men.

Quail don't know if you are new or old. In the eastern marshes of tidewater Virginia, quail learned there was more chance for survival with muck and water than in the airy bowers of the hardwoods or the gentle green fields. So there they went, and there, after them, we went. It could be dicey if you were less focused than you were greedy to kill something. I remember a day Freckles pointed in a marsh hollow. We positioned ourselves north and south, certain the covey would fly east or west. Buddy urged the dog in and kicked the hummock. I can still feel wings graze my head as I look into the barrel of his Browning shotgun. When quail get up they rattle your nerves, like a wall socket's bite. That's one of the reasons why you hunt them, the exhilarating life all the theorizing and preparation is only adjunct to at last. Like writing, it heats up the wildness in a man. You don't think. You lift, you shoot. I knew I was going to die. But I watched him lower the gun, steadily, the discipline of the fathers enabling the sons to live beyond them.

Perhaps in the large scale of worldly matters it's irrelevant that you can read mud tracks, or gauge a bird's age and sex, or know a little the scent that makes a dog hunt until its underside is bloody from briars. And who cares if you find the way farms have been fitted together, the way houses are built against certain shoulders of trees, explains the way families have come and gone? Still, if you know the natural history and the chronicled events of your place, you have access to the apparently unknowable fault lines and shifts of our lives. It can tell you why you keep moving and maybe what's needed to stop you.

On Mother's Day of 1960, in my junior year of high school, my father crossed the Nansemond River bridge and just past a grove of dogwood freshly blossomed he was hit by a drunken driver who killed him. Whatever I had had of the so-called nuclear family from that moment fizzled away like a cheap firecracker. My mother, severely injured and seriously scarred, took to her bed for a number of months. Because I needed a friend more than ever, Buddy and I were inseparable to graduation, but I have no memory of those days or their events. Even the hunting of that fall is a blank. Maybe I didn't do any. At some point that year my mother married a sleazy Air Force pilot whose alien presence among us left me turbulent, bitter, divided. But some of that must be accounted the realization, already beginning, that I was not squire material and my life did not belong to the hunting fields. Buddy and I prepared to go to college, the first in our families to do so. Almost by accident I wound up at the University of Virginia; he went to Campbell University, in Buies Creek, North Carolina. Although we promised to write letters, we did not. In fact, during our first three years apart, we saw each other no more than two or three times. I did not go home to hunt with his people in the fall, though I knew I was welcome.

It's one thing to think you can't go home again and another to be unknown when you go there. My mother sold our house and moved. I found this at Christmas break. The day I drove home, I was met at the door by a stranger who told me I no longer lived there. Perhaps it was loneliness that caused me to shortly afterward marry a girl who was, herself, lost. Perhaps it was loneliness that caused her to leave me in less than two years. Whatever the cause, life seemed a swamp I couldn't get out of. I fled to the Speerses' farm, certain it would always be there, then to Virginia Beach where Buddy had a summer job tending bar. He took me in, fed me, got me work in the same bar. A frugal person, he had been putting himself through college and had saved enough for a special day, graduation or job interview, to buy himself a Brooks Brothers suit. In a plastic bag, it waited for his eventual use. Even the name sounded elegant, but I had never seen a Brooks Brothers suit. One night that summer while he was out with a woman, I got drunk and put the suit on, the first to wear it, and then I walked down to the Atlantic Ocean and then into the surf. The God's truth is that he laughed. He wished, so he said, he had thought to do such a crazy thing. When the end of the summer came, he convinced me to go back to college, and he gave me some of his saved money to do it.

Two years later I was a high school coach in Poquoson, Virginia, married again for just three months. My wife Dee and I rented a two-bedroom cottage on the Poquoson River. Buddy called with some problem with a girl and his graduation. He wanted to go to summer school at the College of William and Mary in Williamsburg, only twenty miles from us. He had given the girl all the money he had left and was now strapped. He did not ask and I did not offer our second bedroom. When I had needed his place, I'd gone there. I told him to come ahead and said the door would be open. Moreover,

I'd go to school with him and begin my teacher certification. Williamsburg wasn't yet the tourist mecca, the experiment in living funded by Rockefeller and August Busch; it was a lovely college town among old English buildings. All summer we drank beer in the now-demolished Greek bar that faced the Christopher Wren building across the Duke of Gloucester Street, or talked at a pizza joint near the football and track fields. We made loud plans for books and sermons. My course was the Theory of Running Track. Some days I was actually required to run, and he would toast me with a beer as I passed. He took Marriage and the Family. Trendy boutiques replaced those college bars.

In the next year my grandmother died. My mother divorced, then slipped away to find a life. My sister and her husband separated. My uncle lost his children in a divorce. Vietnam already loomed in 1967, and I had students who enlisted. Deferred as a teacher, I felt a small pressure to do what the fathers had done in their wars, but a friend suggested I try graduate school. I did, heading off to Illinois and leaving behind forever, so I thought, all the deaths divorces, arguments, and bruises. It didn't occur to me that I was escaping from the South, a common pattern among its writers or that periodic, sometimes permanent, returns were equally common. I hadn't written anything much. Maybe I had given up hope I would write anything. Before I moved, my wife and I took the manuscript of what I had hoped was a novel to the town dump.

Over the years Buddy and I exchanged Christmas cards and occasional long-distance promises to get together as heartfelt as they were boozy. I sent pictures of my three children and copies of my books, the postmarks trailing us from Ohio, Michigan, Utah, New York. Every fall I picked up the Model 12 pump in its cracked leather case, but I never bought a license. I thought about hunting and even missed it when wood smoke hung on cold autumn air, but I didn't miss it greatly. Hunting seemed a small part of something much larger that I had lost, something I might never understand. I wrote poems about good early days in the fields I missed. I tried to make connections with words, following my nose the way a dog would.

Buddy's life and history seemed to me as unremarkable as mine. He married Jerri Rawls, the girl I introduced him to in high school, then taught school for a few years, had a daughter, and against all advice went home to Churchland where he opened a copy service business. It grew rapidly; he and his family thrived. Then he was told he had Hodgkin's cancer. He took the brutal treatments at Johns Hopkins Medical Center in Baltimore. He went alone, as he said, because he didn't want to be seen dying. When it was the worst, he hired a black cabbie to baby-sit him in a nondescript motel, probably in Glen Burnie or Dundalk. Somebody would know if he died, as he put it. Five years passed. The doctors certified him cured. But he had lost his business, had mounted up huge debts. Calling in a favor, he hired on with Kodak, proved himself quickly to have the force and charisma of leadership, and was moved to Rochester, New York, where he prospered, and paid back every cent he had owed.

I knew he would sooner or later return to Virginia. I moved to the University of Florida at the same time he left Kodak. Gainesville wasn't home for me, but it was the South. There Aubrey Williams, a crusty and impeccably mannered eighteenth-century scholar, asked me to go dove hunting with him. Dove hunters usually surround a field with many guns and fire at these stupid and terrified birds until no more fly over. I think because it involves no cooperative effort with a dog and no adaptation to landscape and no comprehension of birds or their behavior, it is mostly redneck shooting by men who surround an open field that leaves the brown carcasses to rot. I had done that years back.

Aubrey Williams hunted doves as the grandfathers might have. He placed us under a lone tree in the middle of a field whisked of all but the last bristle of soybeans, the October sun boiling overhead, and we waited for birds. With no free fire driving them, doves came few and far between, so there was with us plenty of time to talk and speculate about the sagging fences, odd trees, gouged and rutted field roads, even the changes to old manners and ways of behavior. I thought we understood the hearts that had beaten up and down on this hot dirt. Aubrey, one of the fathers, said to bring my son along. So I had. His first hunt.

In that year came an unlooked-for chance to teach in Virginia. My Florida job and future were superior, but I believed something called me home to Richmond, the capital, and I would be near my old and true friends. Did I envision myself with Buddy and the dogs hunting quail? I don't actually recall that, but I was certainly aware that my children might come to know much that mattered to my heart. I knew, nevertheless, that this move was rank sentimentality, but I could not blink away the chance. At Florida no one understood what I was doing or why. Except Aubrey Williams.

There had been a place called the Speers farm in a village called Churchland in a county called Norfolk. My grandmother and my grandfather and

my father were buried in the Baptist cemetery under honest-to-God vault-
ing oaks and beards of pines. It was tranquil and green and you could think
the good life would always find a way there, yet no reasonable person would
have held this village void of evil. Its dominantly white population throve on
racism, poverty, ignorance, greed, the usual aches. But, there, people knew
your people, your histories, even your convictions, if you had any. There were
certain continuities. Hunting was one, though I do not mean the killing.

Probably some developer knows how many tract houses he squeezed
onto the Speers place and why they squared the roads to handle neon shops
that surround the cemetery where what used to sound like breeze now roars
and guzzles. I don't know why. When I got back the Speers farm was gone.
The county was gobbled by the bankrupt City of Portsmouth, just across
the Elizabeth River. Churchland and its hunting fields became condos and
parking lots. It could have been called Snopesville. There are more shops
now than people in our 1961 high school class. The attentive eye is dizzied as
it passes over the neon phalanx. Yet if you take the old bus road west toward
Newport News, maybe five miles out, you can find patches of last farms.
Most of them are owned by something called Chicago Bridge and Iron Com-
pany, which has placed a lot of little pink ribbons on a lot of trees.

Buddy and I, by then, lived an hour apart. W did not much see each
other. He had come home to manage a German firm's local business, and
he seemed to be headed for the big numbers. Money mattered to him and
to Jeri. He said there wasn't time to hunt. There were no birds anyway, ac-
cording to the *Richmond Times-Dispatch,* at least not on public access lands.
The writer of that article said the cause was not clear: it could be acid rain,
altered weather cycles, unreported atomic fallout, or land developers killing
the habitat. One Christmas on the phone, Buddy told me a Virginia com-
pany had sent him to a quail ranch in South Carolina where they had hunted
from golf carts and killed baskets of birds. The newspaper report I had read
never said we hunters were the problem.

Twice, I think, I went hunting with my son. We walked National Forest
land in Powhatan County, west of Richmond, carrying the guns as uselessly
as if they were staves. But we actually talked to each other, listening and
playing around and dreaming out loud. I was a poet by now, with published
books, and I knew I was hunting for poems.

My wife and I sometimes chattered about moving to a farm. But where?
Why? We liked movies, museums, libraries. Writers are loners, but I didn't

want to be that lonely. I read for-sale ads. I began to suspect the hunting I
missed was a symptom, not a hurt. I had no time for the time a farm re-
quires, no inclination to raise dogs. I didn't really want any life but the one I
had. If I was a writer, my job was to write books, not find ways to avoid that
work. When I felt nostalgic, I counted on my children to raise objections.
They never failed. They had, after all, their home ground and they meant to
stay. Still, I thought about moving.

Late in the summer of 1988 my mother called. She had heard at a bridge
party that Buddy had lung cancer. People say of cancer patients, "You won't
recognize him," and we scoff. His face lay in my brain's wrinkles, familiar as
my own, having been with me in all those first moments of adult life—smoke,
booze, sex, fear, and joy. But when I stood in that Norfolk General Hospital
room, I stared at a stranger whose once red hair now spiked in only a few
white wisps, whose skin was fissured and freckled and scaly as my grandfa-
ther's. His toenails were yellow hooks. I could leave, I told myself. The crea-
ture slept. Then the head lifted slightly, as if I had made some noise in the
silence, and the watery blue eyes took some depth, grinned, and the back of
my skull went light with love and despair. I cried as we talked, not loud, just
tears slipping warm down my cheeks and drying on the back of my hand.

One Sunday morning in November, as if no time passed, I stood, suitcase
in hand, to leave for the airport and a week of poetry readings in New Eng-
land when the phone rang. Nobody had told me the end was near. I should
have known. They said he had made them let him work his way with a chair
through the house to the car for a visit to the doctor. It took all of a morning.
Finally, they thought, he had just worn out. Then he was gone.

The preacher had to shout over bulldozers moving just below the cem-
etery's edge as they knocked down the last bricks of the junior high school
walls where Henry Willet taught us. I could see the basketball backboard
and the little concrete court where we'd taken that photograph, Buddy, Billy,
Paul, and me. Puffy faces, tear-streaked and just recognizable, kept telling me
nobody ever had a harsh word for Buddy Speers. Usually it was just breath
filling awkward space, but I knew what they said was true. They filled the
Churchland Baptist grounds as they had when I was barely seventeen, crowd-
ing the hole for my father twenty yards off, the sun blinding that May. Buddy
had been next to me then, shoulder to shoulder. I saw, past his casket silver
in the thin light, people passing in and out of a new Wendy's. That had been
a pig field, gagging us in the fetid summer heat when football practice made

us, as poet James Wright said, gallop terribly against our bodies. There had been two very tall grain elevators and men named Peanut and Bootsie and Old Joe who worked there and laughed as they watched us learn to be violent.

Where were they? All the others? Those who had been? The family? The hunters? Driving back to Richmond, I held in my mind Big Bruce's face, curiously serene. He had lost the farm that was everything. He had been killed in an automobile accident, but had recovered and lived. Now Buddy's dying was done. Big Bruce seemed almost glad, a father's gladness at helpless pain's end. He was still called Deacon Speers, but he was smaller than I remembered him, and he was all that was left. I did not know how much I loved all of them until now, in the fullness of broken connection to a place, a family among whom so long as they lived I would never be an outsider. Where were those missing—brothers, fathers, and friends? I felt lost.

Not long after Buddy's funeral I received an invitation to hunt quail with C. Edward Russell, Buddy's lawyer and a high school classmate I hadn't seen in almost three decades. What I remembered of Eddie was that he was proud, intense, tiny, well-off, and once, as we played touch football at the beach, he had thrown sand in my face, an unnecessary and a dirty gesture. I remembered thinking I would never forget that; I had not forgotten. We arranged to meet in Suffolk, a part of Churchland that had been annexed to Isle of Wight County. That was how we dealt with desegregation orders; the county was dismantled, given away.

I arrived first at BJ's Family Restaurant, for no reason I knew called "Bunny's." Johnny Ellis, Buddy's insurance man and fellow church member and friend, settled into the Naugahyde booth. His hunting clothes were stained, tattered, frayed like buckskin, just like the ones I wore, which were mostly the ones Buddy had passed on to me at one time or another. Eddie, smelling and sounding like he had just opened a box of hunting togs from Orvis, slipped in beside him. We ate eggs, ham, biscuits, grits, and coffee, and we laughed at old stories. Men in ties and men in padded vests and farm caps sat mingled in fours or fives at tables. Often as one left he would stop, introduce himself to me, greet Eddie and Johnny, then ask about Charley Russell, Eddie's father, who had given friendship or groceries or money in hard times. Charley Russell was an Alzheimer's victim in his eighties. Eddie assured each visitor his father was just "somewhat forgetful." One said, "and a damned good thing, too." I hadn't known Charley Russell had treated his only son like a bad drop from a very good bitch.

We walked all day in fields, along hedgerows, through swamps. Houses, many under construction, surprised me everywhere. The dogs nosed the ground as they always had, not caring the Chicago Bridge and Iron Company and its MBAs and its pink ribbon crew were erasing the old farm names. Where we went would be Oakdale, Queen's Mill, King's Crown, or Azalea Shores—one more Anglo-phony subdivision name. We should have grieved for the changes but we didn't even when we traipsed inside a wobbly unused farmhouse where Eddie said he had spent considerable hot summer nights. A sink pump worked as stiff as our legs; a busted table might be the one an uncle used in the Depression to hang himself. Eddie thought the bulldozers would surely take down his grandmother's house, which was where we stood, before Christmas. I didn't know that Eddie had made the deal that sold off the land. It wasn't mentioned.

The country store we drove to for lunch might have been A. W. Johnson's, the heart of Churchland. We admired its boot-worn plywood floors, gawked at rare gizmos on sagging shelves, and drank a beer at the potbelly stove. We said "Yes sir" to the patriarch at the cash register who noted he had plenty for us to eat, who asked after Eddie's daddy. Eddie said "plain forgetful," and the storekeeper's remark was too soft to catch as he touched Eddie's shoulder gently.

We stopped hunting at dusk and put the dogs into a cage in the rear of Johnny's wagon and sat on the tailgate and sipped Buddy's favorite drink, Wild Turkey bourbon. We had raised only two birds. I had not taken a shot, but we made toasts anyway from scarred pewter cups Johnny kept in a paper bag. The Nansemond River bridge rose to the northeast, and raw wind slapped the cold at us over whitecaps. We had parked in that last field by a bluff, and behind us now the new California-style house shells looked mean and tooth-ragged until the night that swallowed us also turned them invisible.

On the road home I thought about fathers who were now our obligations as much as we all along had been theirs. We had behaved, sometimes, in courtly ways they taught us. I remembered Allen Tate's friend, the West Virginia poet John Peale Bishop had written that southerners understood manners existed to keep people "comfortably apart, to preserve between them and keep whatever distance is necessary both for their integrity and yours." Manners had something to do with hunting, and Bishop's seemed the right words to describe what was realer than I could say, but I was tired. Everything was so jumbled in my head I was not sure of anything but that dimly glowing farmhouses passed me by and darkness lay ahead.

It had been a day of endless tales, remembering and weaving histories, years covered by a sentence like a dog's lope. We killed many hours in words and comradely wandering. Was that why I felt I understood and even loved this ground, these men? Maybe like our fathers I was a little wild, a little unbroken. I hoped for that. Maybe while I thought it was bird hunting they taught, it was also hunting for the right men, and the rightness in men— what they had been in the history and debris of our place and what we might yet become. I knew without saying it that my way of writing a poem was shaped by that hunting, and something in the men I most loved was danger- ous, unpredictable in the way poems could be. Maybe hunting was a form of consciousness, of knowing sons and fathers and brothers, even when they were gone, dead, or just forgetful, continued with us and were what Buddy had long back meant by civilized. Civility and hunting wouldn't solve social problems and wouldn't put meat on the table, but thereby you could know a few valuable things.

Pulling into the driveway of my home where, inside, the Christmas lights flared around my children and wife, I thought of my father. My mother had found and given me some long-forgotten home movies of him. I'd spent hours watching him, on my living room's white wall, walk toward me, squint- ing, just awakened from a nap in his hammock. Twenty-nine years ago in that spring he had been one of the new men of the South, and his face wondered what I, holding the camera, was up to. I could almost hear him ask that ques- tion, as I turned off the car engine and watched shadows pass back and forth inside the well-lit house. Sitting alone for a moment I could see all that merge with his image on that wall, brief, distorted, each moving with some purpose individual and, to me, invisible. I was cold and apart, and I wanted to go in, to hug them as I had hugged Buddy Speers the last time I saw him alive, as my father had held me when he had seen the rabbit bolt and I had not shot it and had been ashamed and had thought I would never be one of the hunt- ing men. Way back, before I was a poet, before I was one of the new men.

THE QUAIL MEN OF CHURCHLAND
for Jeddie Smith

They loved Cary farm, or Everwine's, that hadn't been Everwine's
in memory. Its harvested rows flew up coveys like dust

as Big Bruce's blue truck, wobbling, conceived one battered body
we spilled from, lying as men do to find things alive among us.

Somebody's joint they stopped in, back-whacking jokes, whistled
hellos, hustling bets. Then chair-scrape, fingertip on a boy's arm.

They'd whip out the two-lane, all piled up with red beans, bread,
potato soup not soup, maybe not even potato. They bragged,

cast bird dogs, read mailbox names, walking like gents, telling all
that couldn't be explained. I'd bounce in front, say tell me again

about birds arrowed up the air, black Peanut's trailer Bruce paid for,
Peanut drunk, knife in hand, begging work, begging cash, crying

for Robert, his boy, gone, Vietnam, or prison, that never came back.
Now behind my tall son, shade-drowned, dog-wag close, gun

broke, I remember when I was the boy they fell behind, path gone
blank as knowing, chill night where I walked on fern, stars,

their breath blooming loud last dreams. Afraid, I want those growls
of love, words hearts lived for, a woman's touch and a tall son.

Save us! George's boy screamed, in the Sea of Japan again. Quiet
hurts, Uncle George would say, firing if stalk shook, no houses

squatted yet. I'd say, *bird's down!* If woods or swamp gulped it,
I'd say; if dogs went weird in ice or snow, I'd say. Big Bruce cried,

Bird won't go in no hole! My dog did. George sighed, *Careful,
careful!* Then wham, a blood shot. *My bird!* Bruce down, grabbing,

bent old grandfather, me dreaming I'd done it, feathers tumbling.
Day would come at last to not much, voices, words failed

as souls do, weightless, waiting for what happens. They'd stand
at Peanut's trailer, light somewhere, and soon silver bourbon cups,

clink-clink, everything divvied, Bruce holding Peanut's hand with
jokes until tears freckled them. Wanting to be. How little I knew.

Now, game bag heavy, I hear my feet pad where my son leads,
stars hung cold over pines. My throat burns with dust, so I ask,

if birds blow up like children, and we drink the last midnight air,
oh Lovies, what cry keeps alive in the fields? Cry it again.

The Trail of Obligations

SUAREZ: In a relatively early piece, "The Spring Poem," you use Louise Gluck's remark that "Everyone should write a Spring poem" as a catalyst to put forth your conception of poetry. The poem responds to Gluck's statement with the lines, "Yes, but we must be sure of verities / such as proper heat and adequate form. / That's what poets are for, is my theory." Has your opinion changed?

SMITH: When I wrote "The Spring Poem," I was a little more smug, as young people tend to be about what they know. At this point in my life, I am less sure what I know and how firmly I know it. Still, I would not change radically my opinion about what constitutes the virtues of poetry. I believe feeling is the primary spring of poetry, but I also think feeling has to be trained; it has to be shaped. It must emerge from discipline. I don't think feeling and artistic discipline are independent of each other but rather are codependent, the one enhancing and making possible the other. That's what the argument of any sonnet says. People who write sonnets tend to argue that they couldn't have said what they said if they hadn't had the form nudging them. I don't take it that far, but I believe in the enabling capacity of form to realize the potential for feeling. Without feeling, poetry wouldn't interest me. Regardless of how finely crafted or sophisticated the formal expression might be, if it didn't move me, I would find something else to do with my time.

SUAREZ: Your poems possess a narrative base, coupled with precise formal control. How do you negotiate the relationship between those things? Do you decide on a form first?

SMITH: Part of me would answer no, but part of me would qualify the answer. I'll try to say both at once. I think the form chooses me. I usually don't know prior to writing a poem what form I'm going to write it in. That is, whether it's quatrains, tercets, stichic lines. Most often, I don't know until the poem evolves, until it begins to manifest its chosen form. The poet learns to listen well to what the poetic experience seems to want. But having said that, it sounds a bit disingenuous. Surely somewhere in the recesses of the imagination I am making choices. It doesn't happen that automatically one writes tercets rather than quatrains. In my collection *Fate's Kite* the form of the poems was decided before the poem was written. I began writing thirteen-line poems with eleven-syllable lines. I did that for almost every poem in the book. Clearly that wasn't happenstance. One created another and another and another, and it became a form that I was comfortable working in for a while. It didn't prevent me from writing other poems, which I did in parallel to that book, poems I hope to complete for another book.

I also think that there's something of what happens to a poet that's inexplicable, even unsayable. It's in our nature to try to explain some of the things we did and why we did them, as if rational consideration is behind our actions. But the choices one might make in a rhyme or a syllable or a stress pattern may simply fall out. Maybe it happens because of something in our biology. Maybe it happens to us because something happened to our great-grandparents that we don't know about. There are reverberant forces in our lives that we are but dimly aware of, if at all, and these may have an effect on what we think we've decided. So part of me thinks I do choose form and part of me thinks that I don't choose form.

I'm never sure what I want to say about narrative. Southern poets are accused of having narrative in the way blacks were stereotyped as having rhythm. Blacks were quite properly distressed with that label. I think southern writers are distressed at having been told that they have narrative. Which is why Charles Wright would sit here and tell you he can't write a story, which he very well can. Ellen Bryant Voigt would do the same thing.

It's a false distinction to argue that there are narrative poets and there are lyric poets. Now, this may say only that I am more comfortable moving through space and time than some others are. If that's so, then that's so. I don't require everybody to write as I do. God forbid. Nor do want to write like everybody else. But I do require a tale, as Warren says at the end of *Audubon*. It would be difficult to cite great poets who did not depend on human tales to interest readers. I don't know who they would be. I've heard people say Emily Dickinson is a purely lyric poet. But I think Miss Dickinson is one of the great storytellers of all time. They happen to be small stories in structure, but they are still stories, and certainly stories of the utmost intensity of human experience.

I argue that anybody who writes more than two words in sequence is already engaged in telling a tale of some dimension. The next question is what kind of tale, how long, what elements are emphasized, etc. You know my poem "The Roundhouse Voices." I could tell you what happens in that poem in about twenty seconds, but it would take me twelve minutes to read it properly. What's the difference? It is language and what I call orchestration. I like the way language loops in and out of linear narrative and asks you to care for things other than plot events. But that doesn't strip the poem of a plot function. I don't care for plotless writing. I am almost uninterested in language for language's sake. L-A-N-G-U-A-G-E poets, and I regard that as a contradiction of terms, have no interest for me. Poems which are purely lyrical, if such a poem could be said to exist, don't interest me. Perhaps this is because I am drawn to the story every poem sets out to tell. I will accept the notion that form, as it has been used in my poems, is narrative to the extent that the tale is serving some interest. But I'm far from satisfied by what literally happens in the unfolding chronology of a poem, mine or that of another poet. It's a combination of—I really want to say vectors—musical or lyrical vectors and narrational or plot vectors, but all of them working in a co-dependency.

SUAREZ: What, exactly, do you mean by "orchestration?"

SMITH: I mean the elaboration of imagistic constructs which reinforce each other in such a way that the reader is led to perception by repeating signals. This can be done by varying image patterns. In the first line one mentions a kind of bird; in the tenth line one mentions another bird; in the twentieth line or the second poem one mentions a nest. Some kind of pattern has developed which the reader comes to be aware of if not necessarily to focus on immediately. It could be repeated very closely, directing reader attention. I prefer to repeat, to make a pattern, through variations which are tangential rather than immediate, and, it becomes orchestration rather than exact repetition. The same thing, it seems to me, happens sonically, in phrasing, in stressing. My interest lies in a fairly heavy Anglo-Saxon language, particularly with a lot of stresses in a line. I think of it as a muscular quality of language.

SUAREZ: The physical quality.

SMITH: Yes. I like that. It is my practice. First drafts tend to be much plainer, more idiosyncratic American speech. I try hard to get through to the end of what is being spoken to me before I revise, so the most utilitarian language works there. But this language never quite pleases me, so I twist it by shoveling in more stresses in the revisionary process. Over the years this has tended to excess; it comes out more Anglo-Saxon alliterative and jammed stresses now than it used to. There are those of us who have a taste for thickly textured speech, and there are those who don't have that taste, who prefer a more conversational American idiom. One of the ways you can create intricacy and interest in the working of lines lies in variations of stress and phrase and vowel and consonant. That's orchestration, the weaving, the looping. For me, far more effort goes into that than goes into what happens in the poem or why. I'm often not very good at why things happen. You couldn't look at my poems, for example, as a guide to behavior. Or even a clear presentation of dramatic scene. You wouldn't go very far. But if you don't mind a certain kind of sonic practice, and the chance of vagueness, then you might find my poems interesting.

SUAREZ: Your poems tend to accent several emotions that are at odds with each other.

SMITH: That kind of complexity is something I would like to have. It's what I admire in other poets. I have said before, and have believed it true, that what I write about is "obligations." This is an Horatian ideal. My poems pay attention to things done for which one feels some obligation toward change, and to things not done that should have been done. Also to events and to people for whom one feels the obligations of complex emotions. It tends to be an elegiac stance rather than an ode stance. Complex emotion offers the character of poems I want to write; it is also the source of poems I want to write. I admit I may be confusing subject and effect here. Maybe it has to do with the nature of my own experience. In the course of my life, poetry has often been the way that I could both record experience and come to some understanding of it that otherwise was inaccessible to me. I mean inaccessible either to the understanding or to the knowing. I have a poor memory. It's curious. Many of my oldest friends have almost photographic memories of what we did together. I don't. But the more I write, the more I recover even deeper memory that they don't have. And because I work to claim it, perhaps I can bring to the surface an emotional complexity that their memory for facts, details, evidence doesn't encounter. It makes me nervous to think how like psychotherapy this sounds. But a poem really does help me to recover my own life. Literally, re-covering it in some sense. I think this goes to personality, insofar as I can speak of personality with any accuracy. All of us have opinions. There are people who feel I am opinionated. I don't see myself that way. I think, in fact, that I am mostly befuddled and uncertain about almost everything. It doesn't, therefore, surprise me that some of the poems of mine I like best wind up in a state of interrogation but no conclusion. Or if they take a position, it's a position that the poem seems to be undermining or countering in some way.

Warren talked about the necessity of a poem's enacted experience. It took me a long time to understand his meaning. I don't remember the essay, but he speaks of the poem as a laboratory for, literally, human living. He says that when he writes a poem, he wants to try human experience, to see how the virtues that we say we believe in come out again. Right off the bat you must feel, it seems to me, things are going to come out the way you write them, that what happens is predetermined. That's the way you see events and poems. Yet, it doesn't really work that way. Warren, when he talks about a poem as an enactment, tries to suggest a neutral observer waiting to see what will happen, given the forces that are at play with full power to reveal what he doesn't know he's going to reveal. Whether my poems work out that way or not, that's how I want them to work. It's inconceivable to me that you could write a good poem, as Milton does, knowing the answer: I'm going to justify the ways of God to man. He knows already what he's going to say. It's not a surprise.

I don't know where I'm going, or if I know, it's only in the most ditheringly vague way. It's not the arrival that's important to me, but the quality of the journey. The journey is always fraught with uncertainty, with suspicion, with duplicity. All of which is an attempt, in the largest possible way, to establish some kind of scheme of values. I've convinced myself this is true. There was a time when churches we all went to, whether Baptist or Catholic or whatever, said this is the way things are, the way they will always be. People were raised to that, accepted that, and lived by that. But then, for whatever reason, we didn't accept it any more. Or we resisted it. It doesn't mean that everything faith stood for disappeared, but it all got more complex. When we talked about it or thought for ourselves about that experience, we tried to understand things that became increasingly mysterious to us.

I'll try to illustrate it this way: one of my favorite poems is Philip Larkin's "Church Going." I think it's the best of Larkin's poems. It may well be an anthem for contemporary generations. A man goes into a church and powerfully feels everything that's going on within it, although it's empty, and although he has no stated sense of what it all adds up to. That sense of emotional drifting and disenchantment and yearning is very real to me. This is what leads me to the theme of obligation. The sense of trying to find within a scheme of a life enacted in verse some of the few things that matter. I wonder how often individuals overtly ask themselves, as I do, what really matters to me? Richard Hugo used to talk about what he called the knowns and the unknowns. He said poets worked with all the knowns they could muster to try to discover a few of the unknowns. That's close to wobbly New Age talk. But it points to something of value in poetry. I do not say this is what other people should expect of poetry, but it is what I often experience in poetry.

SUAREZ: You've spoken about poetry's ability to help you recover your past, yet you could not be called a "confessional" poet.

SMITH: I don't know about that. Robert Phillips wrote a book called *The Confessional Poets,* one of the earliest and most interesting employments of the term. When I was in graduate school I read about "confessional poets" just like everybody else, and I'm sure I used the term. But I don't think it means anything. I have difficulty knowing exactly what people point at when they say it is the raw human experience that confessionals write about. Foucault says Christianity is confessional because in worship God demands the speech of innermost secrets. It seems to me if you discount contemporary idiom, idiosyncratic practices of contemporary writers, you wouldn't find Donne very far from confessional. I don't understand, finally, what the distinction is. Everybody writes about his or her life. Some of us put less realistic and realistic-seeming details in than others. What we're talking about is not the difference between facticity in art, but the difference between one person's elements and another's formula. Just a different compound, a different arrangement of particulars. The ultimate truth is probably Lowell's truth, who says that he's writing a spiritual autobiography. That's what Chaucer did. I think that's what we're all doing. The idea of confessional writing as only a recitation of unassimilated and unassembled personal facts is, I think, a misapprehension; no good writers do that. Well, maybe some very immature ones do, but we wouldn't be talking about those people anyway. We're talking about people whose work has been tempered, put to the test of reasonably experienced readers, examined, and held to demonstrate those attractions which art has always mustered. I think confessional is now a word used by lazy critical minds. It's one of those terms which is a baggage that outweighs its value. As for me, from the beginning, I wanted to speak to people's lives. I work from the assumption, right or wrong, that whatever I write about, if it's true for me, it's also true for you. Or equally true for the tribes in West Africa or in Puerto Rico or the woman in Australia. Whitman says exactly that in "Song of Myself."

The great writers are the ones who have illuminated moments of definition most fully. Please understand that I am not making a case for personal greatness, only trying to establish a benchmark. No one is capable of illuminating all the moments in the same way or with the same intensity. But in the greatest writers, you get greater wattage. You get greater intensity than with others. It can be argued that this is writing as mythmaking. I would only resist that term in the sense that mythmaking is lying. Myths don't necessarily lie. They do, and necessarily, attempt to explore our experience in comprehensive shapes as a way of understanding what has transpired around us.

This brings me back to what a poem does. A poem, by my definition, creates a little life, a little conception of what a life in time and space can mean. This is a very simple, even fundamental thing to know. And if you know it, then you don't have to know much literary theory because that says the same thing: We all live a life, and language changes that life. Language is also the lens through which we see it. There are no good writers who don't know that. Isn't it very odd that academics have spent so many hours and lives and fortunes and quarrels to discover this obvious truth?

SUAREZ: I'm going to switch gears a bit. You spent many years living and writing in Virginia, and you've used rural and coastal Virginia as the setting for many of your poems. Now that you've lived in Baton Rouge for five years, has that impulse changed?

SMITH: No. It's clear that in my deepest sense of self I am a regionalist. My appreciation of what life means or could mean, whatever I know about life, stems from a sense of place, a sense of the ghostliness of meaning in that place where the apprehension of meaning was attached to visible realities: an ocean for me always represented something. I never thought of it growing up; I never thought "there's the ocean; it means X." But when I'm not near an ocean, I don't feel complete. I have what I think is a historical sense, a historical imagination. In the state of Virginia every rock, tree, river, creek, every physical surface and shape is possessed of some kind of historical spirit. This is probably a primitive kind of imagination, but it isn't difficult for me to see a stand of pines or hickories outside of Cold Harbor, where the great Civil War battle for Richmond was fought, and see in them the terrible and ceaseless violence of that battle, of all battles ever fought, men dying uselessly and painfully and leaving something of themselves in that ground. It isn't difficult for me to see slaves standing before the auction block in Shockoe Bottom, the market area of old Richmond, nor to imagine the horror in a man's breast as he sees his wife sold off one way and his children another way, and him knowing there's nothing he can do; he'll never see them again. That kind of reality, ever tied to physical landscape, is not something I look for. It just happens; it exists. Why else would people go to the very place where England's Princess Diana died in that automobile accident? My wife and I saw them pile up flowers there when we lived in Paris. Why would people want to peer into Edgar Poe's old room at the University of Virginia? Place is magical with the spirit of unknowns and knowns. I had this sense of place when I started to write, and I've never not had it.

Interestingly, it is only somewhat portable to landscapes where my personal life is not in some way engaged. I lived for a short time in upper Pennsylvania, near the New York border, very fine country, but I wrote weakly about it. I lived in Florida for a bit and hardly wrote a word about that. When I went to Utah to teach in the middle 1970s, I found that landscape, maybe because of the austere mountains, most congenial. I wrote some poems which responded to that landscape, and this is the dominant scene of my collections *Goshawk, Antelope* and *Dream Flights*. I didn't continue that response, however. In poems after those books, I went back to my own region of origin no matter where I lived. Since I've been here in Louisiana, which is physically, topographically, very like my native Tidewater Virginia, I have written almost continually of that Virginia landscape I lived in until about the age of thirty, off and on. That is not to say I haven't written about Louisiana. There are a handful of poems about this area, perhaps more, and they come more and more frequently as I grow older and more settled here, but I know that the same coastal landscape which is mine by historic gift will continue to be what I write about. I once had a professor who asked, "When are you going to stop writing those swamp poems?" That was in graduate school when what I was doing could be called writing only by a serious stretch of the truth, and yet my subject was already determined. Swamps didn't particularly interest this man from Illinois, but you know that's what was given to me to write about. Swamps and the character of people made by that place as surely as the tides and winds determine what sort of trees and grasses flourish there. I haven't exhausted my swamps yet.

SUAREZ: In many of your poems—for instance "A Tire Hangs in the Yard"— physical objects serve as psychological centers, psychological cynosures for emotions.

SMITH: Given that I am aware of this historical sense of the life-spirit in things and trees, then it's possible for me to believe in the living quality of almost anything. And, conversely, to distrust the abstract. As I do. It's not that I oppose patriotism and loyalty and love and virtue, the concepts represented by such ominous words. But I see them embedded in tires that hang from trees or reflected by old men sitting on porches, and women washing clothes. I see the world, it seems to me, very much like the old lady in Elizabeth Bishop's poem "The Moose." Riding through the Nova Scotia twilight she sees exact things native to her way, lupins and a dog, for example, but she also looks beyond the light to see those things.

I have a religious reverence for the natural world—though to say so makes me wary of New Age sinkholes here. I dislike poems that gush over nature's glorious spots, overlooks, and pull-offs as cute as puppies but fail to recognize the threat that nature inevitably holds. No threat, no poem. The natural world will bite you in the ass if you're not careful. Maybe even if you are careful. I do have a sense of this livingness, this historical life in things, and it's very important to me to make the poems physical, as well as to make them honest, in precisely the sense that you describe.

SUAREZ: You've written and spoken about another Virginia writer, Edgar Allan Poe, who was concerned with form. What's Poe's significance to you?

SMITH: Professor Daniel Hoffman has a wonderful book called *Poe Poe Poe Poe Poe Poe Poe* in which he says many American writers begin with an enthusiasm for Poe which they think they'll grow out of, and maybe for a while they do, but then they come back to him. Poe somehow speaks to us about what it means to be a twentieth-century spirit, while at the same time he retains, specifically in form but in his thinking also, a connection to the nineteenth century. He's both backward looking and forward living, if I can use that terrible metaphor. Having been a student who walked past his dorm room on my way to class every morning, and having been a moody young man who loved "The Raven," like so many others, I had Poe always, it seems, in my consciousness, and I kept discovering him in ways for which I was unprepared. For example, I grew up in what is called Tidewater Virginia, a metropolitan area nearing two million in population. But it is composed of distinct towns, many of which were once self-contained villages. To get to the Atlantic Coast area of Norfolk and Virginia Beach you must cross water called Hampton Roads. To the east of that bridge there is an Army base called Fort Monroe, clearly visible to travelers. As a youth I spent time there with my grandparents; we went crabbing and fishing, and I didn't know that Edgar Allan Poe had been a sergeant major in the Army at Fortress Monroe. But there he had been. I didn't know that Poe did his last public reading on the steps of the Hygia Hotel at Fortress Monroe until I became a would-be scholar reading about Poe. Yet I read Poe as a boy and he was always part of my thinking, a presence without name or shape I was aware of. This may be true of Americans generally. Even T. S. Eliot recognized it, though he certainly didn't care that much for Poe. Eliot said there was a magic in Poe's poetry that maintains its hold on us.

With respect specifically to form, Poe is defiantly nineteenth century. Poe thought that "The Raven" was, as we would say of dishwashing suds, "new and improved" form. He was wrong on both counts. It was certainly not new. It was certainly not improved. My own belief is that Poe had probably a fairly pedestrian ear for metric form. But he had steeped himself in what he thought made excellence. It's interesting to note that the writer who would change forever the sense of poetic form, the only American writer to attend seriously to Poe, was Whitman. Poe didn't have an inkling of what Whitman was already about, and he would not have been comfortable with Emily Dickinson's vision or weird ballad form, although her gender would have sustained his interest. Poe wanted to hang on to a kind of orderly universe mirrored in his metrical theory or metrical form. But inside that theory, his poems are trying to break through to the twentieth century. I don't think he made it, but the fact of the struggle is apparent to people who continue to feel the power of "The Raven." And they do feel it, in every language. That's astonishing. That poem has been in print for more than 160 years. No other American poem can claim that or can claim the number of foreign languages in which it has been published and read and admired. There is something in Poe that speaks to all poets, but I doubt that many living American poets would argue that he's a very good poet. He's not a poet's poet, but he's certainly, on the other hand, a poet we can't live without.

SUAREZ: Two poets that you have cited as influences on your work are Warren and Dickey. Do you see similarities between them or do you see them as very different poets?

SMITH: Warren and Dickey are first of all united by a southern sensibility, a regional commonality that is more pronounced in the South than in any other part of the country. That's not to say a New Hampshireman and a Vermonter don't have something in common, and very intensely in common. They do. But they might not have much in common with say a downstate New Yorker or a New Jerseyman. Whereas the South is 1,200 miles long and 800 miles wide at minimum, and the people in it generally feel more culturally in common with each other than with what's outside. Warren and Dickey, in lots of ways, had a common matrix to begin with. Their ancestral nation was defeated and dismembered and occupied. Additionally, they were educated to the same kind of literature, the same kind of values, the same kind of destiny and past. They share a cultural heritage in many ways common, if not seamless. There are other commonalities. They are both gifted and compelling storywriters, tellers of tales. That ought not to be forgotten. They are both robust men who lived long and full lives, very intelligent, intellectual lives; lives of the flesh and lives of the mind as well.

There are also substantial differences. Consider this perspective: Warren published his first poems when Thomas Hardy was publishing his last. So he spanned the Modern age. But Dickey is a contemporary. Perhaps the single most important difference is that Dickey is finally, as a thinker, a positivist. Warren is not precisely that. Warren always stops at the point of being unconvinced. He is a skeptic who yearns to believe. In every poem with Warren, there's resistance to what he called the single-answer system. No matter what it was. This accounts for a complexity of experience and emotion and vision which resists any kind of glib answer to anything. This resistance creates a tension in Warren's work that I find credible and attractive.

Dickey, on the other hand, has given himself, from early on, to a single answer, and that is essentially that the momentum of the natural world is the true force in all experience. You may contradict it, contravene it, resist it, but in the end, Nature runs over you. And he glories in asserting we are part of natural cycles, even to the extent in some of his poems that he believes in reincarnation of our spirits. Dickey celebrates our part in the natural process. Not religiously speaking, but practically speaking, he accepts ashes to ashes. He and Whitman are in agreement about cycles, maybe even about human progress. Warren doesn't accept it, but he doesn't not accept it either. That's a huge distinction between them. I used to think they were two of a kind, but I don't believe that is so. Warren is significantly and substantially darker in his vision of human reality than Dickey's worst doubt. I don't mean that Dickey doesn't face up to the problems that human beings bring upon themselves. I mean that ultimately he is far less troubled by the dark nature of human suffering, less concerned about moral and social dilemmas. Far less anxious that there be an answer other than that we live, we seek a certain joy, and we die. It might even be said that the difference is that Warren is desperate for enlightenment and Dickey doesn't care about enlightenment in the literary sense of that word. That's such a fundamental difference between them as to make trivial the argument that they are two of a kind. I think Dickey has recognized this himself in the few things he's written about Warren. He's very astute, it seems to me, not only on others' work but on his own work.

SUAREZ: They both explore experience from every conceivable angle, an approach that in many ways typifies your work.

SMITH: It is true what you say of them. I will hope that it may be true of me. The poet may take anecdote in some direction that allows illumination to come about; otherwise, it would have simply remained gross anecdote. Certainly in that respect Dickey is an impressive writer. Warren, too, although he's less plastic in that sense than Dickey. Dickey masters poems of intense feeling. I could name a number of poems in which Warren does the same thing. But Warren accepted after a certain point that his poems were about himself. Even the poems about Dreiser or one about Flaubert, which is scandalously not about Warren. I think if Red were here, he would say "Well, yes, in some regard that's about me. I'm in there with him."

I think Dickey has leaned away from that more than Warren has, particularly in the later poems where it's so hard to see the outlines of factual events in his life. Even a set of problems such as the *Puella* poems present is murkily veiled. I suppose someone could completely annotate the *Puella* poems, and we'd know who did what, where, when, and so forth. And I suppose that's of some scholarly value, but it's of very little value to people who want to experience the poems as poems. Dickey has made those poems so oblique it is difficult to read them at all. Those poems are internal; they exclude narrative. Yet readers see Dickey as a wholly narrative poet. He was, at different times, very different poets.

SUAREZ: Comment on your own writing in relation to Warren's and Dickey's.

SMITH: I don't belong in a mix with those two. I simply don't have the work done and don't have the quality of work, nor does it appear likely at my age that I will manage to stand with either one when all is said and done. So I don't really think about it that way. After a certain point in my life I couldn't read Dickey. And I didn't read him until I did another essay on Dickey last year. Because he was so compelling to me, I could not help wanting to write like Dickey. Obviously he can do it better than I can. Too, there was a side to Dickey that I did not trust and did not like, a bluffing aggressive man who demanded to be so much the center of all attention that no betrayal, whether of a person or principle, was out of bounds for him. I just resisted reading him. I realized that my allegiance, though this word overstates the case, had turned to Warren. I think it was a matter of maturing as well as coming to know what I actually thought. This would have been maybe ten, fifteen years ago.

SUAREZ: Around 1980, I would say.

SMITH: Well, perhaps even a bit earlier. I found I read Warren with an imaginative profit, but I wasn't echoing Warren as constantly. Unfortunately, it happened that after a certain point, I assimilated Warren so much I began to sound like Warren, so I had to leave his work as well. I stopped reading either one of them. I could tell you who I read, but what would be the point? I think all poets choose or have chosen for them a kind of guide figure; Yeats has always been one that I read that way. Another way to say this is that I graduated from both of them, as they had each graduated from someone earlier. I had to make my own language, to make my own sound. Your question, taken properly, concerns what I learned from both of them. I learned from Dickey what I think you learn from good fiction writers too, which is, you've got to get something happening, get on stage efficiently, make the action of interest, and make it have moment. Then get off stage. Dickey was very good, particularly in the middle poems, about teaching you those kinds of things.

Poets do not learn from the atmosphere, but they learn constantly. I well remember even little things I have learned from poets. Richard Howard's essay on Dickey taught me about what Howard called "the gerundive mode." I wondered what in God's name was a gerundive mode. Howard's essay shows you how Dickey does more with the gerund form than any other poet. It is a window into Dickey's formal approaches. I saw things that Dickey did that I'd never seen anybody do. He fools around with adjectives, transforms them to adverbs or nouns; he reverses roles of syntactic units, of verbal units. Had he no respect for the rules he was breaking? I asked. Of course, he had respect. That permitted him to see what working against the grain and the rules might offer. His results were another lesson for me. There are poems of mine, unpublished apprentice work—and, embarrassingly, even published work—that sound more like Dickey than Dickey. I'd like to think that what I take from him, at my best, are lessons that enable me to find my own sound, not to sound like him. If I had come to Dickey only during the time I was writing later poems, I would not have learned from him because I wouldn't have understood what he was doing or why. His way would not have been pertinent. He was important to me early on in a way he is no longer important to me, though that doesn't mean at all that I do not greatly admire his poems. I do.

When I read Warren, I learned a new syntax. I learned sonic devices, ways of pressurizing the experience in the poem, ways of making it syntactically and tensionally more interesting. I learned to write a language of scrutiny, whereas in Dickey I learned to write a drama of adventure. As anyone who has had the remotest acquaintance with Warren must testify, he was among the most admirable, pleasant, and generous of people. He was a man's man in every respect Dickey wanted to be. Warren was not a saint, as I may be in jeopardy of suggesting, but he taught me, too, that a soul's intense inquiry was still possible in lyric poetry. That is, there were yet ways to ask questions of magnitude, to achieve discourse in poetry that could make sense and appeal without being sententious or boring. One did not have to fall into Ashbery's rhetoric of disconnect or pile up a perfect house of cards in the manner of Merrill. Probably I have no business characterizing myself among such people, and it is at best unseemly, but I see myself as more like Warren than like Dickey. Temperamentally, I am more tuned to Warren's harsher vision of what the world does to us, of what people are, than to Dickey's. Dickey's poetry is comfortable in the world in the same confident way of the southern good old boy who is not, basically, introspective but who can nevertheless get his furnace fixed, his rabbit skinned, and his book reviewed by the right editors.

SUAREZ: You are a very distinctive poet.

SMITH: It would please anyone to hear you say that of the frightful adventure of writing poems. Without necessarily agreeing, I'm especially pleased because so many people want to lump us southern guys all together. You probably can also see the presence of James Wright, who was every bit as important to me as Warren or Dickey. Wright represents, more than either of them, the pure lyric, which I never mastered, but I admired enough early on in the 1970s and early 1980s to try to write such poems. If you follow Wright's work, you know he went through his own troubles with lyric poems and came out on the end of writing longer tale poems. He never abandoned his lyrical quality. But he moved in a direction he wanted with those later poems that are, roughly speaking, fifty lines long and tend to have a story that they develop, one with a very blunt, personal, lyrically emphatic language. I admired that. I could point to poems that echo it in books of mine. I could also show you, were I so inclined, the marks of Philip Levine on my poems. I have said previously that I was influenced by an English line of elegiac and thick-textured poets beginning with the Beowulf author and including Hopkins, Housman, Hardy, Yeats, and Dylan Thomas.

Perhaps that is why I think no one today excites me, teaches me, more than Seamus Heaney. He has the same lyrical quality I have always loved in poems. When I read poets, I'm not looking for answers in any kind of philosophical or religious or worldly sense. But there's a pleasure in the sound of language that is provocative, an energy that startles the stilled surface of the pond. I hear it in Heaney, and I like that a great deal. I once felt it was there in Wright more so than anybody else. But you won't find it at all unusual, I think, that Wright found the same thing in Warren that I found. He said so in his essay called "The Stiff Smile of Mr. Warren." And he told me on at least two occasions that he thought James Dickey was the best poet in America. He was aware of Dickey's abilities and appreciated them intensely.

SUAREZ: Warren, Dickey, and Wright are all storytellers who remain attuned to language's nuances, particularly in regard to sound.

SMITH: In the middle 1980s, Stanley Plumly wrote about a form of poetry he called the "prose lyric. " I think he was after something like what those poets did with the lyrical tale. He said a smart thing that Warren tried to say earlier in his essay "Pure and Impure Poetry"; it was that the prosaic imperfections of the world had to be somehow employed in lyric poetry. The beauty of lyric language could be fused with story to face up and manifest the rawness and ugliness of human experience, not merely to exist as a kind of distortion the ear likes.

SUAREZ: You just described your poetry.

SMITH: Perhaps. When Plumly wrote that, I thought he had named exactly what some of us were after. I thought that, in the late 1970s, I was one of the few people who were trying to write this kind of poem, which is a variation of the prose-lyric poem. People, as far as I could tell, thought that I was a little strange. I mean in the poems, although it may be true outside the poems as well. That kind of poem wasn't the trend; it wasn't fashionable. Then Norman Dubie was writing it, or his variation of it. He saw my poems, wrote to me, and out of that brief correspondence we became very good friends. The same thing happened with Larry Levis who, I now think, has made the best poems in this form. Since the 1970s Robert Hass, C. K. Williams, and others have worked in this direction.

The so-called neo-narrative poets, who have married the so-called neo-formalists to become the so-called and self-named Expansionist poets, have made the gross mistake of arguing that they have resurrected narration in poetry in the 1990s. It is typical of the shoddy scholarship of people like Bruce Bawer, David Dooley, Annie Finch, and Dana Gioia to simply ignore the dates of publication of poems, or to distort date sequence, so that evidence fits exactly their stated history for a "new" poetry. If you wish to identify a list of poets who have written in narrative directions, before any of these who protest were born, you could begin with Warren and leap to Robert Lowell and Allen Ginsberg, and you would not want to ignore Adrienne Rich, Donald Hall, W. D. Snodgrass, Philip Levine, Galway Kinnell, Richard Hugo, Carolyn Kizer, or among younger poets Dubie, Levis, Sharon Olds, Yusef Komunyakaa, Garrett Hongo, Terry Hummer, Bruce Weigl, Henry Taylor, Laurence Lieberman, Lynn Emanuel, and—well, you see the point. To declare a reality that is so blatantly contradicted by easily available evidence is to follow the path of Albert the Alligator who was, and not concerned about it either, lazy, illiterate, provincial, and full of bogus convictions which he roared all too loudly to make himself believe them.

The issue, if one is generous enough to think those people are not merely self-serving literary sycophants, is the relationship of prose matter, not only rhythm, and lyrical form. I don't think there's very much prosy about the prose lyric. I disagree with the verse arguers who want to say it's really prose lined up to look like poetry. I think they have advanced no help in understanding why meter doesn't make poetry all by itself, despite Emerson's caveat. I think what's prose in the form is metaphor; that is to say, we are using the word "prose" to imply the rough, odd mixture of worldly experience that is in some way refined into the form of artifice when it enters lyric language. The language is not so refined or conventionalized that one could identify anything like a pure poetry. The contrary is the case. That rough experience is carried by a deliberate mixture of roughened language, dictions and idioms and syntaxes braided against conventional usage. It seeks to establish a new sound.

SUAREZ: Thematically and sonically, you are aiming at what Lionel Trilling called "the recalcitrant stuff of life."

SMITH: Yes, of course. That's exactly what I mean. I'm not interested in and not capable of thinking in the sort of editorial way that strict verse form wants to mount. If you come at poetry from the point of view of loving the sound of language, but also loving the enactment of human experience, then you're probably not looking to make a point. You do not seek lyric purity or a verse podium. You're looking to engender a verbal equivalent to your own reality. Just be inside the experience. I do not want to use the anecdote to make a theoretical statement. This is not the same thing as saying the presentation of personal experience with abundant clarity and sonic pleasure is sufficient for a good poem. It is not. Poems must make a point; they are acts of discourse. But the subtlety of elements, of form, coheres wholly in the greatest poem only when a significant, often surprising, point is made. If a reader was to speak about whatever could be found of a philosophy in my poems, I suspect he would not speak long and he would discover in me no great profundity. Perhaps there is no philosophy, no synthesis. I don't see any recognizable point by point comprehensive understanding of things. I'm not a thinker in that way, although I would like to be. None of the poets I have loved have been such thinkers. Oddly, one could argue Dickey is a better thinker and a more consistent thinker than Warren in this respect. Perhaps that is one of the things about Dickey that offends his more delicate critics.

"Thinker" is a curious word to use here. Dickey is systematic in what he observes of the natural forces, of the relationship of beings, of the cyclical course of things. He was trained at Vanderbilt University in the pre-Socratic philosophers, and that disciplined thinking undergirds what so many people regard in him as sheer rapture. In the essays he's written over the years, he's been articulate about this, without needing all the buttressing that theory and speculation brings. He isn't, for instance, the kind of systematic gatherer of poetically useful material that England's Ted Hughes has been, a poet I very much admire. Hughes has all that anthropological and mythical buttressing. I don't doubt Dickey has done his own gathering, and a good detective will find the underlying matter at some point. But I don't see footnotes in Dickey. He wants the world made immediate to the reader and rejects the awareness of apparatus. I learned to want Dickey's immediacy in poems but I am temperamentally more inclined to Warren's more didactic style.

SUAREZ: You have also written a novel, *Onliness*. What is the relationship of the novel to your poetry?

SMITH: I don't think there is any relationship between the two genres. I wrote a novel out of greed and envy. Poets, as you know, make little or no money. I have always been a reader of novels, and I thought many that I read were terrible, though they made some money. I told myself to go forth and do likewise, make money. Only I wasn't good enough to write badly enough to make money, and I was too bad to be a good novelist. Still, like many others, the first book I tried to write was a novel. It wound up at the dump in Poquoson, Virginia. The book you mention, *Onliness,* began as a story about eight basketball players on a schoolbus. I can't begin to tell you how that metamorphosed into a the story of a shot-putter who happens to live in a junkyard operated by a madman, or what happened to the guys on the school bus who were traveling around the South trying to play basketball. I do know that at some point I became aware that I was parodying the southern gothic, grotesque tradition, and having fun doing it. I couldn't get it to end. It just kept getting bigger and bigger as another little tale would enter.

I did not, of course, know how to write a novel, and I came to a point where the tale stalled. It happened then that I was giving John Irving a ride to Park City, Utah. *The World According to Garp* had not yet been published, but I had heard him read from it. We were talking about the way novelists write novels. I thought you started on page one, like Snoopy does, and went to page End, and that's that. Irving told me that he had done sections of *Garp* without arriving at the book's cohesive form. Only when he had, late in the writing, invented transvestite Roberta Muldoon and put that story in, having then to seam it through what was already done, did the novel settle into its final shape. At one point our talk turned to observations about madness. I forget the exact connection, but Irving said madness was catching, it was infectious. When I heard him say that, I knew there was something bigger, and to that point still outside my novel, and that's why I hadn't been able to end it. While I was having fun mocking a genre that I admired, I also wanted to say something about the madness of violence and people's obsessions. Maybe that novel is the zany side of everything I write in poetry. Perhaps this means there is a relationship between my poems and that fiction after all.

The novel seemed to me about ordinary events in my characters' lives jacked up, taken to the jokey extreme, but I could not let it end as a joke. So it became about what would happen if you take an obsession too far. My second primary character, a mad old man named Tom Zucold (a fool!), was obsessed with his mistreatment at the hands of the neighborhood do-good-ers, and it led him into violence. This set up a division between him and the shot-putter, Billy Luke Tomson, who came to regard the old man as his surrogate father. Once I understood that was the story, I saw that what mattered to me in all of it, as it does in all of my poetry, was obligation. The big shot-putter winds up with an orphan child at the end; that is an obligation he cannot refuse. I think of it as a positive ending. He takes on an obligation, and it seems to me that's finally what that book wanted to tell me. If I am permitted a small philosophy, it is that life consists of one's obligations, the handling of responsibilities, including the bungling of obligations. But insofar as *Onliness* is different from my poems it's because I was having such fun playing with Flannery O'Connor and Faulkner and Harry Crews and Jack Matthews, writers I admired.

I have started other novels, one I really wanted to finish, about ten years ago. I haven't been able to finish it, and I don't know why. I ought to be able to write fiction, but it's like a chore. I don't feel the pleasure in it that poetry gives. I started out writing things that I imagined to be novels, bad as they were, and I am very reluctant to talk about this because I have respect for those who make novels. At a party once, I was asked by a woman who had actually read *Onliness* if I would write another novel. I started to tell her about the one I was trying to write. The novelist Stanley Elkins sat with a woman on the sofa only a few feet from us. I heard him say, derisively and loud enough to be sure his ridicule was known, "lookit, the poet wants to write a novel!" Elkins was sick, bitter with age, but he had a point. It isn't good form to speak of a book not yet published, done, made an object.

SUAREZ: The poetry lures you.

SMITH: It does. That's a better word for it than pleasure. It does. I've talked to novelists about this and they say that what they like is coming back to something that's not finished; they like the way it waits for them. That aspect of fiction seems to me a job I have to go back to but would do anything to avoid. I just can't get it done. I had fun writing *Onliness,* but I don't feel that work is where I properly satisfy my interests. If I'm ever to be remembered by any single reader for anything, I hope it will be for a poem. It surely won't be for fiction.

SUAREZ: What's next for you?

SMITH: I should take my own advice to say no more. But alas. I have been working on a new collection of poems, four longer, more narrative-like pieces. These have connections to my earliest writing interests and are combinations of memory and idyllic speculation: an invented southern man fleeing the South for work; a memory of attending a Halloween costume party in Washington, D.C., just after racial disaster in Selma, Alabama; a speculation about a woman whose marriage takes her from the South to the North and into a peculiar madness; and a tale of lovers who survive a rogue wave on the Chesapeake Bay. It feels like my most southern book in some respects, if by southern we mean a heightened awareness of the continuous role of region in one's conscious moments. But I feel a strong pull to abandon this awareness, to resist such subjects and interests. I also have a book-length poem whose manuscript is now more than ten years old, and I still hope to return to it with enough freshness to make it right in ways that so far elude me. I am contracted to edit a historical anthology of southern poetry, with introduction, and I hope to get that under way. But these last are only hopes for books, for none of them now exist. To the poet there is only ever one thing ahead, and that is the next poem, the unwritten poem, the poem that may carry the impression of your life, breath, and bone, that is unlike anything you have done. That, I continue to think, is what is next for me.

In Search of the Real Thing

LIFE PIECES

The ancestors from whom I am descended were the grim-faced, pragmatic issue of English wanderers who settled the coal ridges of Maryland and West Virginia. Their people, Lutherans, assumed a man's actions had spiritual reactions. If they were not the sort to hang you for the Lord's sake, they didn't step forth to help you either. None among them ever needed fear any bargain like Faust's for a superior, passionate vision. When the preacher said not to challenge God's knowledge, nobody blinked. These were men in both armies of the War Between the States, some who fought and were not in any army, and women who simply bore the mess and got replaced when they fell like mules in harness. They feared the unknown in themselves and in creation.

They dug coal, farmed, floated in and out of history, and went unnoticed. Individuals and clumps, they drifted and got families in Indiana, Maryland, New York, and Virginia. Probably now one is telling another maybe there are yet kin down in Virginia, but who knows if they've died off. It's a story as American as Yankee Doodle and Walt Whitman, the road out of town into the territory, the restless spirit in search of a promised freedom—who learns to think he has left something but isn't sure what. He wonders when he will know what he belongs to. Some of my travelers set down seed and started legends their generations know as *home*. Some paused and went on down the road. Thomas Wolfe said you can't go home again, but that's what writers do in each poem and story. Our one great tale is exile: the nature of what we had, how we were lost, our loneliness, a possible triumphant homecoming.

Ralph Smith, my father's father, sold tickets for the B&O Railroad in Cumberland, Maryland. He walked to work for more than four decades, then came home to a small, dark, brick bungalow that matched his wife, Xena Mae. My parents left me with her on occasions they visited that home. She once made me go down and pee into the basement drain because she had cleaned the bathroom that week. There was no light there and, being a small boy, I was afraid. They had a boarder, Melvin Holiday, a train engineer, who gave them the house. He was diabetic, as I am, threatened me with his needles, and told me he kept fishing worms in the apple sauce I loved. Their daughter married a liquor store in California. Xie and Melvin are long dead. Ralph at one hundred died in that house. I have not been back there since boyhood.

Harry Cornwell, my mother's father, son of a carpenter, grandson of Asham Buckner, captain in the Grand Army of the Republic, a Yankee, married Mary Alice Folks, sixteen, by hauling her away on his Indian motorcycle. He had graduated high school and done well as a draftsman apprentice with the B&O Railroad. They had two children, Catherine Mary ("Kitty") and Harry Jr. Then the Depression came. No job. Harry Jr. in bed for a year with a mysterious sickness. At last, because somebody knew somebody who knew Harry Cornwell was a hard worker with some vision, he got on with the B&O in Baltimore. He commuted by free train to that home, took classes at the Johns Hopkins University, learned some engineering, passed a civil service test. The job offer came to work for the U.S. Navy in—"Where, Harry?"—Portsmouth, Virginia. My mother, Kitty, stayed in Cumberland to finish high school, then she went by rail pass down to the house my grandfather had bought in Glen Sheila, a worker's suburb, 226 miles and cultural light years away. My father-to-be, Ralph Gerald ("Jeddie") Smith, followed, a draftsman apprentice working for my grandfather in the Norfolk Navy Yard.

They were working-class families who took up chance's road and went south on it. They lodged by salt water, in Virginia. You could hardly fail, there, to look out a bedroom window onto beautifully green land, as nearly unspoiled as when John Smith had sailed up to nearby Jamestown. For love and for opportunity, they gave up hills and home. They valued education as the path to the middle-class life they wanted, but they had time only to work. My grandfather became a naval engineer. At fifty, with very bad eyes, he taught himself to fly and then abandoned the matter because he knew he would never be able to afford an airplane. He transformed himself into an aeronautical engineer, an early worker on the NASA projects at Langley Field. Then an Army test engineer in the Fort Eustis transportation command. No degree.

My father took extension courses, as they were then called, at the College of William and Mary and the University of Virginia. I mean in rooms at the Norfolk Navy Yard. He never set foot on a college campus except for MIT, where he once spent a full, government-paid summer. No degree. But it made him hungry and restless.

My mother married him in her teens, took work as a telephone operator and civil service secretary, a brunette with simmering red streaks in the sunlight. Smart and tough, she might have made a biting lawyer or politician (is there a difference?). One of her cousins became an engineer. There was no money for her to fund college. No degree.

My grandmother kept house. She was the most tender, most solicitous human being I have ever known. I have seen her sob when waiting for a late bus while shopping because she knew supper would not be on the table at exactly six when my grandfather walked in. Maybe it wasn't tenderness after all. Her holiday dinners filled the house with family and tales of the old times in places I would never know. But to me she was the heartbeat of summer. I'd always find a free nickel in her pocket. She cooked pancakes at midnight. I'd lie in bed with her and watch late movies on the Truetone television. She walked with me to the waters of Hampton Roads, waiting, hoping for an imminent storm with the waves pounding in.

This was the famous tidewater area of Chesapeake Bay, where the *Monitor* and the *Merrimac* fought the first ironclad naval battle. I grew up around and on water: the Elizabeth River where they'd once brought in the head of pirate Captain Blackbeard, the waters of the York and the James Rivers, and many smaller ones, and creeks, all sweet and salty at once, with black bottom steaming in the sun and scuttling fiddler crabs and the tangy smell of swamps. You walked under redwing blackbirds and over skeletons of boats so plentiful they might have conveyed an army that failed miserably and sank. Sometimes your family might drive south to Nags Head, North Carolina, and spend a night on the ocean beach, but more likely it would be nights in the sultry, humid glitter of Virginia Beach or Buckroe Beach. No one had air-conditioning, and the streets would fall silent after a while and you could lie thinking of the moon spread on a creek, a path you might walk. Some nights there would be the reek of the "factory" that turned crab shells into fertilizer or the droning silhouettes of U.S. Navy ships against the horizon. Today the small waters float a stew of trash even the Green Peace honkies ignore; the mighty Chesapeake has the worst de-oxygenized dead zone ever; oysters are almost gone. Houses so big my wife calls them "monsters in a field" stand shoulder to shoulder where water is, each one flushing into the Bay.

In Glen Sheila we lived in an apartment rented from my grandfather across from a dock where men kept work boats. From there Uncle Harry went to war on the *U.S.S. Croatan,* came home safe, and then scandalized the family when he fled to Florida with a married woman who became, finally, one of my favorite aunts, until driven from us by divorce. My father, too, went into the Navy. A training accident landed him in a naval hospital for leg surgery, and he was discharged honorably to live.

Two images dominate our family pictures. One is a house and one is a car. My great-grandfather, "Big Daddy," built a small house on Douglas Street in Cumberland, but few of my ancestors were so fortunate as to own a house. Those we have had may be understood as the language of my family history, a search for solidarity, security, the future America was supposed to mean and sometimes did for its peasants, its yeoman class—but only with the GI Bill after World War II. For the Cornwells and the Smiths, it meant identity.

My parents left Glen Sheila for a small postwar box in Loxley Place, near the Craddock area of Portsmouth. It must have been a tiny suburb, but it looms large in my mind. Portsmouth was home to shipyard laborers, toughs of all sorts. It caught spillovers of sailors from Norfolk, the world's largest U.S. naval base. I grew up aware of pawnshops, streetwalkers, fleet arrival times (don't get caught with a girl when the fleet has just steamed in, unless you want to fight). If we were not at the bottom of the housing tree, we were close. Bare ground, a box. Pain, that was the house. I accidentally pushed my mother into the floor furnace which was open for cleaning. I can still see blood running down her leg. Once she whipped me until I sobbed myself asleep because Lynette had pulled her pants down to show me what a girl had. Not far away there was something being built and it was very muddy and I got stuck to my waist and some men pulled me out. I never told my mother this happened.

We moved to Simonsdale. How lovely suburban names are, the promised consolation. In Tidewater, green ordinarily means the tall, girlish loblolly pines and the family of yellow and white pines that, closer to the ground and thicker, create a permanent shade in the air and leave on the earth the brown blanket that absorbs the sound of your footsteps. There may be nowhere else on earth so thicket-beset with exploding azaleas each April or the astonishing blue heads of hydrangeas that filled my grandmother's yard in her first owned house. That green is the message in names like Glenn Sheila and Loxley Place and Simon's idyllic "dale." It wasn't exactly so. When I was in college it took me a long time to understand what poets like Milton meant by the word *bower*. Real-estate developers have known it all along. We stayed in Simonsdale one year. My father had now begun his adventures with cars, and here came the hull of a 1932 Ford he would transform into his little deuce coupe.

A civilian working for the Navy, my father was, as yeomen are, reliable and ambitious and did well. Promotions kicked him into the middle class, where my mother believed we belonged. They built a small house in Sterling Point, an Anglicized 'burb that expanded Green Acres, the oldest bedroom community for Portsmouth. We were bounded by soybean fields, a thick susurrus of pine trees, and the western branch of the Elizabeth River, then blue-green, not today's chocolate.

The house was typical of the 1950s in its brick rancher style, low and dark. It had my father's touches in its utility layout. My bedroom was designed in the middle of the house, with pass-through doors so that it might become a den when I had grown up and gone. It meant there was never privacy; there was a fold-out sofa but no bed. One pink-tiled bath, a fireplace unused because it would have to be cleaned. The trees in the yard had, most of them, been bulldozed down and replanted. I could jump over the pines in the front yard. All the yards-to-be here were still just brushy spaces, and over the years we would have to shift our homemade baseball plots each time a new house got built. Two blocks away there was a lake with bass fishing, an owner said to be terrible if he caught you at it. I never saw that owner.

This was 108 Bridges Avenue. Some awful things happened there but it remains, often veiled to me, the place inside the place of my poems, one of the homes of my soul. Sometimes I remember almost nothing of the place, and then images come flooding back. I water-skied in the river, danced in basements of girls' houses, rode the team bus home after football practice, dreamed while I listened to Johnny Mathis and Ray Charles, and watched the moon through pine needles. In our back yard, about fifty feet apart, stood a pine and a pecan tree. I nailed homemade basketball backboards up on each, one too high and one too low. I played one-man basketball there so much that years later the clay had to be plowed up and replaced before grass would grow. When my father died I found in that attic his cache of pornographic photographs, Navy uniforms, and athletic medals. But it is cars I see when I think of that home.

He owned a 1955 Ford convertible, blue and white, the family car. Also a deuce coupe. By then that jewel gleamed bright red in our gravel driveway where I frequently pulled away the oily tarp to expose the completely chromed Mercury flathead V-8 engine. I sat and shifted the gears and pretended. What did I pretend? Going fast, I think, but not really going *anywhere*. I never drove that car, though I always expected it would be mine. By my fifteenth birthday, when I took and failed the license test (I passed it the next day, nerves vanquished), the 1955 Ford and the deuce coupe were gone. He bought a 1957 lime-and-white convertible. He also brought home a 1930 Model-A and challenged me to get it running. When I did, he sold that, too. He claimed it was unsafe. Maybe it was.

Whatever I felt when he sold the A-chugger went quickly when, one Saturday morning, he brought the puke green 1949 Ford Coupe, with teardrop spotlights. Together we lowered it, decked and frenched it, painted it gleaming black. At Christmas he surprised me with rolled black-and-white Naugahyde seat covers. Then we painted the inside with white lacquer. Then I had a father. Randall Jarrell wrote that "a man polishing his Mercedes is the last link in a chain that goes back to Achilles patting his divine steeds Balius and Xanthus." My Ford coupe wasn't speedy or agile, but it was mine. It was freedom. In it I discovered manhood, time, distance. I learned you couldn't go fast enough to get anywhere except alone.

Maybe that loneliness, uncaused by any specific I am sure of, led me to read. We were not a literary family; we owned few books, subscribed only to the daily newspaper and two magazines, *Sports Illustrated* and *Hot Rod*. I have occasionally been asked what influenced me to become a writer and the truth is I don't know. How did I manage to read, and today remember, a biography of Simon Bólivar in that home? In high school English I memorized Robert Frost but would never have admitted that. I belonged to the jocks, and no jocks read poetry. I wanted to belong. When I told my girlfriend I liked Thomas Hardy, she thought he was the hero of a boy's mystery story. Maybe she was right. I think those magazines had something to do with my becoming a writer.

My father built bookcases around his fireplace and there he stacked the months, then years, of *Hot Rod*. I dreamed through each issue. *Hot Rod* was a vision of life with ease, speed, power, and confidence. It featured photo layouts of outrageous cars men created at home. One hundred coats of hand-rubbed crushed-oystershell paint, tufted leather upholstery, ingenious gizmos, the ubiquitous engine's bright muscle. There was, to make the editors' point, always a girl in skimpy swimsuit. Often, she cupped her hand on the shift knob. When I had devoured the photographs, I chewed through the technical essays that explained how to chop, to channel, to lower the bodies; how to scallop paint; what made Holley carburetors and Edlebrock manifolds the best. I learned what "blowers" (turbochargers) did. My head reeled with overbore specs, torque grids, disk brakes, and speed-injector tricks.

Everything seemed to be happening in California. Was that why *Hot Rod's* language jumped with an energy I couldn't find in anything we read at school? The message was that a life was out there somewhere down the road. I was excited to read *Great Expectations* and *Macbeth,* but also dulled by my teachers, who asked nothing more than rote memorization. If they loved the sonorous greatness of Shakespeare, nobody knew it. They taught me to divorce literature, which was only pretend words, from actual life. Still, I throbbed with whatever was inside the words about Isky camshafts and jet dragsters. I don't confuse journalism and Shakespeare, but I know the energy of dreaming takes many forms. Dickens would understand why with *Hot Rod,* especially, a boy feels the need for passion's expression. I had no idea this would lead to the speech of the inner life that is poetry. What was poetry?

In 1974 I started a novel about a grotesquely big and inarticulate young man who fell in with a wizened old junkyard mechanic named Tom Zucold after "poor Tom" in *King Lear.* The youth's one passion was cars. Yet he had owned none. Having no language of his own, he borrowed the lingo of cars and spoke that to Zucold, a crazy man who understood. My hero, called "the Grip," liked to say a woman's eyes were "Oldsmobile Marina Blue" rather than simply beautiful. He did not speak poetry, if he spoke at all, but I think he made the world newer as he shifted, shaped, and dug deeper for his true speech. To him words meant, first of all, experience—love, sex, hate, pain, hope, loyalty—and he wanted not merely *adequate* words but especially *appropriate* words. Cars became a song of reality. For him language was a kind of music, but he had no awareness of this.

Coming to an awareness of music's importance to my early life took a long time. Writers often make eloquent testimony to music, usually to the classical tradition or to jazz, and they are musicians before becoming writers. My father gave me the choice of playing football or being in the high school band, which was no choice. Because I have steadily regretted I play no instrument, and have whined about this, my wife gave me a violin several years ago. It lies in its case, untouched. Nevertheless, music played its role in my coming to be a writer, the outlaw music and the rock, both hymns to the life of the body.

At thirteen, I fell in love with a Baptist girl named Celia and with gospel music she and her mother sang. My parents were nominally Lutherans whose worship at the Church of the Holy Suburbs meant sleeping late and cutting the grass. With no other way to be near her, I went with Celia and her mother to service and was finally baptized at the Churchland Baptist Church. She and I had some good nights as we rode in the dark back seat. Once, my oldest friend, Buddy Speers, and I sneaked out, hot-wired his mother's blue Studebaker coupe, and went joyriding. Sex, cars, gospel music, the frailty of men, the incredible sound of the King James Bible all came into my growing awareness of language simultaneously.

It was more or less the same pattern for rock-and-roll, my music. I am a World War II baby boomer. In the late 1950s, I kept my head next to the radio while I read *Hot Rod*. I can hear an oldie even today and it's as if my first life, with all those partners, has danced right up beside me. There were two kinds of rock then, almost legal and not. Norfolk Virginia's WGH played the bubble-gum pop songs. Dion, Fabian, Neil Sedaka, Paul Anka, the city boys, are embedded in my memory, with long weekends of the top thirty and coded dedications. A kind of syrupy save-the-last-dance-for-me, which never comes. Even then, it seemed trivial.

Yet before and behind this music was what we called "nigger" music. It thumped and strutted and wailed a blend of African rhythms, gospel passion, and street innuendo. I can't summon call letters, but I know the station was way down on the low end of the dial. That music was rhythm-and-blues, and it would breed Elvis, the Beatles, the Rolling Stones. I remember a few of the names—Joe Turner, Fats Domino, Little Richard, James Brown—criers, bards with hearts broken and thin allegories of sex, exile, hunger—things they made into my Church of the Night Air. They were all black singers. Even the songs from our Baptist church weren't the same if they sang them. So foreign and unreal to me was that speech, interrupted with snappy hair-straightening commercials, that it might have been beamed down from a black planet. I was helplessly drawn to its incandescent intensity.

Even now if I think of my father he is shaving to "In the Mood," his music. He loved that swing style; he loved all music. That's why he gave me permission on my fourteenth birthday to go with Lonnie Evans, who already drove, to a concert. I doubt my father had heard of Little Richard or that he

suspected Lonnie would sip an illegal beer as he drove to Norfolk's civic au-
ditorium. It turned out this was a black dance, we whites allowed as specta-
tors only. We were herded to an upstairs balcony and all evening we watched
black dancers below us swirling and singing. They were penned in, but we
felt wronged because strolling cops would not allow us to dance.

Little Richard is still in my mind's eye, night black and a moon of elec-
tricity, screaming "Long Tall Sally" and plaintive "Lucille." Other songs are
blurs, not words, sounds that swallowed me. Was it real or something I have
dreamed, something odd and hormonal enough to make that night a mem-
ory? In my mind now, and I *think* in fact then, we watched in astonishment
as Little Richard, howling, piece by piece hurled his costume to an audi-
ence as frenzied as hatchery trout at feeding time. When he glowed in white
briefs, we whistled and shouted like everyone else. We wanted, if briefly, to
be black with those who loved *that* music, a cry of freedom, as we stepped
back into the soft night air. (Years later in a movie about Little Richard's life,
I would see this strip scene performed and grin for all it affirmed.)

If I think of music and cars as images of passion's language, a car also
leads me to something else. On Mother's Day, in May 1960, a glorious morn-
ing, I delivered my usual present to my mother, a yellow climbing rose.
Then my father offered to drive my mother to her mother's house for lunch.
Harry Cornwell had built his rancher forty miles away at the western edge
of Warwick, not very far from Williamsburg. My father's offer surprised us.
At thirty-nine he had become unpleasant and moody, given to what we now
might recognize as depression. He had dreams. And he had us. We were
blocking them. He growled, scuffed golf balls, tinkered with his new white
Alfa Romeo Giulietta Spider. Probably that afternoon he simply wanted an
excuse to get out and drive.

They drove to Menchville Road, stayed a few restless hours, then back,
crossing the five-mile-wide James River and scooting toward the gentle S-
curve just past the Nansemond River Bridge, fifteen minutes from home.
He cruised at a leisurely forty-five miles per hour because the car in front
of him could not be passed on the two-lane road. Suddenly an oncoming
sedan, its elderly driver not wearing his glasses and maybe drunk, pulled out
to pass three cars, lost control, struck the first car, glanced left as if in a game
of bumper cars, ploughed into the rear of the car ahead of my father, then
smashed into the Alfa. Poet William Heyen once remarked to me it was odd
how many poets have early on lost their fathers. My father's head opened on

the windshield and its mirror post. He went into shock, was ineptly treated by a poor emergency-room doctor, and he was dead before dusk.

I remember little of that year or my senior year in high school, although by the archeology of poems I acquire broken pieces which have made a kind of life. I graduated without distinction, was a modest athlete, playing football, basketball, and golf. I spent long nights wondering what I would ever be good at, why I was who I was. Wherever I sought answers, there were none. My sister and I were shadows, falling apart. Did I read? I remember mostly *The Rise and Fall of the Third Reich* and *Macbeth*. I was inseparable from a cheerleader named Marilyn. My mother began dating, trying to live, and perhaps as consolation she gave me a gold 1958 Chevrolet Impala in excellent condition, electric everything, power everything, Hydra-Matic transmission, a stately vehicle. All it lacked was air-conditioning.

I did what my father would have done. I swapped that slick transmission for a used four-speed Corvette box. I bartered for tri-carburetors, a magneto, special camshaft, wheels, tires. I was ready to race away my troubles and I nearly did. Churchland High School's fight song echoes now ("I'm a Trucker born and a Trucker bred / And when I die I'll be a Trucker dead") when I remember I meant to hit the road. I would go to college like everyone did. Except they would go home, at least temporarily; I would leave forever. I have gone back rarely, and only to visit graves. My grandmother, my grandfather, and my father are buried in the Churchland Baptist cemetery. Where what I remember is silence, wind in pines, weeping.

"To hurt the Negro and avoid the Jew / is the curriculum," Karl Shapiro wrote in "University," and we did not doubt he meant the University of Virginia, where I entered as a first-year-man in 1961. We thought we were gentlemen because we wore coats and ties, drank bourbon prodigiously, were faithful to our ugliest prejudices. We were, we said, men of "tradition," our catchall for snobbery, racism, provinciality, and meanness. When he was at the University, Poe claimed he had seen one student bite off another's arm in a fight. Because I wanted badly to belong, I embraced the worst and the best.

I joined Phi Delta Theta social fraternity (which turns out to have been also the fraternity of James Dickey and Reynolds Price). Their study monitoring kept me in school when I was a poor student, but I learned how to blackball on sight anyone in white socks. Once we spent a long night wrangling how to keep blacks out. Of both fraternity and school. Most of my fellow Phis became doctors, bankers, engineers, architects, and, dominantly, lawyers. I took the law boards still intoxicated from a late-night party, the thing we liked to say we did best, but it hardly mattered. There was no money for law school, for which I now thank the powers. I don't doubt I have been the only poet ever in that organization, but I know Poe would have preceded me in membership if that had been possible in 1826.

Most of us were southern boys raised racist. Sometimes we weakly rebelled. One Christmas my mother and I had a violent argument because I claimed blacks were certainly capable of success in a university. I was, she pronounced in frustration, "educated but not intelligent." Those were the days when civil rights demonstrations were drawing college students into the defense of human liberty and into danger. Some of us muttered sympathy, but that was as far as we went. The University would change, officially. But at UVA an attitude of smug superiority is endemic, caused by both a fear of inferiority to the Ivy League schools and an old-boy system that only verbally welcomes the "unwashed." I have no trouble believing, as they claim, that despite difficulty in citing specifics, black students and women, both admitted only in the early 1970s, feel unwelcome. They probably are.

Coming from a family with no college experience, I had little idea what this culture represented. But I loved the green English lawns, the stiff class-engendered formality, the unforgiving honor system (it selectively forgives now). When the cheerleader and I married during my first year, both out of loneliness I think—her parents had left Virginia for Cleveland—we moved into a stone cottage on Rugby Place. When we found a lemon pie on our doorstep it led us to our neighbors, Professor and Mrs. James Southall Wilson. He was the founding editor of the *Virginia Quarterly Review* and a scholar whose knowledge of Edgar Allan Poe was rumored to be unsurpassed. Their decency and gentility was Jeffersonian, and I found it among some others such as Dean I. B. Cauthen.

I, who had dismissed school as serious endeavor, learned learning with teachers whose passion for books so communicated itself that I wanted to become a professor of English. After my second-year English survey course, I asked my teacher, John Crisp Coleman, how I might do that. He coolly replied that I was not smart enough. His was the less Jeffersonian and, to my mind, more typical attitude toward undergraduates at the University. But I was honored to have learned from David Bevington, Douglas Day, Robert Kellogg, and others. Still, not everything you learned at the University of Virginia was worth knowing.

In my third year the cheerleader and I divorced. My fellow students, none of whom I was ever to know well, included Henry Taylor, who won the Pulitzer Prize for poetry, and the medievalist Stephen Barney, who was working beside me in Mincer's Pipe Shop the day John Kennedy was assassinated. At Mincer's I sold records to famous visitors, opening and playing whatever they wanted. I most remember concerts by the Kingston Trio (about which Henry Taylor wrote a fine sonnet), Peter, Paul, and Mary, and Miriam Makeba. That was where I began the unequivocal piece of trash that intended to be a novel, then a handful of poems quite as bad. I watched William Faulkner as he strolled the University's grounds.

During my first two years I had been a woeful student, constantly on the edge of failure—except in literature and writing. Then it was June 1965, and I was abruptly the first college graduate in my family. Only my Cornwell grandparents, befuddled by it all, came to the ceremony, driving quickly home afterward. I'd learned the Hamiltonian iciness inside the noble Jeffersonian values. I'd left Mincer's to work in Red Roman's sporting goods shop. He had once beaten the great tennis master Bill Tilden. I learned to string tennis racquets while I dreamed. I read medieval epics, Kafka, Joyce, Faulkner, Conrad, Margaret Mead, Boethius, and Robert Penn Warren's *All the King's Men*. In those days I mostly avoided poetry in fear I wouldn't see the message teachers seemed to want from poems we discussed.

In the spring of 1965 I had other fears. Certain I'd go to Vietnam, I applied for Air Force Officer Training School, having failed the physical for the Navy and the Marines. I was accepted, but my OTS class date was delayed. My draft board did not recognize that as sufficient, and I was told to get a deferment or be drafted. I was lucky enough to find a job teaching English and French and serving as a coach at Poquoson High School in Poquoson, Virginia. In December, my friends Mary Linda and Billy Carmines arranged a blind date for me with Deloras "Dee" Weaver, a freshman at Christopher Newport College. Three months later we drove to North Carolina and were married. When my OTS class date came through, I declined and taught another year. The U.S. Air Force did not forget that slight.

Somewhere in each of my book titles there is a house. I think of it as the soul's lodging and the emblem of a place. It may be implied or actual but is where I have felt, temporarily, I belonged. No place is more home to me than Poquoson. *The Fisherman's Whore,* my second book of poems, and *Onliness,* my novel, are set there. A village of about four thousand people then, Poquoson is called Bull Island by natives. It is not properly an island but a peninsula surrounded by the Poquoson River, Back River, and the Chesapeake Bay. So much apart from the cultural life of William Styron's nearby Newport News, it may as well be an island. Its citizens have always been watermen, American renegades with hard hands, bowed backs, salty tongues, a tribal capacity for loyalty, courage, and admiration for the work a man or woman could do.

If at first I felt as exiled as the Roman poet Horace, in Poquoson I found a family. Everyone seemed somehow related and all knew their ancestry cold, but a man was not defined by his old school tie, by his station wagon with an estate name on the side (as in Charlottesville), or even by the books he had read. This rough breed of people made, for me, an antidote to the University of Virginia. Walt Whitman would have loved them. I know how racist, provincial, and even desperate they were, and may yet be. If you live on what the sea allows you, it is a lonely, severe life. But often enough it is heroic, human, firsthand life. Even now I but dimly understand how the opposition of Poquoson and Charlottesville forecast the long, unresolvable struggle of the physical and intellectual in my poems. It is reflected in the choice of form, speaker, subject, and each poem dramatizes a case for ultimate belonging. In Poquoson I began, really, to write. I also came to miss the bookish life I had glimpsed in Charlottesville and decided to go to graduate school.

With Dee I felt equipped to do what I might never do alone. We left for St. Louis, arriving in late August 1967. Dee worked for McDonnell-Douglas Aircraft. Lured by a friend from my undergraduate years, I was an M.A. student at Southern Illinois University in Edwardsville, probably the only place that would have me with my record. St. Louis had a proud tradition of jazz and blues, but I had not known it was the birthplace of T. S. Eliot and Marianne Moore. I knew nothing of poets there, John Knoepfle, Donald Finkel, and Philip Dacey, all of whom proved generous in their friendship to a beginner. At Washington University, Dee and I saw poets read: James Dickey, Richard Howard, Robert Bly. Slowly, I became interested in writing poems. I heard encouraging words from my first mentor, Dr. Daniel Havens, professor of American literature, bird hunter, and jazz musician. Professors Nicholas Joost and John I. Ades taught me in excellent courses in Whitman and Milton, respectively. I was made editor of *Sou'wester,* the student literary magazine, though I had no idea what an editor was to do. All of it seemed a very exciting form of play. Then one day Dee handed me the letter that said I had been drafted.

The U.S. Air Force gave me a delayed enlistment, the Marines and the Navy having once more declined my poor eyes, and I finished my master's degree writing a thesis on the poetry of James Dickey. I entered active duty January 1, 1969, at Lackland Air Force Base, Texas, certain President Nixon would quickly get us out of Asia, as he had campaigned. After accounting and finance training at Wichita Falls, Texas, I was posted to Langley Air Force Base, Virginia, four miles from our old house in Poquoson, where we stayed until September 1972, when I was honorably discharged as a staff sergeant. During this time I tried to learn, working at the base during the day, teaching in local college evening classes at night, then reading or writing poems until three or four in the morning. I remember it as a period of exhilaration and fatigue.

I think I knew from my first poems that my subject would be the heroic spirit. Like all poets I had to learn necessary skills, strategies, and structures. My poems began appearing in little magazines, and in 1972 *Mean Rufus Throw Down* was accepted by Basilisk Press, in Fredonia, New York. The title, too clever, came while I drove the Washington beltway and listened to a baseball game. The book was immature work. If I had had the guidance of a mentor at the time, or a kindred community, I might have waited for poems and intellect to mature. Or I might not have. As an enlisted man in the Air Force, my only community was in my head and in the school of the mail. I wrote, mailed, was rejected; revised, started again, remailed. Dee and I published by hand a little magazine we called *The Back Door* and, with clandestine help from a Navy print shop technician (she then worked for the Navy), we published ten *Back Door* chapbooks. Of 250 copies of *Bull Island*, my own 1970 chapbook, I gave away some 50 and took the rest to the dump when I was discharged to return to graduate school.

In 1973 we left home again. I had been rejected at one program but accepted elsewhere. Undecided about whether to study for an M.F.A. or a Ph.D., I decided the Ph.D. meant I could probably teach as I now wanted to do. I chose Ohio University because it was hospitable, and someone had recommended it. Athens, Ohio, in 1972, was a dull burg, and I was bitter toward uniforms, and I resented the "enlisted" status of the graduate student. Jack Matthews, teacher and friend, told me I ought to leave if I could find a job. And he suggested I send a manuscript of poems to the Ohio University Press. *The Fisherman's Whore* appeared in 1974 when I was to be an instructor of English at Western

Michigan University in Kalamazoo, joining poets Stuart Dybek, John Woods, and Herb Scott.

In Michigan I wrote continuously. A long essay on John Woods's poetry taught me about lyric skills. Woods introduced me to the poetry of James Wright and David Wagoner. As always, I sent poems out for publication and placed some. Most were rejected. The elegant *New Yorker* rejection slips dominated. Then a letter arrived from editor and poet Howard Moss, two pages, saying he admired "Cumberland Station"; he would be glad to see others. The poem was not among those returned. But he hadn't said directly he'd accepted it. Had he? How soon would he read others? I waited—it seemed like years—and sent more. He was clear, then. Yes, he had bought "Cumberland Station" and now bought others. *Bought,* he said.

In a small magazine called *The Lamp in the Spine,* which someone at the University of Iowa had published, I had found a perfect replica, with one important difference, of the *New Yorker*'s rejection slip. It used to say, I think, "Thank you. We are not currently accepting this material." The one printed in the Iowa magazine said, "Thank you. We are not currently eating this shit." I had taped the parody rejection slip of *The Lamp in the Spine* to my office door and now, without hesitation, I took it down. I wanted to belong among the poets who published in the *New Yorker.*

In a dozen years I saw Mr. Moss on two occasions for a total of less than three hours and spoke with him on the phone perhaps five times, all briefly. He picked my poems from a pile of manuscripts and made a life in poetry possible. I have been read in Bombay and Big Stone Gap because the *New Yorker* goes where few poetry journals do. Mr. Moss died recently. There are many, like me, who will miss his kind support, who know how childish and self-serving are the complaints by critics such as Charles Molesworth that you had to know somebody and do certain things to be a *New Yorker* writer. Mr. Moss was the most considerate, helpful, and genteel of literary men I have known, and the shyest.

Laurence Lieberman was similarly generous. He had written encouraging letters when I was doing my thesis on Dickey and we'd kept in touch. He knew my position at Western Michigan University was terminal and suggested me for a sudden opening at Cottey College in Missouri. I was invited as an assistant professor and accepted, probably imagining life at a pastoral liberal-arts campus to be perfect. Cottey College turned out to be a tiny two-year finishing school on the Kansas edge of the Missouri plains. I wasn't right for them, and I determined to finish the doctorate. We returned to Ohio where Jack Matthews, Bob Demott, Hollis Summers, and Carol Harter helped me to push hard enough to graduate in June 1976.

During that year in Missouri I wrote day and night, urged by acceptances at good journals. I began to believe in myself. My imagination moved from Poquoson's waters and home, to mountains in Maryland and Virginia where my family began. I was reading Thomas Jefferson's *Notes on the State of Virginia* when I discovered he had believed the Potomac River, navigable from Washington, D.C., to the Chesapeake Bay and the Atlantic Ocean, might actually be connected to the Ohio River, then the nation's frontier. I had heard through family lore that our ancestors arrived by the ocean, settled inland in Lynchburg, Virginia, then migrated to western Virginia, headed north to the mountains, and at last arrived on the same coast, completing a circle. I arranged a book of poems I called *Cumberland Station,* after the railroad station where so many kin had passed, in a mimicking circle of passage.

Cumberland Station was published by the University of Illinois Press in 1976, the year I became director of creative writing at the University of Utah and a new assistant professor of English. I'm not sure I knew Utah was a state until I arrived in Salt Lake City. As in St. Louis, poetry had been alive and well there with Brewster Ghiselin, Henry Taylor, and Robert Mezey. Ghiselin had once run a writers' conference that hosted Allen Tate, William Carlos Williams, Vladimir Nabokov, etc. Of the many faculty writers, I was most welcomed and befriended by poet Richard Schramm, whose capacity to know and say the exact value of a poem exceeds almost any critic I have encountered. Utah, like nearby Idaho, Wyoming, and much of Nevada, is predominantly Mormon, a culture whose unconditional and programmatic answers to life's problems seem to prohibit significant writing. But the University of Utah, under President David P. Gardner, made deliberate efforts to be a national institution, open-minded and progressive. It strongly supported the arts. With that support, and good luck, we attracted truly wonderful student writers, many of whom have had fine careers as academics, poets, critics. They remain close friends. It would have been hard for me not to learn there.

So I was happy and I wrote. The western landscape, sooty brown as a deer's first horns, contrasted sharply to eastern mountains. These mountains were craggy, higher. Air was brighter. People laughed easily, fished, skied, ran, lived the West's informal way. Dee and I got lucky. Our landlord, the father-in-law of fiction writer Ron Carlson, then living in New England but spending the summer in Salt Lake, decided he couldn't after all convince Ron to manage his string of rental properties. When we told George, all I have of his name, we someday hoped to buy a house, he virtually gave us the one we were renting. If that was the best of times, it was a little damped by discovering I was an insulin-and-needle-dependent diabetic. And though we loved our house (with its living room built to accommodate a professional pool table) I was still restless. We moved to a house on a spectacular Wasatch mountainside 5,000 feet up. I was already writing the poems of *Goshawk, Antelope.* I had seen Wyoming only from Interstate 80 but began to have a dream of a Wyoming ranch. A small child played in the yard, throwing handfuls of dirt into the air, closing his eyes before it dusted over him. A sorrowing young mother watched in an upstairs window. She could see miles of empty miles but watched her son. At one point she opened her mouth as if to scream off some hurt near the child, and he, seeing her, forgot to close his eyes and they filled with dirt. Taken with this "snapshot" of a larger story, I wrote a sequence of poems to pursue an absent father, family deaths, loves, intrigues. When the sequence began to feel willful, I abandoned it. But poems I kept seemed to some readers to make my best book. I hope they captured something I felt about the fierce severity of the western landscape and maybe something I had brought there that, so far, imagination had not revealed.

They also led directly to the longer poems of *Dream Flights.* I thought *Goshawk, Antelope* was more opaque than I wanted it to be and I wanted to clarify my poems, but I also expanded them as I worried over technical problems of staging them. Teaching poets as good as those in Utah's graduate program meant every day was a struggle to know and say the right thing in the face of very sophisticated questions. The poems in *Dream Flights* had shorter lines, more overt plots, expanded spaces, a dependence on repeated imagery, relaxed rhythms. Too, I was going backward in time to my childhood and in space to places I had loved. These poems were flights in dreams and dreams of flight—but from what?

I told my students it was important to write something when poetry wouldn't come, even letters. Now, between books, I took my own advice. Poems came from remembering, but I invented a fiction in drafts of *Onliness,* a novel published by the Louisiana State University Press in 1981. I wrote review-essays for the *American Poetry Review* and other literary magazines.

In a journal I put something down every day after I finished work on poems. It became an argument, a forum for ideas I didn't know I had, a confronting of problems, notes on writers and their new books. I typed more than three hundred single-spaced pages. These, squeezed to forty pages, became the title piece of *Local Assays: On Contemporary American Poetry.* The University of Illinois Press published it in 1985, my fifth book with the press.

Just as I was preoccupied with clarity, something nearly impossible to achieve in a poem, I became concerned with two other issues. The first was the gulf between memory's version of events and imagination's. The second was homesickness. *Local Assays* was begun, perhaps, as a way to get at the first problem, one I had long worried. One afternoon I was chatting with Terry Hummer, a fellow southerner. I told him about a racial incident that had happened at a strip shopping center in my hometown. Photographs of that incident appeared in *Life.* The more I talked about it, the more an idea for a poem pressed up. Terry and I walked to the library, convinced we could easily look up the photos so clear in my memory. But we did not find them. That night I continued to recall images like snapshots.

I wrote "The Colors of Our Age: Pink and Black," and the *New Yorker* bought it. Later the magazine's fact-checking office told me which *Life* issue carried the photographs. I was stunned to find them not violent at all, as I had thought, even radically unlike what I had described—in fact, if not spirit. Yet I hadn't intended to "invent" anything. I meant to be *clear.* Often enough family members and friends have told me what I presented in poems as factual was not the fact they knew. When I wrote about this problematic gap, I became interested in how language and reality do not comfortably coexist. I had been writing about it in poems like "The Perspective and Limits of Snapshots." Perspective is, I think, a central issue in my poems, one that remains unresolved. For writers, perspective has many aspects. One of them is a necessary self-regard which permits accomplishment but does not overvalue the self when prizes and awards come, gifts as much serendipity as those of the muse. I have been fortunate to have been awarded fellowships by the National Endowment for the Arts in 1976 and 1981, a fellowship from the Guggenheim Foundation in 1981, a fellowship to the Bread Loaf Writers' Conference in 1976, and a Lyndhurst Fellowship in 1987. I was honored to receive in 1979 an award for excellence from the American Academy and Institute of Arts and Letters. And as grateful as I am, recognition from those who have worked at the writer's trade is the best support.

In 1981, prompted by novelist John Gardner, I moved to the State University of New York at Binghamton. Here, poet-novelist John Vernon told me, "It's like Hopper country come to life." Gardner suggested we try Montrose, Pennsylvania, for a place to live. Why had I come east? I was homesick for this coast, for my family. I believed if I stayed in the West much longer I would never go back to the South. Moreover, my children would never know family or family's places. It was four days by car from Utah to Virginia. Or Pennsylvania, where most of Dee's people were. These were inept excuses.

Montrose, south of New York's SUNY-Binghamton, is a lyrical country town of just over two thousand souls, the Susquehanna County seat. Houses were not available for rent. I scoured the real estate on that hot August day when we arrived in the Endless Mountains. Dee and the kids walked. I found them talking to Sue Smith, daughter of the late Judge Edward Little, whose three-story Victorian was for sale. Sue had steadfastly declined to rent it. Sue's house and her father's stood next door to each other. Dee waited, nothing else to do. Sue's girls had just gone off to college. Our girls played with Mitzi, the dog. A certain inevitability, I guess. Sue relented. We rented. I wrote a book of poems called *In the House of the Judge.* I felt as much at home in that house as anywhere I have ever been. But, as John Vernon said, SUNY was Hopper country. To me that meant gray and implacable.

That spring I was invited to be director of creative writing at the University of Florida. Meanwhile Ted Solotaroff asked if I might be interested in publishing poetry with Harper and Row. I left a fine press to become an entry in Harper and Row's catalog. *In the House of the Judge,* with the judge's house on the cover, appeared in 1983, was never promoted, and was remaindered within two years. *The Roundhouse Voices: Selected and New Poems* appeared from Harper and Row in 1985. Solotaroff wooed me with a destiny I wanted. I thought poetry was always deciding and undeciding, a good editor helping in the process. But Solotaroff, with no explanation, decided to abandon me. The next manuscript I sent was returned in a week. No phone, no mail answered.

We moved to Gainesville, Florida, with the intention of spending our lives there. In January, at Virginia Commonwealth University to read poetry, I was asked if I might be interested in coming home to teach. Instantly, I thought, I knew why I had left Utah. Just as in the circular passage that Jefferson imagined possible and that I had felt in *Cumberland Station,* I was circling back where my family began. But VCU asked again. My wife and

I knew we could not pass up this opportunity. I thought it was a decision smartly made for my family, but hindsight shows it was nostalgic and not very smart.

In 1982 I moved my family to Richmond, a city I had passed through countless times, though never spending a full day. We settled just an hour distant from my grandfather Harry Cornwell, now in his eighties, from my mother and her husband, from Dee's parents, brother, sister, and their children. Virginia Commonwealth University, once Richmond Professional Institute and just decades old as a state university after its merger with the Medical College of Virginia, was the only urban university in the state. I would be a professor of American literature and creative writing in a new MFA program, soon discovering talented students Ron Smith and Elizabeth Morgan. Restless enough to move house three times in our first six years in Richmond, we continued to look for home. I published a small book of poems, *Gray Soldiers,* in 1983, concerned with local history. In 1984, a small press did a limited edition of stories and poems called *Southern Delights.* In 1985, I was the first nonmedical Distinguished Scholar of the University, an honor as well for the courage of my grandfather, who did not remain bogged in Appalachia's Depression, who moved on, throve, alone, with imagination.

There are poets who proclaim an intention to avoid literary life. Whitman stands in that line. But what is literary life? Is it serving on prize juries? Cocktail parties for writers? Book tours? Brokering books, grants? Traveling as literary ambassador? Entreating younger poets to write favorable review-essays? Battering suspected enemies in print? We all know those who this description fits. It sounds ugly, and it may be. But poets work in many ways to serve the art, to keep imagination alive. Their partnership with each dreamer, reader or not, sustains the ancient pulse of community, which is imagination and its moves. Our poets have not yet become comfortable with imaginative words as honorable labor. Robert Frost claimed he was a "farmer." Wallace Stevens was a lawyer. William Carlos Williams was dedicated to obstetric medicine. Poets struggle with self-doubt and also with doubt in the value of the art. They work hard, mostly, to make the best poem, poem after poem, and to see it published, to find readers. They suffer when it is dismissed by the malicious and inept, the often woefully ill-informed, agenda-driven critics and gunslingers eager to make an impression. Some poets do little in husbandry of the art except to declare innocence and their love of the poetry of the real thing. James Wright said a good poetry demands a good criticism, yet he, like most of his generation, wrote little about poets or poems, leaving the dirty work to the least among us, the ambitious pretenders, the editors who, overwhelmed, no longer edit with taste, vision, or truth.

Is there, then, a "real thing," a poem independent of vagaries and fashion, a poem that fuses the felt life and the percolating significance always shadow to life's events, a poem in which the self stands forth like Whitman stating, "I am the man, I suffered, I was there"? The poem of the "real thing" will have to embrace the moving targets any man or woman is in time. I am what my people were not: educated, devoted to books, music, painting they would not think worth anyone's time. I am, to them, an intellectual creature. My life is literary. My daily activities consist almost entirely of reading books, writing books, writing about books, with teaching, public readings, conferences, and even visits to Gotham City. As a result my acquaintances tend to be writers, editors, teachers, students. We may fish, play tennis, garden, but what we do for our deepest pleasure we also do as our life's work. We are constantly, directly engaged in what seems the real thing, though perhaps never completely certain what it is. I belong to a competition to say life's secrets outright. Randall Jarrell praised the poem that distinguished between real life and "newsreel" life. We want real life, only that.

This has led me, I think, to write of the spirit of place, particular places I might call home. Frost famously said home was where, when you had to go there, they had to take you in. The spirit of belonging, he implies, is not controvertible even if it is unpleasant. Mine is a regionalist's perspective. The provincial voice has interest in local color. The regionalist assumes the immediate object, life, and landscape are alive with the shapes of both historical and transhistorical reality. When I have written of personal ceremonies wherein the watermen of Poquoson buried a boat, I have done so to witness a mystery. But I have written as if no burial or cemetery was ever different on this globe. To know the real thing takes a continuous examination of the past in the present as primary evidence. We proceed with conviction that we may discover an unknown relationship between life and death, a redemptive act.

And what of my actual life, then? I live in a colonial house in a colonial suburb named Midlothian, Virginia. Because this was the site of the first coal mines in the New World, there are extensive tunnels everywhere, some of them unmapped, unsecured, and a dangerous landscape for the unwary. My wife of twenty-two years, Dee, and my children Jeddie, Lael, and Mary Catherine live with me. Our life seems ordinary, like anyone's.

As I write, my son has come into the room to tell me he has a date. He wears the varsity letter jacket of the Monacan Chiefs. The Monacan, one of Powhatan's subtribes, like the Kecoughtan, the Chickahominy, and the Pamunkey, was banished from this earth by the forces that brought the English "Midlothian" here. My son has completed his senior season of basketball. He will probably play on no more teams. He will go to college, to new life. Is this home for him, having lived in ten houses in seven states during his eighteen years? He speaks a soft British-Virginia drawl that last summer, when he studied at the Bennington College Program for young painters, identified him as a southerner.

My fifteen-year-old daughter Lael is a beautiful, bookish freshwoman at Midlothian High School, strangely called the Trojans. There is no clear connection between this place and Troy. But it is deeply American, the wish to possess a great dream-standing in the memory of the world. My daughters sound and act like people who cannot think of Virginia as other than home, even as it reaches with every gesture beyond regional limitations.

Mary Catherine, at ten, really doesn't remember any other place. But they will also depart for college, careers, homes maybe far away. They will create lives more and more unlike those of my grandparents and their grandparents. But in some ways not so different. It is in the intersections of difference and likeness, change and stasis, and in the located stories of our pasts that we will find what we all need: the particulars of home, the real thing.

Poetry has taught me, finally, that home is only inside my head, streets I walked, swamps I smelled, waters I lolled in. It's a place formed of circumstance and contingency. Last fall I returned with my wife for her father's funeral. It was a mild Atlantic day in December, like a sudden happiness, with occasional sharp gusts of cold air. We drove old roads where we had fallen in love, despaired, guessed at the future. I saw the collapsing face of a nineteenth-century house, remembered it spooked me as a kid, and remembered that, older, I wanted a homeplace as grand as that had been for someone. We saw the Hampton Fire Station, a community monument I loved, now a pink boutique shop. Even that was better than farms despoiled by mall developers, none of whom live near their rubbish. No better almost than rapists in my view, they will pave your home if you will sell it to them. And many, for enough money, have proven willing to do that. Frost did not say they have to take you in unless a better alternative can be found. Times change.

Americans place elders in graduated living residencies, nursing homes, human pens. In Frost's day, they stayed in the home until the end.

Poems, however, are not valuable because they recover or describe or yearn for a home to belong to. They are valuable as enactments of the deep reverberations of living which we seek to understand. I once said I would never write about suburban life because it seemed as bland as the Eisenhower era. After my book *The Fisherman's Whore,* I have hardly done anything else. The reason is simple enough, and banal. Life is mysterious and death, with its fellow actor, change, is equally so. The lives and deaths of those one has loved, who meant that *belonging,* are the most natural, the most compelling of subjects. Most of my writing has been about family because it is the source of obligations, my duty, what they made me to be: name-taker and place-keeper. I came to this role when I tried to write about my grandmother's death in 1969. My first published poem was about her, a celebration of her gift of life, though I did not know that was what I was trying to do.

If I sift through all the memories and inventions and dreams, a dark, double-storied, hall-echoing house rises before me. Then we are moving away from it abruptly. The night is achingly cold and blowy and wet. People are about, dressed darkly and heavily, but no lights at the windows; half-shadows are fixed on car headlights. Men, if there are any moving near, wear uniforms. A few carry weapons, a grim look on their faces. It is the holiday season, with hung holly wreaths, mistletoe, and wrapped gifts. The local bars are full of sailors from Iowa and Arizona and Kentucky, places they describe like distant heavens, drinking more than they should. They talk of their mothers, and back home, and girls they belong to. They sing. Then, surprisingly so near the ocean, it snows hard, layering trucks, jeeps, roofs, Quonset huts, even the big house we have just left. This is a thick, special, memorable snow. Our home is not attacked by the Germans or the Japanese that everyone is terrified will come ashore in the blackness. My mother makes it to the Kings Daughters Hospital on December 19, 1942. My grandmother begins the calls home to Cumberland, spreading the word. I am born.

Statements from the Field

AN INTERVIEW WITH TODD MARSHALL AND ROB CARNEY

MARSHALL: You've written short stories, novels, and many "narrative" poems. What do you think the difference is between how narrative works in poetry and how it works in other genres? Exactly how detailed a "story" do you feel compelled to tell in a poem? When does exposition, in poetry, become tedious?

SMITH: There has been a discussion—particularly among lyric poets—in recent years about narrative and lyric as genre definitions. I think of narrative as "what happens," a sequence of events. As a poet sometimes identified with the regional literature of the South, to be called a narrative poet feels to me a limiting jacket. I think any writer is likely to bristle, maybe without justification, at what he or she is labeled. So, sometimes when I speak about narrative it sounds like I am rejecting it. I do not mean that at all. Warren, in his poem about Audubon, says, "Tell me a story of deep delight." He recognizes that experience is organized, made understandable, made accessible when it's given narrated shape. That is a primary reason I write poems, to narrate comprehension. On the other hand, even my longest poems, if distilled to the plot, would take only a few seconds to say, whereas the poems themselves ask you ten to fifteen minutes. They are not essentially narrative but are lyric poems that take narrative occasion to experience language possibility.

I'm much more interested in quality of expression, in the way something is said, than what is said. But I don't reject narrative. Poet Ellen Bryant Voigt, and author of *The Flexible Lyric,* and I have had a running dialogue about this issue. Ellen feels there is too great a propensity among younger poets to move toward narrative. That may well be true. If it is true, I may have anticipated a shift in the mid-1970s when, starting to find my kind of poem, I looked away from the dominant lyric and image style. There were fewer poets then who were interested in what is now called the narrative poem.

I have been amused by a rump movement called "the neo-narrative." What they seem to want to do, I am uninterested in. I don't think Stanley Plumly went far enough in his definition of the prose lyric, but I agree with his principle. He named me as a poet who was trying to marry what Warren called "the imperfection of experience," which he more or less equated with prose, to a lyric orchestration. This was a way of trying to get more into the poem, rather than less. Image poets moved in the opposite direction. It wasn't so much to get more story in, though that was one strategy, but an attempt to reach a fuller, richer, more complete verbal experience in the poem than seemed then prominent. Prose, in the sense Warren used the word, refers more to rhythm and tone than to subject matter, although that is included. At that time Bly, Merwin, even James Wright wrote poems of a lyrical image that some of us didn't want to write. Not that we didn't like their sort of poem, we just didn't want to write it.

Narrative is a way of maximizing experience. One of the firmest convictions I have is that phenomena, the physical world as I can present it, expresses. I need to know not only what to look at and what to hear but how to hear it. I regard the poem as a "hearing" of something being said by whatever is around me, whatever's going on. This is distastefully mystical and yet accurate. I don't minimize the role of the poet as maker. My experience of the poem is that at some point it's being dictated and at some point it's being refined, or made; the turning where the one shifts to the other is different in every poem. Perhaps this is why a poet will write in different forms rather than find satisfaction in only one. On this point I would disagree with Richard Wilbur, a great authority, who regards form, not matter, as art's character. The poet narrating seeks to find a way not merely to manifest but also to make understood the resonant layers of experience. There's a kind of narrative poet—let's say Robert Service—who tells a good story, a story you want to hear at any bar or with friends, but he doesn't concern himself greatly with the language. That's not his primary interest. He's not particularly drawn to the resonant layers of language by which one tries to say secondary and tertiary things; he wants to hurry ahead to what happens. One might write a poem about three old ladies, like grandmothers, remembered from childhood. Roethke did, and spoke indirectly of relationships with ancestors, the past, life's bitter changes. Service isn't interested in that. He's interested in story that leaves you on the edge of your seat with suspense and excitement.

MARSHALL: So you're suggesting there are several types of narrative poetry?

SMITH: Yes. It's misleading to think we're always talking about the same thing under the rubric of narrative poetry, though that's the usual case when lyric poets speak of narration. People assume we all do the same thing, as it's said all southerners have narrative. Perhaps this is the legacy of fiction from Twain to Faulkner and onward. That isn't so. Charles Wright will tell you, "I can't write a narrative." I think that is untrue. As his books will show, he can and does write stories in poems, but he's resisting the myths that diminish what he intends. I believe in the power of the tale for certain aesthetic and structural reasons. It enables the poem I want to write. I do not think of myself as a narrative poet, or a poet who also writes fiction. I haven't vigorously worked at being a fiction writer. Nor do I pretend to expertise in fiction, where my skills are limited and my talent modest. I am interested in what story does to a poem as a formal organizer.

Ellen Voigt maintains—as she said in an essay in *The Southern Review*—that narration and poetry are somewhat contradictory terms. She identifies herself as a lyric poet and, in small ways, this denies her book of poems, *The Lotus Flowers,* which is more narrative in style than her other books. But it is a book of poems, still. She says, "It was just an experiment; I wanted to see if I could tell stories." I'm suspicious. She knows what she can do, and she does it very well. Her strength, perhaps, has been in understatement, vignette, tone. I have tended to write longer poems, and these require developing other strengths, notably action, character, and scene. Recently, however, I determined I would not do those poems anymore. My new book is formed entirely of thirteen-line poems.

CARNEY: "Terrible" sonnets?

SMITH: Some readers will no doubt think them terrible. But they are not sonnets. There is a shadow of the sonnet's operation in the background. I don't claim I am uninformed about what the sonnet does, but I only wanted to write short poems, and I wanted to write them in such a way that they might echo other forms in miniature. It was an arbitrary decision, the desire to do something different. I have written short poems previously but not so determined as this work.

CARNEY: One of the things you mentioned is the formal matter of a poem. What kind of formal qualities do you give the most attention to while writing, or is that something that comes secondarily when you're revising the poem?

SMITH: I want to say yes and no at the same time. The most honest answer is that over a period of years you train what might be called "literary" muscles which know what to do before you ask them to do it. My first sense, without being conscious about it, is to seek form. In this new book, once I knew that I was going to write in a thirteen-line form, I only twice sought a fourteen- or other-numbered line poem. The form was given, the arena I would work in was set, and decisions I had to make about thirteen-line form were different from the decisions you make when you see the blank page and know only that you are going to start to write.

People begin poems in many ways. There are poets who habitually write whatever comes to them in prose, then shape that into a recognizable poetic form. That's never been possible for me. Interestingly, Warren's drafts of *Audubon* show that is how he began that poem, though it was not his usual practice. My pattern has been to respond to an image, a visual image of place. I seek verbal representation of what I "see." Often what comes is puzzling to me, incomplete, or surplus. This is where the shift to narrative happens. I tend to invent a story to explain what has come to me, why it matters.

In 1972 or 1973, an image came into my head of six men buried head-to-head in a circle so they lay like wedges in pie that had been cut—they were buried that way. I knew that they were related, and I knew they were significant to me, but I had no idea who they were or what they meant. It was a twenty-two-line draft poem at that point. Short lines, short poem. I put it in my desk drawer, as I habitually do, and took it out a few days later. Nothing happened. I couldn't budge it; it wouldn't talk. I continued to do that periodically, shuffling through other drafts, looking for something to write each day, and then something else happened. I realized this poem was linked to softball. I cannot tell what the connection was, but once I knew it I began to see the poem wanted to remember an uncle of mine. When I was a child, on at least one occasion my family went home to Cumberland, Maryland, to bury one of the kin, and my uncle took me to play softball inside the B&O railroad roundhouse where he worked. From that came a poem called "The Roundhouse Voices," a ninety-one-line poem, that relatively speaking, is a "narrative" poem. It's a funeral elegy, a traditional form with most of the characteristics of historical practices. When I first saw that little image, I had no idea I was writing a funeral elegy.

To return to your question—it's a puzzle to me how I turned to a form centuries old. Where did the narrative and my interest in funeral elegy merge?

I had read such lyrical poems, of course, but I was not consciously aware of attempting to write one. I couldn't then have told you I knew the form's characteristics. Probably my habits of reading had something to do with my "discovery." It may have been I made the leap when reading "Lycidas" or even Thomas Gray's "Elegy in a Country Churchyard," poems I had frequently studied. But what led to my own loosening of the form, or forcing it to be mine, I don't know. It's probably buried in biography, if I may pun.

To come at it another way, existence of form is not something, even in terminology, everyone agrees on. To a neo-verse writer, form means verse and anything else is imitation. Poet David Middleton said in a Louisiana magazine recently that there is verse and there is all the other stuff that is not poetry. I do not agree that form is a synonym for verse. Whitman is a poet, but he is not a verse writer. Dickinson is a poet and sometimes is not a verse writer. What of Wordsworth? Neruda? Sylvia Plath? I think that poetry is synonymous with form, but there are different kinds of form and they do different things, and the responsible intellect tries to understand how form can be employed to produce desirable results. If that's correct, as soon as the poet puts the first word on the page and adds a second word, there is movement toward form. It's part of the poet's responsibility to equip himself with a sufficient knowledge of form to know, when the tool comes to hand, what it permits and does not permit you to do. That is how you prepare yourself for the opportunity to write a poem. I don't say that will produce the poem, only that you now have the tool and the chance.

The best poets are those able to make form maximize whatever is given to them to write. There are no poets who write outside of form. There are some who write sloppily, poorly, but if it's poetry it's form in some way. If not, it's not poetry. A good deal of what gets published is, of course, not poetry. Looks like poetry, acts like poetry, talks like poetry, but isn't poetry. Unfortunately, contemporary training of scholars and writers doesn't equip them to distinguish the false from the real thing. This is one of the effects of democratization of art, a relativism which values art's accomplishment less than a quota tote for all who make the attempt. This is one reason why applied criticism is so poor. Poets certainly are aware that without good criticism the art of the poem languishes, poetry grows weaker.

MARSHALL: You've written about Robert Penn Warren and Edgar Allan Poe—a postmodernist poet and one whom many would point to, because of his relationship with Symbolism, as a significant "pre-modern" poet—however,

I can't recall anything you've written on any of the modern poets. I was wondering if you had any favorites or felt any particular indebtedness to any of them or if you feel your relationship with them is more antagonistic.

SMITH: You point out something that surprises me. One of my Ph.D. examination questions asked something like, "Who is the better poet, Eliot or Williams?" One had to explain. My answer was Yeats. I haven't written about modern poets, and I'm not sure why. I certainly feel close to Yeats and the Yeatsian sense of what poet and poem are. Less so to Eliot, although I don't think you can be close to Yeats without being close to Eliot; they share a preoccupation with keeping form alive, awareness of historical sensation and place, the fragmentation of experience and the necessity of poems as ways to examine what the soul knows, the poem of intuition and impression. This is so for Pound, as well, but I confess I have never had much interest in Pound, whom Gertrude Stein called "the village explainer."

Your question forces me to think about why I do not find much of modernist art (it is not only poetry but also painting and music that sometimes fails to compel me) attractive. I just did the 32nd Wallace Stevens reading at the University of Connecticut—it's not just a reading; you have to talk a little bit about Stevens—and it caused me to reread all of Stevens, a poet I have not been devoted to. In fact, I was just yesterday on a thesis defense that dealt with Stevens. I still don't warm up to him as I think I ought to do. Perhaps you can feel me dividing up these poets into teams, Yeats and Eliot, Stevens and Pound. What do I do with Williams? I put him with Eliot and Yeats, although many poets would place him with Stevens and Pound. Maybe he's a utility man. But what do you do with Frost, to whom I feel closer than to any of them. Modernist or pre-modernist? A good argument, perhaps, either way.

So what is a modern poet? I return to Robert Penn Warren. He begins as a modern poet, if we speak in terms of literary history. Warren was publishing his first poems as Thomas Hardy was publishing his last. It's interesting to think of them as overlapping, an overlapping not that far from Gerard Manley Hopkins. With Hopkins you ask again is he modern or is he not? *The Norton Anthology of Modern Poetry* begins with Walt Whitman, in the middle of the nineteenth century; it's an arbitrary categorization to say what is modern poetry and what isn't, but I think you mean a kind of poet who wrote a kind of poetry in the early part of the twentieth century, a poet marked by contradictory or ambiguous attitudes toward form. Allen Tate, one of the definers of modernism, recognized the impossibility of settling on adequate or appropriate form in any uniform way. He knew the reliance on an individual intuition which had led to and then collapsed Puritan culture in America, which was also responsible for the democratic juxtaposition of the one and the many as the central character of our government, would create a potential chaos of forms. That has proven exactly so. And in our time, with a dearth of critics able or willing to read poetry well, the result has been both to diminish form and to claim form value in what is often the least accomplished writing. Tate's sense of uncertainty, for these poets and others like Marianne Moore and H.D., that range of people seeking form in different directions and seldom finding its common ground, though politically, economically, and historically they had it, seems to me remarkable.

Maybe among poets of my age that range of exploration isn't as great, although there seems an entirely open field, as may be seen in a virtual disappearance of inhibition, not to say critical prohibition, with form's limits. In any case I am not unaware of the modern poets and not hostile to them, with some minor exceptions. I don't care for the Olson project at all. I respect but have little enthusiasm for Pound's poems, and Dr. Williams, as pure as his image work may be and as congenitally American as his vision is, lacks the texture I desire. There is another texture and strategy in Stevens, by whom I am less moved than perhaps I ought to be. I admire him but have little affection for poems of such artifice, poems so antiseptically removed from human rawness that I do not trust them. On the other hand, Frost never loses appeal. I never lack interest in Robinson Jeffers, D. H. Lawrence, and Edwin Muir.

One of the most interesting poets I have read, Jeffers saw himself as antimodernist, by which he meant he preferred traditional poetic sounds, forms, values. But there was more. He saw himself as a lingering Anglo-Saxon. This should be understood to mean both the harshly alliterative and stressed line texture and also the heroic isolation of man at the edge. He saw himself connected to a tradition behind the moderns rather than with the moderns—a line of classical connections that he felt profoundly. There's something even more antimodern in his sense of poetry as the expression of individual passion that he felt the moderns resisted. He must have known Eliot's argument in "Tradition and the Individual Talent" and Joyce's in *A Portrait of the Artist as a Young Man*. Though much of Jeffers seems to me severely flawed by willingness to make the poem a soapbox for political and social opinion, I feel connected through him to origins of English idiom and western thought. "The Seafarer," that Anglo-Saxon elegy, is a point of connection.

Most American poets don't speak much of Anglo-Saxon language. Perhaps they no longer know about it. It used to be commonly taught in graduate literature programs and alluded to, if not taught, in courses in the history of the English language. The curriculum reforms of the 1960s and the further relevance reforms, as well as diversity pressures, tossed out such courses; this means that often younger poets have no idea why their language operates as it does. I feel acutely a connection to the Anglo-Saxon power in my language. There's a line that runs from that language that was fully alive until about 1066 directly to English Romanticism; then there's a hiatus. The muscle of the language begins to dissipate; its characteristics wane. I mean the vocabulary and rhythm of English speech, the cadence of our expression, changes some. But I also mean a disposition to a core of poetry, something we might think of as internal or intuitive form, starts to shift. Poe experienced this in America before others. Poe was important to me, and Mr. Tate called him "our cousin," not only because he was a southerner. One doesn't avoid Poe; he is always there. Yet it isn't exactly the poetry, which is suspicious if not bad as a rule, but the simultaneous acceptance and tweaking of language at that core. This enterprise Mr. Whitman would advance, although he moved away from Anglo-Saxon toward a plain idiom closer to American poetic "sound."

The modernists Yeats, Hopkins, Lawrence, and Jeffers manifest a strong Anglo-Saxon sound (excepting Pound's finger exercises). As the line fragments under the explorations of the Romantic poets, Whitman and Dickinson and others, an older tradition passes through Hopkins, Hardy, Yeats, and somewhat through Frost. Those poets, as *The Norton Anthology of Modern Poetry* implies, may be called modernists, and I feel a visceral connection to their practices. Of course the definitions of modernism are many, and my answer may not satisfy your question.

MARSHALL: I guess when I was asking about the modernists, I was asking about the early-twentieth-century group—Pound, Eliot, Yeats, Stevens, Moore, Williams, Crane—poets who generally produced their great work in the period David Perkins refers to as "High Modernism," poets who were very interested in formal experimentation, the use of the fragment, making the poem a very dense textual object.

SMITH: At the risk of taking up psychoanalytic criticism, one can say the sons reject the fathers. Bly and Wright and those working with image in the 1960s were early inheritors of that fragmentation, that elliptical poetry. I suspect I have rejected those choices, though neither entirely so nor deliberately so. I never rejected James Wright's lyricism exactly, because there's this other condition in Wright which is the so-called prose lyric that he ultimately settled on. You can see the same process occurring in other poets of Wright's generation, Robert Lowell for example. Early Lowell is all that embedded, literary, Eliotic stuff—and a lot of his early poems are fragmented and elliptical in the shadow of that greatest collection of fragments, *The Waste Land*—and there are the poems of *Life Studies,* which seek to be more unified, narrating, open, to create formal "wholes" rather than fragments. I responded favorably to that Lowell. Maybe what happened in the 1970s when I was learning how to write my poems was a response to the fathers that were still around. Maybe I selected those that seemed to offer what I wanted and rejected those that didn't.

There is a possible third answer. The modernists I read and admired and was first influenced by were fiction writers. Faulkner foremost, then Conrad, then Joyce. I started out trying to write novels. As an undergraduate I would have killed to stay out of a poetry class. I was terrified of poetry. Or, to be specific, of teachers who seemed to expect a single answer to their Socratic vacuuming of a poem. I never had that answer. Others, maybe. I felt intimidated well into graduate school; I didn't understand the secrets, the arcane language everyone got except me. Fiction was my access to all kinds of formal theory and structuring. At the point when I was able to come to poetry, I was twenty-eight years old, married, a father, in military service. I then had self-confidence enough to question teachers, poets, and poems. I was able to look at the moderns through a formed character, with aesthetic and political values of my own. Perhaps the revolutionary impulses of the moderns were not so revolutionary to me by then, although the mysterious push to make the poem "new" does not lose its allure or its evasiveness. It is there in Frost, abated, there in Yeats, restrained, and there in Eliot, liberated.

CARNEY: It seems that Frost and in some ways Yeats are doing what you're talking about—they're storytelling, but they're not. Their work is not strictly narrative, but there often is that narrative beginning or narrative catalyst in the poems. There is, especially in Frost, that storytelling impulse, but with an attention to lyricism.

SMITH: Exactly, and I'll add, for lack of a better word, "regionalism." Both Frost and Yeats are close to a local world. They are valuable because they transcend the local, but they begin, firmly, in that local landscape. From the first, that strategy interested me. I wanted to write about what was around me; it took time to understand that wasn't enough by itself, that the artist lifts the work to a more transcendent expression. The modernists, of course, had all done that. They tended to be universalists rather than regionalists, and almost by virtue of their impersonal aesthetic and disorienting structure choices. Many of Stevens's poems, by design, are unlocated; they float in the art world of the imagination. This we must understand as an emphasis, not an absolute characteristic. Eliot is the poet of London very specifically, in the twentieth century, as no one else is. But most of us read *The Waste Land* as a poem set in the mind's landscape, one London cabbies do not have on their famous licensing test. Is there a local place in Stevens? In Pound? Williams even writes the history of Paterson, New Jersey, and that is the specific gravity of a poem whose intentions are clearly mythological and universal. The moderns understood they sacrificed a ground, a grounding, for the gain of ideological representation; this was part of making the poem "new."

CARNEY: Richard Hugo's poetry and James Wright's poetry seem very centered in a specific place—the Northwest and Ohio. I see, looking at your work, a sense of place as central, whether it be the Virginia coastline or Utah.

SMITH: If James Wright had given us only vignettes of Polish drunks in bars and football stadiums, we would not remember him. He'd be as forgotten as Edgar Lee Masters is. What Wright does transforms the Ohio River valley into a contemporary, nearly mythical, equivalent of the classical underworld, the land of the barely living and the dead. Wright's poetry forms a human history and a myth in much the same way Joyce's *Ulysses* is an overlay of Homer's *Odyssey*. The power in that is the presentation of recurrent truths outside of the restrictions of time and place. But there is also the power of the local and known story, the songs we sing in time and place. You can read Wright at either level, and at levels within those primary organizations. I had a wonderful teacher, Robert Kellogg, who showed me how Dante's *Divine Comedy* developed four consistent levels of expression, the first of which was as regional as Florence. I am certain that lesson tells me what a good poem tries to do.

Richard Hugo, a poet I admire, did not have the success that Wright did. But he was certainly trying to accomplish the same mythical power in the local landscape. Hugo became the undisputed voice of Montana, Idaho, Washington, reflector of a huge and harsh expanse of country where people, simply put, did not survive and did not accomplish. What good is such a life? his poems ask. Then, as in "Degrees of Gray in Philipsburg," they tell us the good is in a meal, a woman's red hair, a powerful car, time to live a little. Horace would understand.

CARNEY: What about Philip Levine?

SMITH: I have written a little about Levine, and I have great admiration for his poems. I have also had reservations. Levine is a more formal poet than Hugo or Wright, surprising as you may think that opinion. He has always made a pre-writing decision about form. I don't think you find much variety in his form, and Americans have a false idea that variety means excellence. Few of us would fail to recognize a Levine poem after perhaps a dozen lines, its stichic repetitions, its plain vocabulary, its masterful and guiding syntax. Then there's the democratic feel for laboring people, sometimes rhetoric, the scenes of a life we feel we have literally walked in. He is a fastidious crafts-man. Also a religious poet, meaning an awe before the mysteries of life and the bigness of existence. He is also an anarchist, and I would not want him as president. Or mayor. Interestingly, Levine has a special strength with the po-etry of anger. Nobody can write anger poems like he can. This talent places aligns him with Old Testament prophets, acerbic judgment and righteous indignation scalding us for transgressions.

It is not unusual for Levine to be spoken of as a poet of place. While that is certainly accurate, there is room for some question as to whether he is less a poet of place than a poet of social and religious ideas despite the placement of many poems, in all of his books, in urban Michigan, especially a book like 1933, which more or less happens in Detroit. He does not, as some say, write all his poems about the hard life of work in a Detroit transmission shop. It's worth remembering that he worked in such a shop only a few years and has been a practicing professor of literature and writing for more than forty years at Fresno State University. My point is that Levine has made good capital out of biographical and regional experience. He likes to begin a poem very lo-cally in details and scene, but what he can do then is often astonishing. For instance, "They Feed They Lion"—a poem intensely about black people who are hungry in an urban American city. This poem emerges from the 1967 riots in Detroit, but Detroit is not specifically mentioned, and indeed the movement over diverse and distant landscapes which details the migrations of hope is not locally identified. Levine turns the landscape into a Biblical apocalypse. Who else in this country has the power to do that in poetry? He is unique.

But it is possible, too, his is a narrow talent, as it is in many of us. Does Levine have range to take his poems beyond anger at bad luck and hard times among America's poor? Perhaps the question itself is suspect. Richard Hugo's range was limited, I think. Every time Hugo tried to get away from a poem about coming to a small town and learning how miserable that life made him feel, he wrote less successfully. Please understand, I would take that talent, that poetry. I think I would say that's enough for me.

Levine, the great voice of anger and intense representation of silent victims, has tried to be funny on occasion. He is not a successfully funny poet, not good with light moods. When he tries to be overtly satiric, he fails. I said of him in the *American Poetry Review* that his book *The Names of the Lost* is compromised by a simplistic political stance. It's like a Charles Bronson movie, or Eastwood's *The Good, the Bad, and the Ugly.* If you don't agree with him, then you're the bad and the ugly. I think that is a weakness. It's a unionist mentality, divisive and violent. When he attacked Helen Vendler and Marjorie Perloff in a shameful essay in the *Kenyon Review,* he revealed his anger without grace of poetry's form. He did, let me say quickly in fairness, clean up the essay for its book appearance, though the same spirit of knocking off the enemy remains. While I have not suffered the privations of urban or union life and, on the whole, academic life has been wonderful to me, Levine's response seemed ungentlemanly. I think he can be worse in poems that threaten anarchic personalism as the only view tolerable. But maybe this is an impertinent position. I would trade anything I've done for Levine's best poems. Any day of the week. I think his poems are as important as any American's in the last fifty years.

MARSHALL: Besides being interested in James Wright, Dickey, and Levine, what other contemporary writers do you find yourself returning to, following, having an interest in?

SMITH: I tend to read those poets who seem to me helpful in the manipulation or wielding of a tool in the time that I need that tool. If I were trying to write about abstraction, I might read Anthony Hecht because he is very good at combining intellectual abstraction and physical reality. I don't want to get far from the physical world, so I wouldn't seek a poet of abstraction only. It wouldn't help me.

I use certain poets as touchstones when I am having difficulty in moving a poem ahead. I feel close to Robert Lowell for propulsion through details. It's been written that I was influenced by Dylan Thomas, and I did read him as a young man. I was attracted to his texture. Dickey is another poet of propulsion that I like. Warren, another favorite, is more compelling. He can frame a story quicker and more efficiently than any poet I know. He turns ordinary events, anything, into stories, and they will be intense because he can read the depths latent in those stories better than anyone. His language is brutal and true. As Levine's can be. I keep Levine on my desk shelf. These poets are my reference books. And Wright for his tenderness, his ability to say something that seems expressed not so much by the mouth as by the heart.

I like Galway Kinnell's big exuberance, a Whitmanic energy in language. I like that a great deal. But for the last number of years I've most enthusiastically read Seamus Heaney. I love his lyrical feel for the world, his local map and the resonant human landscape. I admire the way he puts feeling into language that's different both in vocabulary and syntactical expression from what is ordinary to me. When Seamus Heaney speaks about what he calls "slub silk" I am charmed by the sound; I don't know what it is, but I am drawn to it. The feel of Heaney's language, the glide and twirl of it, became important to me as early as 1973 when I heard him read in Michigan. He can concentrate the image and allow it to speak as few can. And he has become, as I've followed his books, an introduction to other British, Irish, and Scottish poets. The Scot, Douglas Dunn, is important to me.

I like very much the rough presentation, the guttural sound, and the immediacy of life-struggle in the poems of Ted Hughes. There's a great vitality in Hughes that I think American poems could emulate. In many of his poems, Hughes does seem to bark at the world, and this isn't necessarily likeable. Still, few write more delicately than he does in a poem like "Roe Deer," which is among the most graceful and mystical poems in our language, a poem smaller than but very like Elizabeth Bishop's "The Moose." In it a deer appears at the road in a mist as Hughes is driving a car; the deer seems to be not there, then there, then it's gone. Like an angel. If these deer came in a Philip Levine poem, they would be angels. Hughes manifests and transforms and translates the natural world without diminishing its reality or its threat, its nature.

CARNEY: Do you read William Stafford for that as well?

SMITH: I don't read William Stafford so much recently. I did earlier on. When I was a young poet, Stafford was the consultant in poetry to the Library of

Congress; he was what is now called the American poet laureate. I didn't know what that title meant. I thought he was the head poet for the U.S. government and, therefore, I could go and ask him questions. I didn't know better. I was on active duty with the U.S. Air Force, only 150 miles away from his office in Washington. So my wife and I decided we'd go see him when I had time off. We drove up, called him, and Stafford, being who he was, said, "Sure, come on in." I took a tape recorder and asked a lot of questions. He was the cagiest human being you'd ever want to meet. Being much puzzled about the free verse line, I said at one point, "Do you have a line theory?" He paused in his grave way, then he said, "Yes, I do." Then I waited and I waited and it seemed he wouldn't give it to me, so impatiently I said, "Well, what is it?" He put on his grin and said, "Well, when I'm typing along I know that I'm going to come to the edge of the page and have to start over." That was it. That was his whole line theory. Of course, I thought then, and I think now, that Stafford was a good bit more deliberate than that. I learned what I think you can learn from Stafford. To read him is to see more than anything else an honesty of expression. Stafford relentlessly asks himself what he feels about a scene, an event, a place. Then he says it as baldly as he can. His poems find equivalent language for being in the moment. For him there is nothing too plain, too solid, too simple for the idiom of a poem; anything can go in if it helps the poem be comprehensive. That is a great lesson. He lowers the threshold of form, or he makes form more usable, less threatening, without making us feel we need a degree or arcane instruction. That doesn't mean his poems are not complex, or lack form; it means he insists on us all having competency to write and read. This, too, is a great lesson. If poets don't believe they can do it, they don't do it. I asked Stafford what he did for writer's block. He said he didn't have it. He said, "Writer's block means you are afraid to write, and I'm never afraid." There is truth in that. He wasn't afraid.

CARNEY: You mentioned some international poets—Seamus Heaney and Paula Meehan. I wonder if the Eastern European—Herbert, for instance, or Salamun or Milosz—interest you. I ask because I don't see translations appearing nearly as often in *The Southern Review* as in other journals.

SMITH: As for the poets you mention, I find some of Milosz dazzling. Much of it remains, for whatever reason, distant from me. Many of his lyric poems are transparently beautiful. Some of the poets you've mentioned have not been of particular interest to me. Herbert and Miroslav Holub, whom I have read, I have liked very much. And a Yugoslavian, Janos Pilinszky, who wrote a more narrative poem than the others. Ted Hughes is the only western translator, I think. His book was not widely available in America. He may be dead now.

I should note that I am only the co-editor of *The Southern Review*, and I edit only two of its four annual issues. I have nothing to do with the other two. *The Southern Review* has never printed much translation. It isn't in our expertise or our interest. We have done some translations as they have come to us. Our recent special Irish literature issue turned out to have a focus on the importance of translation to emerging Irish poetry, and surprised us. We didn't set out to foreground translation, but it kept appearing in essays. Particularly in the exchange between Irish and English, the relations and the hostilities, but also in the ways that non-English poetries have had in influencing Irish writers and their deployments of language.

MARSHALL: I think Rob [Carney] speaks to the vogue or intense interest in poetry that has come out of international contexts of oppression or suffering, best exemplified, perhaps, by Carolyn Forché's book *Against Forgetting* and the impact, influence, and what Seamus Heaney calls the "shadow challenge" that these poets' work has upon poets writing in the West, how this work has shaped many American poets. I'm interested in whether you've felt a "shadow challenge" from poets or if you have a response to the "poetry of witness."

SMITH: I'm made nervous by what Forché has advocated. I have both ambiguous and ambivalent feelings about such poetry. Heaney, who is a poet and a man about whom I have strong feelings, has been a friend of mine since the early 1970s. I knew him before he was "famous Seamus," as the Irish say. But I would not be the first of his readers to raise the issue of whether there isn't in both his thinking and writing something of a naive hero-worship. I have heard Seamus speak almost adoringly of Milosz for having endured political turmoils and troubles that Heaney sees himself as having not experienced, thus being the less tempered. He has something of the same attitude toward Derek Walcott and Joseph Brodsky. I understand this, I think. I am not comfortable with it. I don't know what to make of Forché's righteous certitude, so I prefer to say nothing.

Americans, it might be argued, have the handicap of no immediate experience with the wide and deep oppressions in the world of a Palestinian or a Chilean or a Hungarian. We haven't had so much world war or concentration camps on our soil, yet having said that—and having tried to say we don't have subjects like those oppressed peoples—we do have the very real and abiding presence of a subjugated black population in this country, which is not merely an idea; it's around us. Here in Louisiana, where I live, we have a half-black, half-white country. The pain of black subjugation, or any racial division, is as scathing to American culture as Israeli-Palestinian hostility is to the Middle East. I have my own poet-heroes, admiring what they have done and written to shed light on oppression, just as Heaney views Milosz. But heroizing anyone risks a blindered reality, and poets can't afford that, any more than they can afford the finger-pointing of victimization.

There's a temptation on the part of serious people, who happen to be writers, to take on the biggest human subjects, particularly those where we see the engagement and resistance of oppressions. This is entirely appropriate. But there is a danger in becoming a "subject hunter"; one can become a romantic of moral righteousness. It is a good thing to be careful of what subject one takes on, what moral position one celebrates, even demands, careful that one doesn't fall into sermonizing, into stating righteous ideas which are not necessarily grounded in experience. Heaney knows this is a problem; he's written an essay about it, one published in a journal but not included in his American prose essays. It chronicles the danger of falling into the trap of being an *authority* whereas others only struggle for simple, inevitable truths.

In America, because we don't really have the overtly political subjects writers in other cultures live with, some poets tend to feel we don't have a subject at all, that one must go on tour to "take up" victim causes. But we do, in fact, have real problems. Racial division and its violence subdues every American city of any size. Ethnic components of American society represent, in various ways, individual stories that need expression within the entire culture. The question is how a poet deals with the largest moral issues we all face. I once asked James Wright about his poem "The Morality of Poetry." He grumbled that a poet's only moral duty is to write well. That seemed limited to me then; now, I think it is the only possible answer.

I think it is incumbent on us to take up the largest issues each is capable of handling, but only to the extent of not becoming false to our individual truth and experience. What could I say about the Romanians or the El Salvadoreans or the Israelis? Only the most tentative, general, and therefore useless observations of the tourist, since that's all I could be, and I have not even been that. Conscientious concern is necessary, but so is humility. If you know the prose of Mr. Milosz, you know he has spoken against people who, with little or no direct experience, assume the right to speak of troubles in his country. I don't think his attitude is defensive or even possessive. I think it recognizes the validity of "knowing" something close and well. The *witnessing* act of poetry does not require international voyeurism to be permanent and powerful art. It may be, as Mae West said, focused on what's lying around the house.

CARNEY: In *Local Assays: On Contemporary American Poetry* you said that you ask workshops three basic questions: What is the poem doing? How well does it do it? Is it worth doing? I'm especially interested in the third question about significance. I think people frequently bring poems to workshops without considering the question "Is what I've done worth doing? Is it significant? How do *you* know that the poem's subject is worthwhile?

SMITH: We may be talking about the most important aspect of poetry. That is its moral relation to the individual and, perhaps, to a community. The simple answer is that anything you choose to write about, to care about, is significant. Conversely, in another sense, nothing is very important in a poem. It's a chicken-and-egg conundrum. The reason I raise the questions as I do is that poetry ought to be more than acquired skills or shocking life events. We can learn skills without learning what matters about poetry. We have all read books of poems that were perfectly competent, maybe better, but they estranged or disengaged us from anything we have felt in a crisis. The fault may have been in us, that we were not capable of recognizing the reach of the poem. But let's say that our reading apparatus and instincts are right; they say the poem is trivial. Is it possible to write well-executed, even admirable, trivial poetry? Certainly, it is. Some poets write without intensity, engagement with life, discovery we readers want. In my view this is exactly so with Language poets. They are not stupid; they are trivial. It isn't easy to say to students, "You wrote a trivial poem, now go write something serious." This hurts their feelings. But not to tell a student the truth is to deceive and harm.

If you wrote what I thought was a trivial poem, I would try to tell you why it was that. I might say, "Look here's a poem about vulnerability, and it's much more important than the one you wrote about how many bottles of beer you drank last night, and how you lay unknown in a bush." Vulnerability is a good subject but by itself not enough for a serious poet. That poet will always up the ante, making the poem a window through which more is to be seen. There's a lot of jargon talk among teachers, writers, reviewers with respect to the poet's *risk*. This or that one takes big risks! Poetry, despite what Hopkins says, isn't brain surgery, the sort of thing where the reader might say, "Go ahead and write the sonnet, Dave, I won't make it if you don't!" There are, however, risks that must be transcended in writing a successful poem, and their presence has a lot to do with why we admire Whitman, Heaney, Komunyakaa, etc. If the poet is not willing to risk failure in honest treatment, accurate expression, to be and to appear silly, sentimental, or worse, the poet is likely to come only to competency, or skilled poems. The poem we want is always built around a threat, employing guises and strategies to avoid sentimentality and glibness, but ultimately giving itself to disturbance, provocation, challenge. I take those actions to be primary values of poetry.

There is a sense in which a poem is, almost literally, a laboratory for testing values we say we cherish. In the dramatic enactment of the poem, values can be tested, we can see what history cared about, what maybe remained the same or maybe changed. Consider the quality of courage: is it valuable in a man? If so, in what way? The poet might portray a man in circumstances that require inner courage (not bravado) and see what happens. We may think that because the poet knows how the experiment is supposed to come out, the answer will be inevitable. In my own experience, however, that has been rare. When I have tried to project what I might do, or not do, or did or did not do, language has taken over. I never knew how the poem would end. That's the surprise. When Sylvia Plath throws the reins onto Ariel's electric neck, none of us know what's next. The risk pays off one way or another.

There is another consideration. If you argue that poetry does not help us to identify, dramatize, and deliver knowledge that enables us to live, then you have removed from culture the ethos for poetry as a civilizing agent. A. E. Housman, Latin scholar and poet, left an essay called "On the Nature of Poetry" in which he said—he uses the curse of Isaiah—and I can't get this exactly right, he says the curse is that a people's eyes shall be blinded, their mouths shall be stopped, their ears shall be closed up so that they can't see, speak, or hear. They can, otherwise, go on living, if you call that a life. He then says that poetry exists to take away the blindness, the blockage, and the stoppage. I believe he means we participate most completely in living by employing the senses, employing what we have to make expressive what we know of life—that we live it and see it and hear it and speak it. The poem, therefore, has civic function. Not that it moves masses to change anything, but that it can refine the individual, help him to know, be better through the agency of the most concrete articulation of values.

Your question was, nevertheless, "How do *you* know the subject is worthwhile?" That's the heart of teaching, isn't it? The answer is that *I* paid attention. Absorbing the poetry of the past, reading the poems of men as laboratory experiments with evident results, living the examined life, enduring years of stunted and lame and immature drafts—mine and others—compiles knowledge useful in approaching the judgment of worth.

If you accept the poem as a made thing, both skill and inspiration, then you can say to students some things are more important than others, and part of what education ought to do is help the student see what matters beyond self-interest. This doesn't mean any of us wouldn't help ourselves a little when we get the chance. It doesn't mean—I don't know—that Milton didn't like a joke now and again, even while writing *Paradise Lost,* that forty-year project. It doesn't mean the poet should not relax. Still, if your eye is on becoming the best poet you can imagine, then you ought to know what being serious means, the highest kind of serious. My task is to cause students to respect the art and their potential as fully and completely as they can. That is a *seriousness* all the giggling and mockery and small-mindedness of our kind can never diminish, surely what Philip Larkin meant when he described an abandoned church as "a serious house on serious earth it is."

I am afraid I have very little tolerance of people who want to be a class clown, a show-off. Such people can exist only when teachers permit that. We do not study poetry to indulge a hunger for attention. I have been lucky over the years. I've had students who believed they could learn to write important poems, who were committed to the struggle to do that, and, as a result, more than you might imagine have written fine poetry. When you deal with serious people who are trying to know how to become an artist, even if they studied the art of laying bricks, you find what you study is how to be more fully human than you might have been otherwise. It is amazing how much joy and laughter and pleasure that releases. And why else would anyone write a poem?

St. Cyril's Dragon

THE THREAT OF POETRY

In fact, when I know what is meant by "mamelon" and "ravelin,"
When I can tell at sight a chassepot rifle from a javelin,
When such affairs as sorties and surprises I'm more wary at,
And when I know precisely what is meant by "commissariat,"
When I have learnt what progress has been made in modern gunnery,
When I know more of tactics than a novice in a nunnery:
In short, when I've a smattering of elemental strategy,
You'll say a better Major-General has never *sat* a gee—

You'll say a better, etc.

                      —W. S. GILBERT

Gerald Stern, a garrulous, savvy, upbeat poet, on his way to do a poetry reading took a wrong turn in New Jersey and at a streetlight was shot for his trouble. Although this might be poetry's threat, there is a more necessary threat in every poem. Threat, to a poet, is a very good thing, a tool, a strategy, a necessary medium. Indeed, no threat, no poem, I tell students. Most shake their heads or gaze away at Nature. They are already enrolled in the audience raised to believe real poetry is beautiful thoughts in rhymed quatrains, or at least the swooping flourish of bright hope even tough Hopkins gave himself to in his 1877 lines "No wonder of it: sheer plod makes plough down sillion / Shine, and blue-bleak embers, ah my dear, / Fall, gall themselves, and gash gold-vermillion." Two years later, Gilbert Sullivan rocked the house with parody, spoofing the poet's mastery, control, knowledge, and strategies of art. Buyers of poetry, excepting poets, like books with ornately poetic statements that affirm permanent "realities" they need to believe in: God rules like the American president; heaven waits like a country club lounge; each of us is seductive and sublime inside, if not in our plain outward wrappers. Weak poems, pruned of thorns, barbs, and threats console and soothe us; we all want the beatific promise. If it were not so, ever-positive Walt Whitman would have little appeal for us beyond verbal postcards from the travelogue of his imagination. Threat, various as a heartbeat, is the weight, complexity, difficulty, problem, resistance every poem draws energy from as it seeks resolution.

One form of threat is simple tension, controlled within artifice, the glanced-at thing Whitman often juxtaposed to his buoyancy, as the knife-grinder in his 1871 lyric "Sparkles from the Wheel" bears both procreative powers and deadly inflection:

> Where the city's ceaseless crowd moves on the livelong day,
> Withdrawn I join a group of children watching, I pause aside with them.
>
> By the curb toward the edge of the flagging,
> A knife-grinder works at his wheel sharpening a great knife,
> Bending over he carefully holds it to the stone, by foot and knee,
> With measur'd tread he turns rapidly, as he presses with light but firm hand,
> Forth issue then in copius golden jets,
> Sparkles from the wheel.
>
> The scene and all its belongings, how they seize and affect me,
> The sad sharp-chinn'd old man with worn clothes and broad shoulder-band
>   of leather,
> Myself effusing and fluid, a phantom curiously floating, now here absorb'd
>   and arrested,
> The group, (an unminded point set in a vast surrounding,)
> The attentive, quiet children, the loud, proud, restive base of the streets,
> The low hoarse purr of the whirling stone, the light-press'd blade,
> Diffusing, dropping, sideways-darting, in tiny showers of gold,
> Sparkles from the wheel.

A poem is a test of expectations. Like anybody's life. At some age most of us begin to have conscious expectations for a future. We begin consciousness. My father was killed in an automobile accident when I was seventeen. My mother shortly remarried. I went off to the University. The semirural community of Churchland, Virginia, where I had grown up, then changed drastically in some respects and in others remained as it had always been. I did not think about that, and I did not think about returning, ever. Within four years I would marry, divorce, remarry, graduate from college, teach high school, go away to graduate school, enter military service, and begin to write poems. It seems to me not one step was predicted by any expectation, though I am sure others would read my life differently. To me, things happened; I responded.

My turn to poems came at the age of twenty-five. I began to want something I will call a life with a shape, a purpose. I had lived, as most people do, through a sequence of crises, lesser and greater, but I had not realized that the formative pressure of threat, as well as any harmful force in fact or potential, already and inevitably shaped in me some unrealized meaning and purpose. Belief, here, would be too light a word, for I mean the tougher, more personal recognitions of cause-effect, contingency, and unavoidable dilemmas each man, if he lives at all, learns on his pulse. I mean what I am certain Gerald Stern felt at the moment he saw that gun in his face. This is what a man is, or isn't, when painful choice arrives.

In the engagements with human crises, we discover selves. Each of us needs and seeks identity, the self able to know and act with intention. This "self" acts according to conviction rather than in mere response to the manipulative rhetorics of commerce, religion, politics, any of the one-answer systems. The self is a process, not a nice waistline, a new car, a top medical school admission. Yet we are all walking closets of false selves, living adopted images, eating and drinking to attract others, wearing what our fantasies implore, hopelessly wanting and almost helplessly responding to desires. The consumerism that makes American business and psychotherapy hum has not lacked the worried attention of poets, largely because among its worst effects are the fragmentation of self and community. *The Waste Land* appeared long before T. S. Eliot possessed it. John Donne, one of Eliot's favorite poets, famously deplored the self exiled where no bell rang. Edgar Allan Poe composed ghoulish parables of men left to live alone. Herman Melville isolated Ahab and Ishmael to frame his moral fable. Whitman spent almost seventy years asserting the indivisibility of self and selves, and he took much of his view from the essays of Ralph Waldo Emerson and their early New Age saintliness to which Melville, the ex-seaman, said, "what stuff for one who has been around the Horn." Genius that he was, Whitman's Kiwanis good-speak remains to many readers a tainted gassy rambling, little match for the threat of a looming raven or an avenging whale, that Nature reviled beyond anger, according to poet Ted Hughes, upon which we rely for our very breaths.

The story of the imperiled self, social fragmentation, violence, fear, all
the good fictive elements, swallows us every day. Texas debates whether a
child of twelve may marry the father of her baby. Louisiana passes one law
to prohibit minors from buying alcohol and with another permits stores to
sell it to anyone; a third law legalizes concealed weapons. You can carry a
bazooka in Baton Rouge if you want to, so long as your coat is long enough.
One elderly lady from the most elegant part of New Orleans told me, at a
summer writers' conference, she doesn't drive to the grocery store without
her pistol. Increasingly we cannot remember unlocked doors, neighbors who
walk sidewalks or speak openly, and woe to anyone who would willingly help
the injured. My son, a lawyer, says that such help is good for the litigation
business. What values resist our divisions? What good is the past in a swamp
of snapping lawyers?

I don't know a single person who now speaks without apology and cavil
about moral behavior. I don't know a man who would overtly praise honor.
Ernest Hemingway, who was said to be stripped of faith in big words by the
horrors they propelled in World War I, wrote, glibly I think, "moral is what
you feel good after." This standard of ethical conduct lies solely in the self, a
self which may be only the product of advertisers, consumers, governments,
all a mob of ugly actors waiting for the next command. When things go
wrong, responsibility for failure is not what we reach for. We phone up law-
yers. We whine that we are victims, we blame and attack until it is the only
way we know. Neighbor, school, church, race, we blame. I knew a waterman
in Virginia who lamented the decline of fish he had spent a life catching. He
did not blame sophisticated boats, with arrayed technology as complex as
aircraft carriers that made them seagoing vacuum cleaners, or question the
wisdom of decimating an industry, let alone the morality of that business,
for they were fishermen like himself, just bigger and better. The cause, he
claimed with rising anger, was "bums in Argentina." When I asked what he
meant, he said "You know, them nuculer bums that's always getting blown up
on TV." The Argentinian in his mind was an abstraction, nothing he could
see except by the imagination. But not less real for that.

Knowledge, to us, is always partial, inadequate, dangerous in precisely
the ways Pope knew it to be, and just as necessary as ever. We have an infi-
nite need to see. Joseph Conrad's admonition to the artist was put as a self's
obligation in his preface to *The Nigger of the Narcissus*: "My task above all is
to make you see." That sight is the obligation of the arts, liberal and applied.

Seeing means what it says, too, simply the presentation of pictures, though it resounds as perception, the invoking of all the senses into a harmony of awareness. We are, through poetry, made to feel and to know what feeling is for self and community. The artist restores living and perception; he makes a self emerge from contending selves.

But how does the making of a poem, work that is, as I have implied, moral, ethical, honorable, as well as aesthetic, produce its effect? The simple answer is that the poem gives an honest, recognizable picture of human event, the self and the other engaged. Without such pictures we can imagine no destiny. The nature of destiny is what we yearn for, the source of our beliefs, convictions, superstitions, and expectations. A poem, like all high art, proposes that in dramas of crisis, human the same generation after generation, we are permitted distance and objectivity sufficient not simply to see what happens but also to *perceive* much more. History, which performs in similar ways but tells less, and less quickly, informs us that some 12,000 American men were left dying on the battlefield at Fredericksburg, Virginia, at the end of December 7, 1862, many frozen in the following days of brutal cold. The historian might add many evocative details, such as the presence of Christmas decorations in houses along the Rappahannock River, where Confederate sharpshooters from Mississippi sang as they assassinated Union boys trying to rig a pontoon bridge, and Union boys not yet assassinated sang along, for the carols bound them even as bullets tore them asunder. Some, on opposite sides and in uniforms of different colors, were brothers. Whitman, who saw firsthand the results of that bloody day, snaps all that and more into sharp focus with "A Sight in the Camp in the Daybreak Gray and Dim":

> Curious I halt and silent stand,
> Then with light fingers I from the face of the nearest the first
>   just lift the blanket;
> Who are you elderly man so gaunt and grim, with well-gray'd hair,
>   and flesh all sunken about the eyes?
> Who are you my dear comrade?

This dead man, Whitman knows, might have been his brother George. He had traveled as fast as he could by train and boat, more than two days slogging his way from New York, certain it was George, though the name wasn't right, he had seen in a casualty list in a New York paper. The corpse Whitman looked at might have been an "elderly man," for both armies sent men who were the age of grandparents forth to battle, but he would more likely have been one of the younger men that early in the war (Melville wrote "All wars are boyish" because so many of the dead were youths), and even George was younger than brother Walt Whitman, then forty-three. This dead one is old because Whitman is thinking of himself, and of the soul which is the self so imperiled by all that threatens the democratic America he had imagined.

I was the first in my family to go to college. I had wanted to become an auto mechanic. Like the men of my family before me, I knew the names of no painter, violinist, architect, and certainly no poet. The men of my kin were mustang engineers, railroaders; their women were cradlers of babies. None of either kind spoke of having entertained dreams. They would have scoffed at Whitman saying, "I loaf and invite my soul, / I lean and loaf at my ease observing a spear of summer grass." But then they weren't likely to encounter Walt since there were no books in our houses. If I had been asked about the function of arts, I would have said it usually replaced study hall. That arts enable us to seek out destiny, to consider identity, to affirm a relationship of community and meaning would have been as strange and foreign in my family as an actual oil painting hung on a wall. I recall no such pictures. Almost.

There were, actually, two pictures. One hung in each of my grandparents' houses. My father's father, a lifelong ticket salesman for the B&O railroad, slept nightly under a nude more flawless than a Botticelli, her bright red nipples and matching lips impervious to days that slowly bent him. This was an early color photograph. My mother's father, a hunter who taught me how to sit silent in dark woods and wait for squirrels to appear and be killed, kept an oil painting of a deer above his television, a creature so badly made it looked like Lassie pretending to be Bambi on steroids. Miniature pine trees grew up through its clearly drawn toes. When I had gone as a boy to their houses, I had stared. Were women really like that? Why would a man paint a deer so different from those I'd seen in the woods? Did I ever ask why those dour men kept these images on their otherwise blank walls? When you are young, you question everything. But I did not. I accepted the world as it was. Robert Penn Warren's poem says, "Man lives by images. They / Lean at us from the world's wall, and Time's."

Warren does not, I think, mean specifically images of art but there, heightened and focused, we see who we are, and we speculate why and how we fit into the natural scheme, and we may learn how dreams unfold and kindle us. My grandfathers were men who believed in themselves and not much else. They held to no philosophy, no church, no political party. Each had once joined social organizations, belonging desultorily to the late-nineteenth- and early-twentieth-century fashion of *belonging*—they'd been Masons, Elks, and such—but each had settled into job, house, family, hobby, and that was that. Government, they thought, was useless except to keep crime in check and fight necessary wars. Plainness of speech, dress, and action was almost to each man a Puritan principle, though neither would have known a Puritan from a Raritan. They believed in progress that invented gizmos and better medicines, but redemption and transformation meant burdens they had no wish to lift. They worked and left dreams, as they would have said, to the next man, meaning the romantics. I doubt either had entertained one thought in his lifetime about the arts. Each would have nodded in agreement with Richard Nixon who said in his famous tapes, "The Arts you know— they're Jews, they're left wing—in other words stay away." But these Appalachian mountaineers *had* hung an odd, soft image where their lives passed daily, a nude woman and a deer. Why?

Representatives of Nature, some goodness manifested, these creatures loomed wholly benign, nonthreatening. Life supports, we might even say, surely more than charming, images of a greatness to which, however tentatively, each man wanted to be linked. Still, as my grandfathers must have known, whom I knew to be reasonably perceptive men, each was a false image. No woman had ever been so hairless, unblemished, perfectly, innocently sexual as that nude. No deer was, well, whatever that one was. I think they reminded my grandfathers of something yearned for. The sweetness of poetry I will call it, although they would not have. Both of them died before poetry became my life's purpose. If I had mentioned poetry to either one, I would have been glared at like a man who has pissed himself on the street. But in those days I would never have mentioned poetry, having no idea what poetry might be or that I might want it, or even that I had begun to want to know my destiny, or that thinking about one was thinking about the other.

The imagination, Samuel Taylor Coleridge said, maybe the toughest mind among the Romantic poets, is different from the Fancy, an act of the mind that seeks escape from reality, creates false images, panders to us. Imagination, he argued, dives down into the dark heart of experience and returns with knowledge necessary to selfhood. No form of art does this better than poetry. I do not mean poetry of manipulation, of advertised sentiments, but the poetry that scares those who pay attention. It delivers the truth we find hard to live with, the news, as William Carlos Williams said, men daily die for the lack of. Most of us, most of the time, don't want that anyway. Not long ago North Carolina's Senator Jesse Helms said he lay awake nights in fear of what the arts could do. In my local news, a high school has suspended a child for composing and reciting a rap song someone thought was an overt threat to good order. The imagination's power is precisely to confront, comprehend, and redress threat. That is why the imagination is threat.

Great art intends *threat*. Those images it hangs on the world's wall may appear to take our breath away with pastoral consolation and moral serenity, but that happens only in contrast to the deeper weave we see and learn and respond to. Poetry is subversive of untested, unexamined feeling. There is nothing instructive in a Hallmark card's verse; it has no complexity and none of life's stymies. Most of what people take for a poem is only words substituting for what we are too lazy or too afraid to articulate. Real poems resist the smug, easy, glib, and superficial. The good poem destabilizes, unbalances, stirs up, digs down, demands feeling in exact circumstances. It refuses mass idea, mass truth, mass reality as false to its only client, the individual. No poem succeeds without threat, implied or explicit. Threat manifests what is important to know. Threat engineers the struggle of self to come into being.

Films can be more overt about this redemptive process than poetry sometimes is. *Scrooged,* Bill Murray's wickedly funny remake of the Charles Dickens Christmas fable, touches most of modern poetry's themes, consumerism and greed, isolated selves and social illness, petty principle and transcendent reality, childish innocence and the hardened ignorance of age, the uncertain nature of love and the crippling effects of its abuse. Because Dickens is at the stage, evils will be reversed, the self will shine, the community will be protected. Murray's film, heavy on cynicism and surreal characters, wired with humor, presents scenes in which a determined angel, played charmingly by actress Carol Kane, tries to show Scrooge (Murray), a selfish but successful businessman alone in a community of desperate but loving others, how he had better change his ways, and when he will not she resorts to vaudevillian slapstick, banging him hard with someone's Christmas toaster. The film dramatizes what hurts in life—poverty, relentless labor, indifference, illness, time, greed, lovelessness—but reserves as worst the isolation of self from community, a drama of deprivation and contingency. It's all about threat. Normal life, whatever normal is, sucks. We so want to believe in something better, a progressive destiny, that we are cheered when Scrooge turns beneficent patriarch loved by all near him. Even so, when this stability is everywhere triumphant, the inner eye, Melville's eye, squints in suspicion. Threat that has made meaning refuses to sidle offstage.

In poems, threat has many forms, all composing value. We applaud subtlety in motivation that threatens and subtlety in how threat is dramatized. Dickens liked sinister bullies and board-stiff matrons. His style was exaggeration, as it is in the movie *Jaws* where the white shark is so cunning it defeats the worst and most manly opponents, but in both arts the tone is comic in order to signal the threat is, potentially, maybe, probably, but not certainly, manageable. That's why Sheriff Roy Scheider tells drunken shark-hunter Robert Shaw, "You're gonna need a bigger boat." The threat has to be big enough to make action worthy, and the meaning of action memorable. Threat is resistance, pressure creating drama, suspense, intensity. Good readers have no respect for a poem guilty of "unconditional surrender" to the fantasia of its desire. Such a poem resists nothing, overcomes nothing, and wins nothing; it fails even to marshal contending factors in any struggle for definition of a life moment. Limp poems often unload message—political statement, religious opinion, sexual fantasy—as lineated propaganda, ignoring the reader who is knee-deep in experience to the contrary. This poem requires a reader to ignore what he has lived, what he knows of the world. The reader may turn his nose up, as I do, before Billy Collins when he writes:

> It might interest you to know,
> speaking of the plentiful imagery of the world,
> that I am the sound of rain on the roof.
>
> I also happen to be the shooting star,
> the evening paper blowing down an alley,
> and the basket of chestnuts on the kitchen table.
> (From "Litany")

Resisted motion succeeds by imitating the world we know, even in distortion and dream exaggeration, where what happens is *whatever* happens. The poem wants to make the reader a conspirator, not a judge of the poem's accountability. Any reader counts most in a poem its life on the pulse. There is no pulse without threat.

Threat may be only the nuances of tone, the shifts of voice a deft poet can signal. It may be so immediate and familiar that we fail to notice, as if threat

is only breathable air. Indeed threat is evident in a lyric's brooding aware-
ness of bad weather, a weather we find so conventional in the expression of
our spirits, exactly the method of the famous medieval quatrain "Western
Wind":

> Western wind, when will thou blow,
> The small rain down can rain?
> Christ, if my love were in my arms
> And I in my bed again!

The word *threat,* Old English in origin, probably more than 1,200 years in
use, has from the start meant to force or compel action. Harms, we see in
reading, are imminent and depend on certain things done or not, to be done
or not. Thus, threat is contingency. Driving toward knowledge in the poem's
progress, threat forces change; it shapes response as dilemmas unfold, its
own unfolding proceeding swiftly or in delicious retardation according to
the need of the poet to make us wait. When the German poet Rilke, having
mounted a cloud of tension, writes *you must change your life,* the reader is
ready to add the "or else" and is prepared to entertain meaning.

Flannery O'Connor, short story writer and novelist, favored the use of
threats as large and symbolic as possible. A devout Catholic, O'Connor re-
garded fiction as an instructional art. Her characters, all of them outsiders
in one way or another, are exaggerations in the same way as those of Dick-
ens, and mightily funny; they include the Misfit, a cold killer of Granny; a
Bible salesman seducing Hulga so he could steal her artificial leg; a grandfa-
ther, Mr. Head, whose racial bigotry seems, like so much in O'Connor, sheer
cartoon buffoonery. When asked about her style of distortion and threat,
O'Connor said she spoke louder for the hard of hearing and drew larger for
the poorly sighted. She made her threats seem irrational, illogical, outside
ordinary expectation that permits us to drive a car casually because we think
other drivers will stay in their lanes or the expectation that nothing will,
today, fall from the sky under which we stroll. Her intention was to immerse
recognizable selves into symbolic crises. She liked to quote the prayer of St.
Cyril of Jerusalem: "The dragon sits by the side of the road watching those
who pass. Beware lest he devour you. We go to the Father of Souls but it is
necessary to pass by the dragon." O'Connor was clear about what this meant
to her: "No matter what form the dragon may take, it is of this mysterious
passage past him, or into his jaws, that stories of any depth will always be

concerned to tell, and this being the case, it requires considerable courage at any time, in any country, not to turn away from the storyteller." To Miss O'Connor, life's sweetness was dependent on what threatened it and upon the size of the threat. Without threat, the road of life is only a pastoral walk in the daisies. That is why poetry that fails to reveal and risk the life of a real self is no good to us. The dragons of cheap art are only little lizards.

The corollary does not, however, hold. Bigger threats do not necessarily make better art, as soap opera, melodrama, and television dramas show. Successful threat in a poem is proportionate force and release leading to credible statement made or implied, for any poem is finally discourse. The threat begins by affecting the self and ends by shaking the community. When we do not feel the poem bears such power, all the intricate tatting and experiments in the world cannot save it from uselessness. In *Othello,* jealousy threatens the hero. Desdemona, his wife, is then threatened not only by his jealousy but also by her innocence. That destabilized relationship in turn places the state in peril. A chain of cause-and-effect, each link perhaps a manageable struggle, draws into attention how fragile are even the best selves. We watch, projecting ourselves onto hero and villain, never certain how things would turn out for us, though we enter the theater knowing the already-composed ending, and we have the security of expectation. We know, too, the purpose of narrative is to develop contingency and confusion, then to unsnarl everything. That is what defines a good story. It does its job well without alerting us how the unsnarling will come about precisely. In turn, the presence of a good story prepares for the poem whose purpose, reductively stated, is to make meaning of action and to lodge it in memorable words. We might say in images hung on a wall. There, it repeats as often as we need repetition for the delight and instruction of our natures. I do not mean, of course, the platitudes and bromides distilled to commercially pedaled plaques, put on T-shirts, or abstracted like one-minute Shakespeare plays. The images I mean are those which tell us what is the most durable, which we admire and call Beauty because they summon from in us the will to do and to be good, and in Beauty we see the sorrowful diminishing of what had seemed to us permanent. With the poem, as in the play, when threat is overcome, the durable stands forth, found. For the individual that is always consciousness and when it comes there is new stability in community and the self stands reoriented.

Threat tempers the poem whether it is obvious or hidden. Each poet decides; each reader judges. Poems have, finally, few rules; there are no reliable poetry police. Some poems hold the threat close, as a gambler plays his cards; some flaunt it openly. Milton signals threat in his titles, *Paradise Lost* and "On His Blindness." Emily Dickinson's #435 begins with a muted threat as thesis: "Much Madness is divinest sense—."A paradox much employed by seers, wizards, prophets, druids, and bards, the unknown, she implies, lies couched in the familiar. This poem's province is ultimate reality, knowable in the most eccentric evidence.

> Much Madness is divinest sense—
> To a discerning Eye—
> Much sense—the Starkest Madness—
> 'Tis the Majority
> In this, as All, prevail—
> Assent—and you are sane—
> Demur—you're straightway dangerous—
> And handled with a Chain—

Dickinson's gently rational tone in evoking her paradox causes us to think she means only that ersatz madness maybe be actual wisdom—until that final line. Cruelty, utterly irrational malice, a violent chain-whipping waits for the person who proves not like the rest of us, though as far from mad as a house cat. There had appeared to be no self in this poem, though the final line changes that. Here threat is not the absence of a self but the presence of self's individuality that offends the community average. The poet has inverted the more usual process of the poem's movement whereby an anecdote of crisis leads vision outward to reexamination of self and community. She moves from abstract idea to the self in isolation. In this she tells the god-awful truth; the only resolution she offers is a sudden, literal anger. Be too different, she says, and you are screwed. Dickinson, with paradox, wit, and playful pace, allows the poem's threat to build expectations, apparently to satisfy them, but she doesn't dismiss the threat. Poems help us to that point when we transcend trouble and self-redemption begins. That's why Robert Frost assures us a good poem will tell what we know but didn't know we knew. The best poems have no choice but to recognize St. Cyril's dragon.

Randall Jarrell, who never flinched from threat or truth, bore Dickinson's courage in a world of Dickens-sized monsters. Said to have thrown himself under a passing truck, he died in 1965. Often in treatment for severe depression, Jarrell had a child's sensitivity to harms. He knew what any B horror movie knows, that the obvious threats are usually not the most dangerous. Jarrell, like his teacher and friend Allen Tate, happened to be a fan of professional football which, in the early 1960s, was exploding with television's coverage. The Baltimore Colts were soon portrayed as America's team, each of its players acquiring legendary status that announcers embroidered weekly. One of the Colts was the very large, very imposing black defensive tackle, "Big Daddy Lipscomb." Sports writers portrayed him as devastating Bluto, the bulldozer who knocked down any runner, but he was also described as a "caring" man who always helped his victim rise up. Bigger than life, tougher than time and the fears that whittled the rest of us, he stood with the day's heroes, the Kennedy brothers, Martin Luther King, Wilt Chamberlain. But Big Daddy had a secret drug habit; he had his own self-image problem, his human confusion, and it killed him. Jarrell saw the threat to Lipscomb was not football's brutality, not even drugs or too much money or too much stardom. It was being afraid to fail at living, so Jarrell inscribed the problem of the self who descended into isolation and stood outside the community, the big man in "Say Goodbye to Big Daddy" who finally and helplessly admitted, "I've been scared / Most of my life. You wouldn't think so to look at me. / It gets so bad I cry myself to sleep . . . " Poetry, people think, ought to turn things to the pretty ends we want instead of the blunt reality we mostly suffer. Jarrell understood the sinister well enough and the truth-telling power of the poem that was its ultimate value, and that drew him to the pity and beauty in a remarkable and representative man, a player like all of us in the only game that matters:

> his size
> Embarrassed him, so that he was helped by smaller men
> And hurt by smaller men; Big Daddy Lipscomb
> Has helped to his feet the last ball carrier, Death.
>
> The black man in the television set
> Whom the viewers stared at-sometimes, almost were—
> Is a blur now; when we get up to adjust the set,
> It's not the set, but a NETWORK DIFFICULTY.
> The world won't be the same without Big Daddy.
>
> Or else it will.

Jarrell, as Dickinson had done, portrays one self mourning another self's harm, and here the community from which the self is exiled turns out to be the harming actor. Big Daddy is defeated by isolation, by hypocrisy, by bad judgment, but mostly by fear any child would recognize, the fear of being unlike the others, of being unable to become like others. Today, of course, the networks would broadcast a brief documentary at half-time, eulogize him in his social context, make him appear a triumphant hero, and spin-doctor out with a photographic smiling face of the child he was once. We almost see technicians grin as they make sure we are awash in life transformed, onward and upward, then, into commercial break. But Jarrell doesn't buy easy resolution. His chanted fragments, satiric language, tongue-in-cheek portrait of the big hero lead to the only permanence anybody can expect: Death. In its face, Jarrell adopts the glib final remark of the boyish announcer warbling as the documentary dissolves: "The world won't be the same without Big Daddy." Exactly what was said of Hamlet. A lot of lesser poets would have left it there. Not Jarrell, who deadpans, "Or else it will."

Fear and death, threats whose power is addressed only by Jarrell's framing, resisting words, appear to leave us hopeless. But hope is what poems bring, offering awareness, turning us to read those images on the wall of memory where the struggles of our kind are foretold, where we may understand the aspiration to become a self is beaten down all too easily and all too invisibly. Jarrell knows what literary theorists have newly discovered, what poets always know, that language is the most formidable threat, for it makes reality and semblances of reality with the same skills, in the same images. Like Jarrell's television viewer blinded, so it appears, by NETWORK DIFFICULTY, we have to learn not merely to look but to *see*, which is what threat does in "Say Goodbye to Big Daddy."

My two grandfathers are long dead. Many poets I have known are dead, poets whose work I watched as it emerged to become images of guidance past the dragon's house, Warren and Dickey and Hugo and Wright and Matthews and Levis, all dead. I imagine now I may live some years yet, though the sum is always ungiven and destiny is untold. Except, perhaps, in the images art places before us, in threats contained by and shaping those images. The two pictures my grandfathers kept hang only in my memory, inexpressible without words recovering what they were. Still I find myself gazing back there, speculating about what they offered those old men. They would have said just pictures to look at, meaning some pleasure taken. That is almost enough, of course. I think the pleasure must have been a kind of deep memory, a recognition of the self reconnected to a community fecund as the dream of beginning; it must have been a feeling of peace linking to Nature, that woman, that deer. Maybe even innocence. Those images gave them the nearest thing they could know to poetry, a sweet fable of life permanent among the diminished and vanished, all that they had loved. If art is anything, it is love and memory and union that we call knowledge. The greatest American poet, the most revolutionary poet, Walt Whitman, opens *Leaves of Grass* with a bold and democratic claim of continuity: "I celebrate myself, and sing myself, / And what I assume you shall assume, / For every atom belonging to me as good belongs to you."

Then he adds, for the poet, what the poem exists to do: "I loaf and invite my soul." He asks for the soul's narratives, its threats, its gambles and wiles and strategies and successes. The soul is the self, the sum of character, a process of knowing to be courted, nourished, prepared. Paintings, dance, music, poems give image to the flow of time in which we float, encountering threats that would compromise, confuse, prevent our destiny. In the poem's colloquy of self and community, in tales of how it has been and what pleasures and sorrows being has, we create the patterns, stories, myths, the destiny we hunt for because we cannot survive without it. When I think of those grandfathers and their pictures, I allow myself to dream threats they endured and surpassed. I think of poems that chronicle the passage of men through the place where the dragon always waits. Beauty and Passion and Knowledge and Courage are the names of the roads each poet travels. The horse each one rides is called threat.

Acknowledgments

I am grateful to the John Simon Guggenheim Foundation, the Lyndhurst Foundation (Chattanooga, Tennessee), the National Endowment for the Arts Foundation, and the Rockefeller/Bellagio (Italy) Foundation, as well as to the Virginia Commonwealth University, the Louisiana State University, and the Johns Hopkins University for time made possible to write these essays. "There's a Bird Hung Around My Neck: Observations on Southern Poetry" is a composite of three seperate essays originally published as follows: "Why Southern Poetry May Be a Snipe Hunt," in *The Future of Southern Letters,* edited by Jefferson Humphries and John Lowe (New York: Oxford University Press, 1996); "Cornering the Southern Poem," *Poetry Ireland Review* (1994); "There's a Bird Hung Around My Neck: Observations on Southern Poetry," *Five Points* (1998); "Edgar Allan Poe and the Nightmare Ode," *Southern Humanities Review* (1995); "Ransom's Lyric of the Holy Grail," in *Touchstones: American Poets on a Favorite Poem,* edited by Robert Pack and Jay Parini (Middlebury, VT: Middlebury College Press, 1995); "Warren's Ventriloquist: J. J. Audubon," *Value and Vision in American Literature,* edited by Joseph Candido (Athens: Ohio University Press, 1999), reprinted in *The Legacy of Robert Penn Warren,* edited by David Madden (Baton Rouge: Louisiana State University Press, 2000); "James Dickey's Motions," *South Carolina Review* (vol. 26, no. 2); "The Fat Man and the Dirty Bastards: Remembering Richard Hugo," *Verse* (1995); "The Talking Dick in Stephen Dobyns's Poetry," *New England Review* (1995); "The Good Talk: Stephen Dunn's Ideas," *New England Review* (1995); "Hunting Men," *Sewanee Review* (1989), reprinted in *Home Ground: Southern Autobiography,* edited by J. Bill Berry (Columbia: University of Missouri Press, 1991); "In Search of the Real Thing," *Contemporary Autobiography* (1988); "Interview with Ernest Suarez," *Contemporary Literature* (1996). I am grateful to the editors of these books and journals for originally publishing these works.

"Hunting Men" was given as a lecture for the Conference in Southern Autobiography, Jonesboro, Arkansas, in 1989. "Edgar Allan Poe and the Nightmare Ode" was given as a paper at the Modern Language Association meeting in Toronto in 1993. "There's a Bird Hung Around My Neck" was given as the University Distinguished Lecture at Georgia State University in 1996. "Warren's Ventriloquist: J. J. Audubon" was given as a lecture for the Robert Penn Warren Festival, Louisiana State University, 1999. "Barbaric Yawps: Life in the Life of Poetry" was given as the Lewis W. Britton Lecture at the Catholic University of America in 2001.

"The Quail Men of Churchland" appeared in the *Georgia Review* (Winter 2004) and was reprinted in *Little Boats, Unsalvaged: Poems, 1992–2004* (Baton Rouge: Louisiana State University Press, 2005).

Poems are reprinted in the text thanks to the following sources:

James Dickey, "May Day Sermon to the Women of Gilmer County, Georgia, by a Woman Preacher Leaving the Baptist Church," from *The Whole Motion: Collected Poems, 1945–1992* © 1992 by James Dickey and reprinted by permission of Wesleyan University Press.

"Cézanne and Zola," "Bowlers Anonymous," from *Velocities*, by Stephen Dobyns, copyright © 1994 by Stephen Dobyns. Used by permission of Penguin, a division of Penguin Group (USA) Inc.

Stephen Dunn's "Decorum," from *New and Selected Poems, 1974–1994* by Stephen Dunn. Copyright © 1994 by Stephen Dunn. Used by permission of W. W. Norton & Company, Inc.

Richard Hugo's "White Center," from *Making Certain It Goes On: Collected Poems of Richard Hugo* by Richard Hugo. Copyright © 1984 by The Estate of Richard Hugo. Used by permission of W. W. Norton & Company, Inc.

"Photograph: Migrant Worker, Parlier, California, 1967" is from *Elegy*, by Larry Levis, © 1997 by University of Pittsburgh Press. Reprinted by permission of the University of Pittsburgh Press.

"Driving East" and "Airplanes" are from *Wrecking Crew*, by Larry Levis © 1972. Reprinted by permission of the University of Pittsburgh Press.

William Matthews's "Masterful" and "The Bar at the Andover Inn," from *Search Party: Collected Poems of William Matthews*. Copyright © 2004 by Sebastian Matthews and Stanley Plumly. Reprinted by permission of Houghton Mifflin Company. All rights reserved.

John Crowe Ransom's "Captain Carpenter," from *Selected Poems*, Third Edition, Revised and Enlarged by John Crowe Ransom, copyright © 1924,

1927 by Alfred A. Knopf, Inc. and renewed 1952, 1955 by John Crowe Ransom. Used by permission of Alfred A. Knopf, a division of Random House, Inc.

Robert Penn Warren's "Tell Me a Story" and "Not to Be Trusted," from *The Collected Poems of Robert Penn Warren.* Copyright © 1998. Used by permission of William Morris Agency, LLC.

Index

Note: *This is a selective, not inclusive, list of names, places, and concepts.*